# Two Coventry Corpus Christi Plays.

## Early English Text Society.

### Extra Series, LXXXVII.

1902 (*reprinted* 1931).

Second edition 1957 (for 1952).

PRICE 15*s*.

# Two
# Coventry Corpus Christi Plays:

## 1. THE SHEARMEN AND TAYLORS' PAGEANT,
RE-EDITED FROM THE EDITION OF THOMAS SHARP, 1825;

AND

## 2. THE WEAVERS' PAGEANT,
RE-EDITED FROM THE MANUSCRIPT OF ROBERT CROO, 1534;

WITH A PLAN OF COVENTRY, AND APPENDIXES
CONTAINING THE CHIEF RECORDS OF
THE COVENTRY PLAYS.

BY

## HARDIN CRAIG

*SECOND EDITION*

LONDON
PUBLISHED FOR THE EARLY ENGLISH TEXT SOCIETY
BY THE OXFORD UNIVERSITY PRESS,
AMEN HOUSE, E.C.4.
1957

TO

𝔓𝔯𝔬𝔣𝔢𝔰𝔰𝔬𝔯 𝔍𝔬𝔥𝔫 𝔐𝔞𝔱𝔱𝔥𝔢𝔴𝔰 𝔐𝔞𝔫𝔩𝔶.

Extra Series, LXXXVII.

FIRST EDITION 1902
REPRINTED 1931
SECOND EDITION 1957

RICHARD CLAY AND COMPANY, LTD., BUNGAY, SUFFOLK.

# PREFACE TO SECOND EDITION.

SINCE the publication of *Two Coventry Corpus Christi Plays* by
the Early English Text Society in 1902 the most important contri-
bution, so far as I know, to the store of mediaeval Coventry documents is the issue by the same society of *The Coventry Leet Book*.
This valuable historical document was carefully transcribed and
edited by the late Mary Dormer Harris in 1907–1913 (E.E.T.S.,
O.S. 134, 135, 138, 148). I know of no republication of the pageants
except modernized versions of *The Shearmen and Taylors' Pageant*
in *Fifteenth Century Prose and Verse*, Arber's English Garner
(Westminster, 1903) and in Everyman's Library (1925); also lines
475 to the end in *Chief Pre-Shakespearean Dramas*, edited by J. Q.
Adams (Boston, 1924). This highly characteristic mystery play
may, however, appear in other volumes of selections.

After reviewing my book in prospect of a second edition, I
thought it undesirable to make any great changes in its contents or
composition, although I have taken this opportunity of adding a
Supplement to the Introduction (pp. xxxix ff.) devoted to certain
newer discoveries. Some minor corrections have been made in
the text of the Introduction and the Index of Names and Matters,
and a greater number in the excerpts from the *Leet Book*. That
document was not at hand when I made the selections and I was
dependent on transcriptions by others. It is still convenient to
have these quotations available to students, and the same thing
may be said about the contents of Appendix II, " Records and
accounts of the trading companies of Coventry referring to the
Corpus Christi Play." There is collected in that appendix information about the Coventry plays of which the original sources
have perished, namely, from Thomas Sharp's *Dissertation on the
Pageants or Dramatic Mysteries, Anciently performed at Coventry*
(1825), his introduction to the Abbotsford Club edition of the
Weavers' pageant (1836), and from Halliwell-Phillipps's *Outlines of
the Life of Shakespeare*. These books are of course available in
larger libraries, but Dr. Furnivall thought it a good idea to collect
and publish the materials here; for, in spite of heavy losses, the
Coventry records still furnish us with a great part of our knowledge

of how the English religious drama of the Middle Ages was supported, managed and staged.

The *Leet Book* and the manuscript of the *Weavers' Pageant*, along with a relatively few records of guild activities connected with the Corpus Christi play, are in the muniment room at St. Mary's Hall. There was much valuable material about mediaeval Coventry in the Free Public Library, and no doubt in other hands, that was destroyed in the air raid followed by fire on 14 and 15 November 1940.

It will be noticed that historians of literature and great libraries still go calmly forward under the impression that *Ludus Coventriae* and the Coventry plays are one and the same thing.

H. C.

*Columbia, Missouri*
*24 November 1956*

# PREFACE TO FIRST EDITION.

THE appearance of this volume has been delayed first by the addition of appendixes not at first contemplated, but on second thought considered advisable owing to the peculiar value which has been given Sharp's *Dissertation* by the destruction of most of his sources in the burning of the Free Reference Library at Birmingham in 1879; then again by finding, when the work was almost completed, the manuscript of the Weavers' pageant in the possession of its owners the Clothiers and Broad Weavers' Company of Coventry. In issuing this book I wish to thank Prof. John Matthews Manly, to whom I have dedicated the volume without meaning to involve him in any share of its faults, for invaluable instruction when I was beginning the study of these plays, and for his kind permission to print from his text of the Shearmen and Taylors' pageant. I have also to thank Prof. T. W. Hunt and others of my teachers and colleagues at Princeton for kindnesses more or less closely connected with this work. Acknowledgments are due in particular to Miss M. Dormer Harris, who has been good enough to help me with the Coventry manuscripts; Mr. Beard, formerly Town Clerk of Coventry; Mr. Seymour, secretary of the Clothiers and Broad Weavers' Company, and Mr. Brown, at the Free Public Library, have been extremely kind, as has been of course, beautifully and inevitably, Dr. Furnivall.

# CONTENTS.

# INTRODUCTION.

## MANUSCRIPTS AND EDITIONS.

THOMAS SHARP'S first publication of matter relating to the Coventry pageants was in 1817. The thin volume of 28 + 14 pages, large octavo, of which only 12 copies were issued, has the following title-page : *The Pageant of the Sheremen and Taylors, in Coventry, as performed by them on the festival of Corpus Christi ; together with other pageants, exhibited on occasion of several royal visits to that city; and two specimens of ancient local poetry. Coventry—printed by W. Reader,* 1817. The text of the pageant differs but little from that of the better known edition of 1825, which was evidently printed from the same transcript. All variations except in the spelling of insignificant words have been noted in the text of the pageant in the present volume. The remainder of Sharp's book is taken from the *Leet Book,*[1] and is contained in Appendix III., except the two pieces of doggerel which relate to Laurence Saunders.

In 1825 Sharp published his well-known *Dissertation on the Pageants or Dramatic Mysteries, Anciently performed at Coventry, by the Trading Companies of that City.* His book shows that he had before him at that time, besides the *Leet Book* and the manuscript of the Shearmen and Taylors' pageant, the accounts of the cappers, dyers, smiths, and of Trinity and Corpus Christi Guilds, and other less important manuscripts. Sharp's method was the selection of interesting illustrative details and his object a general presentation of the subject of pageants and "dramatic mysteries." He drew for comparison upon almost everything available which concerned English or continental religious drama, though his chief attention was to "the vehicle, characters, and dresses of the Actors." He published here a second edition of the Shearmen and Taylors' pageant, and added also sections relating to Hox Tuesday Play, the pageants exhibited on the occasion of royal visits to Coventry, the

[1] Coventry Corp. MS. A 3.

processions on Corpus Christi day and Midsummer's and St. Peter's eves, and on minstrels and waits. The matters which relate to the Corpus Christi play are made up for the most part of citations from the account books to which Sharp had access. They have been reprinted in Appendix II. of this volume. Sharp's arrangement has been followed and his own words quoted freely wherever he seems to possess information not directly derivable from entries quoted.

In 1836 Sharp edited for the Abbotsford Club *The Presentation in the Temple, a Pageant, as originally represented by the Corporation of Weavers in Coventry.* The manuscript of this Weavers' pageant had, he tells us, been unexpectedly discovered in 1832. To it he prefixed a prefatory notice based upon entries in an apparently newly-discovered book of accounts of the Weavers' Company. He follows the same plan as in the *Dissertation,* and he had gained further information about the location and ownership of pageant-houses which he also includes in the preface. His comments here are also of little value, but all actual information has been included in Appendix II.

The Coventry manuscripts which Sharp used for the *Dissertation* passed into the Staunton Collection at Longbridge House. There Halliwell-Phillips in his *Outlines of the Life of Shakespeare* made a few additional excerpts from them, which I have also copied into Appendix II. Later the manuscripts came into the Free Reference Library at Birmingham, where in 1879 they were destroyed by fire. The last Library catalogue issued before the fire, 1875–7, shows a full list of *Manuscripts relating to Coventry ;* this includes, besides those mentioned above, a good many valuable documents, transcripts, and collections, but not the Weavers' pageant or account-book. It seems to have been taken for granted by students of English miracle plays that the manuscript of the Weavers' pageant was in this collection ; but Halliwell-Phillips nowhere shows that he knew even of the existence of a Weavers' pageant and makes no mention of the weavers' account-book. William Reader's manuscript history of the Guilds of Coventry, now at the Free Public Library in that city, and other documents there, enabled me to find out that the Weavers' Company still exists under the name of the Clothiers and Broad Weavers' Company. The Manuscript was accordingly found in possession of Mr. A. Seymour, the secretary of this company.[1] It is a codex on

---

[1] The MS. is to be placed among the Corporation MSS. in St. Mary's Hall.

parchment in octavo, consisting of 17 folios, one missing, written by Robert Croo in 1534. It is in fair condition, with ancient binding, boards and leather; the names of the speakers, stage-directions (which in this play are of great interest), ornamental connecting lines between verses, are in red ink. Along with this manuscript were two loose leaves in what seems to be a fifteenth-century hand, somewhat earlier than Croo's hand, on paper, torn, illegible in places, but certainly fragments of a purer and presumably an earlier version than Croo's. The account-book used by Sharp (though there was one there from 1636 to 1735, and others later, and a book of rules from 31 H. VI.) was not to be discovered. The fire at Birmingham has made Sharp's books more valuable than they could ever have been had the manuscripts remained; it has therefore seemed worth while, owing to the extent and importance of the information contained in them, to collect in the appendixes of this volume all matter relating to the Coventry Corpus Christi play.

Besides Sharp's two editions of the Shearmen and Taylors' pageant, there is one in William Marriott's *Collection of English Miracle-Plays or Mysteries* (Basel, 1838); this is an exact reprint of Sharp's text. The pageant is also included in the first volume of Prof. John Matthews Manly's *Specimens of the Pre-Shakspearian Drama* (Boston, 1897), where a great deal has been done to rectify the text and metre. Prof. Manly's edition has been the basis of the text in this volume, though it has been carefully compared with the editions of Thomas Sharp. The Weavers' pageant has been published only once since the Abbotsford Club edition; that is, in *Anglia*, Bd. XIII. N.F., pp. 209–50, under the editorship of Prof. F. Holthausen.[1] Prof. Holthausen's edition attempts to rectify the text and metre of the pageant without the aid of the manuscript, at the time of publication not re-discovered.

## THE CYCLE.

The number of Coventry crafts which supported pageants was smaller than at most places, and combination of crafts and union of pageants seem to have characterized the movement. The following act of the Coventry leet was passed in 1445 to determine the order in which the trading companies should ride in the procession on the morning of Corpus Christi day; and it shows the whole number of companies taken into account to have been 17 : " Pur le ridyng on

[1] See also *Beiblatt zur Anglia*, Bd. XIV., p. 65 ff.

Corpus xpi day and for watche on midsomer even : The furst craft,
fysshers and cokes ; baxters and milners ; bochers ; whittawers and
glovers ; pynners, tylers, and wrights ; skynners ; barkers ; corvysers ;
smythes ; wevers ; wirdrawers ; cardemakers, sadelers, peyntours,
and masons ; gurdelers ; taylours, walkers, and sherman ; deysters ;
drapers ; mercers."—*Leet Book*, f. 122. This was doubtless for the
most part an order of precedence already long followed ; it is repeated
in 1447 in this form : *Et quod le ruydyng in festo Corporis Christi
fiat prout ex antiquo tempore conserverint.* The fullers were made a
separate craft in 1447,[1] and there were doubtless other changes ; but
the number was never very large.[2] An order of leet passed in 1449
enumerating the companies (*Leet Book*, 143 a. ff.) shows a slightly
different list : mercers, drapers, dyers, girdlers, tailors and shearmen,
walkers, wiredrawers, corvisers, smiths, fishmongers, whittawers,
butchers, sadlers, cardmakers, masons, skinners, pinners and tilers,
bakers, barbers, wrights, barkers, cooks. Of course a company
usually included several minor crafts whose occupation was more or
less closely connected. The full list of the smiths' fellowship was
smiths, goldsmiths, pewterers, cutlers, and wiredrawers. Something
of the size and nature of the Mercers' Company can be told from
the following memorandum at the end of their book of accounts
beginning in 1578, quoted by Reader[3] with the date 1566 : "For as
much as heretofore every one of the company sold generally com-
modities belonging to the mystery of mercers, linen-drapers, haber-
dashers, grocers, and salters, the charge of which was such that few
or none could furnish the trade ; in consequence whereof the company
is of late greatly decayed. It is enacted that the company shall be
divided into five parts, viz. :—Mercers, 1. ; linen-drapers, 2. ; haber-
dashers, and all kinds of small silk wares, 3. ; grocers and salters,
4. ; all kinds of hats and caps and trimming thereunto, 5."

The cardmakers, sadlers, and ironmongers, and painters (after
1436), and masons (after 1443) were one company ; so also whittawers, glovers, fellmongers, and parchment makers.

Of the companies enumerated above, only ten can be shown to

---

[1] May 3, 1547. It is also enacted that the walkers of this citie shall hensfurthe be a feliship of themselfs, and have libertie to electe and choose maisters
of their company for the good order of the same and mayntenyng of true
clothyng.—*Leet Book*, f. 400.

[2] W. G. Fretton, *Mem. of Fullers' Guild*, Transactions Birm. and Midl.
Inst. 1877, gives it as twenty-three.

[3] History of the Guilds, one of the valuable and little known MSS. by Wm.
Reader at the Free Public Library, Coventry.

have supported pageants; the others were contributory to companies
so charged, or in a few cases were able to evade the duty altogether,
or for long periods at a time. In the list quoted above from the
*Leet Book*, f. 122, the fishers and cooks were contributory to the
smiths' pageant; the baxsters and milners, to the smiths'; the
butchers, to the whittawers'; the whittawers and glovers supported
a pageant; so did the pinners, tylers and wrights; the skinners
contributed to the weavers' pageant; the barkers supported a
pageant, to which the corvisors contributed; the smiths had a
pageant, as did the weavers; the wiredrawers contributed to the
smiths; the cardmakers, sadlers, painters, and masons had a pageant;
as did the girdlers; and the tailors, walkers and shearmen; the
drapers; and the mercers. The dyers seem always to have evaded
the duty of supporting a pageant in spite of several acts of leet [1]
designed to make all crafts contribute equally. Only ten pageants
are mentioned in the *Leet Book* or any other record, and these ten
are mentioned repeatedly.[2] Another piece of evidence to show that
the pageants were ten in number is found in the fact that, upon the
reception of Queen Margaret in 1456,[3] ten pageants are mentioned.
Now in the *Leet Book*, 'pageant' means the vehicle on which the
plays were acted; and ten vehicles were used. Nine were needed
for the Nine Worthies, and one was left over, and stood within the
gate at the east end of Bablake Church.

It seems then certain that there were ten Coventry pageants.
There were also ten original wards in the city;[4] namely, Gosford
Street, Jordan Well, Much Park Street, Bayley Lane, Earl Street,
Broad Gate, Smithford Street, Spon Street, Cross Cheaping, and
Bishop Street. A good many stations where the plays were acted
are mentioned in the records, and these stations seem all to be in
different wards; so it seems possible that the ten pageants were
wont to be acted at ten stations, one station in each of the ten
wards. Gosford Street was the first ward in point of precedence,

[1] The act printed on pages 75 and 76 mentions the dyers, skinners, fishmongers, cappers, corvisers, and butchers as not bearing their due share of the
charges of maintaining the pageants.
[2] Most of the pageant-houses, too, can be located. Reader places the whittawers' pageant-house in Hill Street, and the mercers' and drapers' in Gosford
Street. The weavers had a pageant-house in Mill Lane, as did the shearmen
and taylors (see p. 108) and the cappers (p. 98).
[3] See Appendix III.
[4] This was sometimes increased to eleven (once twelve) wards in town
representation caused by the splitting up of one ward or another into two.

and it is known to have been the first station of the smiths' pageant.[1]
Jordan Well ward probably had its station at Jordan Well; for
upon the visit of Henry VIII.[2] a pageant was set at Jordan Well
with nine orders of angels. Much Park Street ward seems to have
had a station at New Gate; Much Park Street end is also mentioned,
but New Gate stood at one end of Much Park Street.[3] If there
was a station in Bayley Lane ward, it was probably somewhere near
St. Michael's Church. Earl Street ward had a station at Little Park
Street end, on Earl Street, as there are two mentions of the house
of Richard Woods, a grocer who lived in Earl Street. Queen
Margaret lodged there and saw the plays, and the smiths' accounts
show an expenditure for ale "at Richard Woodes dur."[4] Broad
Gate ward probably had a station at Grey Friars' Church; Henry
VII. saw the pageants there in 1492.[5] The most probable place for
a station in Smithford Street ward is the conduit which at the
reception of Queen Margaret was well arrayed and showed four
speeches of four cardinal virtues.[6] Spon Street ward had its station
probably at Bablake Gate (St. John's Church). Cross Cheaping
ward had its station certainly at the cross in Cross Cheaping. And
Bishop's Street ward (called also Well Street ward) may have had
a station near the ancient hospital of St. John the Evangelist.

The pageants were few in number as compared to other known
cycles, and each pageant seems to have had a whole group of
subjects. The two which have been preserved and are published
here show this, as do the accounts of the smiths' and cappers'
companies published in Appendix II. This grouping of subjects
probably characterized the whole cycle. In the following table I
have attempted in a general way to restore the cycle. In making
up the list of probable subjects I have been guided on grounds of
general relationship by the York (Beverley) and Towneley Cycles
and the Hereford list of pageants in the Corpus Christi procession;[7]
rather than by Chester or *Ludus Coventriae.* For reasons which
will appear later only New Testament subjects are considered:

[1] See pp. 84–5.    [2] See MS. Annals below.    [3] See pp. 84–5.
[4] At the visit of Queen Elizabeth (see MS. Annals below) the smiths'
pageant stood at Little Park Street end; see also pp. 74 and 84–5.
[5] *Qy.* 1493.    [6] See p. 111.
[7] *Hist. MSS. Comm.* 13th Rep. pt. iv., p. 288.

| Subjects. | Crafts. | Contributory and Associated Crafts. |
|---|---|---|
| Annunciation. Visit to Elizabeth. Joseph's Trouble. Journey to Bethlehem and Nativity. Shepherds. Kings of Cologne. Flight into Egypt. Slaughter of Innocents. | Shearmen and Taylors (and walkers until 1447). | |
| Purification. Doctors. | Weavers. | Skinners, walkers. |
| Baptism of Christ. Temptation. Raising of Lazarus. Entry into Jerusalem. | (?) | |
| Conspiracy of the Jews. Bargain with Judas. Last Supper. Agony in the Garden. Betrayal and Capture. | (?) | |
| Before High Priest. Denial. Before Pilate. Pilate's Wife. Before Herod. Second trial before Pilate. Repentance of Judas.[1] Way to Calvary. Parting of Garments. Crucifixion. | Smiths. | Cooks and fishers, bakers, millers, chandlers, and wire-drawers. |
| Mortificatio Christi (?). Burial. | Pinners and Needlers. | Tylers, wrights, cowpers, carpenters; bowyers and fletchers. |
| Descent into Hell. Setting the Watch. Resurrection. Amazement of Soldiers, etc. Peter and John before Tomb (?). Appearance to Mary Magdalen. Appearance to Travellers.[2] | Cappers (cardmakers until 1531). | Painters and masons; walkers, skinners, joiners, cardmakers. |
| Appearance to Disciples. Doubting Thomas. Ascension. Pentecost. | (?) | |
| Death and Assumption of Mary. Appearance of Mary to Thomas. | Mercers. | Cappers. |
| Doomsday. | Drapers. | |

[1] See page 90.  [2] See page 94.

The subjects of the smiths', cappers', and drapers' pageants can be told from the records preserved in Sharp; the pinners' from a document quoted by him, the rules and orders of the company, which speak of their pageant called the "Taking down of God from the Cross."[1]   One of the reasons for assigning the Assumption group of subjects to the mercers is, besides the importance of the subject[2] and the priority of that craft, the fact that when the Princess Mary came to Coventry in 1525 she saw "the mercers' pageant play being finely drest in the Cross Cheeping."[3]   This, although a mere agreement of names, carries some weight when we compare it with the special exhibitions provided for the entertainment of Margaret, Edward, and Arthur.   Besides this, and more important, is the fact that the mercers' seems to have been a fraternity in honour of the Assumption.   Their arms, the same as those of the Mercers' Company in London, which may still be seen painted on a wall in the mercers' room in St. Mary's Hall, Coventry, are—gules, a demy Virgin Mary with her hair disheveled crowned, rising out and within an orb of clouds, all proper; motto, *Honor Deo*.   St. Mary's Guild, or the Merchants' Guild, founded in 1340, had annual meetings in St. Mary's Hall, at the feast of the Assumption.   St. Mary's, St. John Baptist's, St. Katharine's, and Trinity Guild were formally united in 1392; and they seem, with the Guild of Corpus Christi, always closely associated and finally united with the amalgamated guild in 1534, to have been from the beginning in control of the mercers and drapers.[4]   After the union of guilds there appear in 1539 in the Corpus Christi accounts[5] entries of expenses on Corpus Christi day and evening which indicate a pageant of the Assumption in the Corpus Christi procession.   The entries are: first, among several entries for food, *peny bred for the apostells vj. d., beiff for the appostles viij. d.*; then, *to the Marie for hir gloves and wages ij. s., for beryng the crosse and candelsticks the even and the day viij. d., to the Mr. to offer xij. d., the Marie to offer j. d., Katharine and Margaret iiij. d., viij. virgyns viij. d., to Gabriell for beryng the lilly iiij. d., to James*

[1] See Appendix II., p. 103.

[2] There is every evidence of a devoted worship of the Virgin at Coventry; St. Mary's Hall and the Cathedral were both named in her honour.

[3] If this was, as seems probable, a presentation of the regular mercers' play, it is also possible that in the four pageants set forth in honour of Queen Elizabeth the regular plays of the crafts were enacted, since nothing is said in the Annals to indicate that these pageants had anything else set upon them; see MS. Annals below.

[4] M. D. Harris, *Life in an Old English Town* (Lond. 1898), Chs. 7 and 13.

[5] Quoted by Sharp, p. 162; *Coventry Corp. MS.*, A. 6.

*and Thomas of Inde viij. d., to x. other apostells xx. d.* (1541, *xij. torches of wax for the apostles*). With these entries are also to be connected the following items from an inventory of jewels 1493 in the same MS. (f. 53): *a girdull of blue silk harnest with silver and gilt weyng cord and all iiij. unc. et dim., a girdull of rede silk harnest with silver and gilt weying cord and all vi. unc. iii. qrt.* These last entries and several others about payments and properties for the Mary on Corpus Christi day prior to 1534 seem to indicate that the presentation of the Assumption in the Corpus Christi procession had been controlled by the Corpus Christi guild even before the union of the guilds; but the connection with the mercers' company would not in any way be affected.

Two other facts are also to be brought into this connection:

The Smiths provided that Herod, the chief character in their pageant, should ride in the Corpus Christi procession, a circumstance which may indicate that other companies did a similar thing. Then it is to be remembered that the Shearmen and Taylors', as the guild of the Nativity, presented an appropriate subject. More will be said about their relation to the fullers later; at present it may be noted that their seal, impressions of which are still in existence, was (according to Fretton) round, about an inch and a half in diameter, of brass, representing the Virgin Mary seated and crowned with the infant Christ in her lap, receiving gifts of the three Kings of Cologne. These two circumstances might offer clues for the determination of the names of other pageants, if more were known about the Corpus Christi procession, and more of the patron saints of the different companies could be determined.

At any rate, we see that, out of ten pageants, the subjects of six can be told with certainty, and of another, the mercers', with some probability. This leaves three companies, tanners, whittawers and girdlers, the subjects of whose pageants are unknown. An examination of the table will show, however, three important groups of subjects unprovided for. First, there is John the Baptist. The popularity of this saint in Coventry was such that it may be taken as probable that there was a play upon this subject in the Coventry cycle. What other subjects may have been grouped with it is still more a matter of guess; but the four, or some of them, which succeed it in the list are the more probable. It is perhaps too slight a thread to connect the tanners with the subject, because their pageant stood before the Church of St. John the Baptist, and perhaps performed

B

the craft play there, when Queen Elizabeth visited the city. Secondly, the Last Supper is a most probable subject, inasmuch as no known cycle of plays is without it. It could hardly have been a part of the already over-crowded smiths' pageant, and it would certainly have been a part of any Corpus Christi cycle. Then, finally, there is a group of subjects centering in the Ascension, which is also of universal occurrence and would hardly have failed to appear at Coventry.

It will be noticed that this leaves no room for any Old Testament plays at Coventry, a characteristic which would be exceptional. Of course one of the unknown pageants may have been upon such a subject; but one hardly sees in the circumstances how it could have been. The following explanation may solve the difficulty. The Coventry plays in existence, except the Doctors' play, evidently grew up bit by bit with little influence from the outside. The Shearmen and Taylors' pageant and the first part of the Weavers' pageant, the Purification, are mosaics of different metres and hands, and show evidence of having undergone a course of amplification extending through a long period of time. It is still possible, as we shall see later, to discover in each of the three stories the traces of an earlier form, a complete outline, with all essential features, of a very early play. The peculiarity which may account for the absence of Old Testament plays is that the prophet plays and prologues in the two pageants preserved, which are probably the first two in the cycle, contain the outline of a *Processus Prophetarum.* Isaiah is the prologue to the Shearmen and Taylors' pageant, and two other prophets enter at line 332 between the parts of the play.[1] There is no way of identifying these prophets, but the allusions in their speeches correspond in a rough way to the parts usually given to Moses, and there is a reference to David (l. 396) and to Habakkuk (ll. 460-2).[2] The Weavers' pageant is also introduced by a prophet play, and here we have to do with Balaam, Jeremiah, and Malachi (ll. 23, 58, 68). Finally, Simeon refers to the Sibyl (l. 197) and to Daniel (ll. 204, 244). In other words, those familiar Latin quotations, ultimately derived from the Augustinian sermon [3] which is the basis of the *Processus Prophetarum,* appear or are alluded to in the two plays preserved. Besides that, other lost plays appear from the

---

[1] See below.
[2] Note also the reference to Adam, line 20 ff.
[3] Sepet, *Les prophetes du Christ,* Paris, 1878.

records to have had prologues and prophets.[1]  It looks very much
as if the *Processus Prophetarum* had never been developed at
Coventry, so that the prophets did not make their formal speeches
by name as at other places.  At York the play of the Prophets has
been rewritten and so modified that it appears as a prologue to
the Nativity (XII).  In the Towneley cycle, there are several Old
Testament plays, some of which may belong to an original cycle
back of York and Wakefield.  The prophet-play itself, incomplete
as preserved,[2] was an independent play.  The fifth Chester play
shows the *Processus Prophetarum* in a transition stage, with the
Balaam and Balak play formed in the midst of it.[3]  The prophecies
of Octavian and the Sibyl occur in the midst of the Nativity play
(VI), a thing which still further bears out the theory of the origin;
since Zachariah and Elizabeth, the proper node for the growth of
the Annunciation and the Visit of Mary to Elizabeth, occur in the
regular scheme of the prophet-play before the Sibyl and Caesar
Augustus.  There is nothing, then, inconsistent in believing, since
at other places there are such wide differences, that at Coventry the
Old Testament plays never developed at all.

## DUGDALE AND THE MANUSCRIPT ANNALS.

Dugdale is the earliest authority for the belief that the Coventry
Corpus Christi play told the story of both Old and New Testaments.
In order to understand his error it is necessary to consider first a
reference to the plays in several more or less trustworthy lists of
Coventry mayors with annals, some of them still in manuscript.
The annals have some bearing on the plays in general, so it is well to
transcribe all of the references which they contain to the Corpus
Christi play.

There are at least four of these books of annals still to be found
in manuscript.  Two, A. 26 and A. 43, are among the Corporation
Manuscripts at Coventry.  Neither is of very great age, and both
contain pretty much the same matter.  A. 26 has more references to
pageants, and it, with Harl. 6388, have been used as a basis for the

---

[1] Adam and Eve and probably other Old Testament characters were in the
cappers' pageant and would appear always in the Descent into Hell ; what use
was made of the three patriarchs in Doomsday is more puzzling. See Appendix II.,
where the three patriarchs, Jacob's twelve sons and the Children of Israel are
seen to have been represented at the reception of Prince Edward.

[2] *Towneley Plays*, p. 64.

[3] See J. M. Manly, *Specimens Pre-Shak. Drama*, vol. i., introduction, p.
xxvii ff.

following collation. There are two also at the British Museum, Harl. 6388, and an octavo manuscript, presented by Mr. Joseph Gibbs, 11346 Plut. CXLII. A., which is of no great value as regards the pageants. Harl. 6388 was written by Humfrey Wanley, and bears the date Dec. 17th, 1690. He says: "This book was taken out of manuscripts, the one written by Mr. Cristofer Owen Mayor of this citty which contains the charter of Walter de Coventre concerning the commons *etc.* to Godfrey Leg Mayor 1637, the other beginning at the 36 mayor of this citty and continued by several hands and lately by Edmund Palmer late of this citty, Counsellor, till Mr. Yardly late Mayor $\begin{Bmatrix}1689, \\ 1690,\end{Bmatrix}$ and another written by Mr. Bedford and collected out of divers others and continued to Mr. Septimius Bott. And two other collected by Tho. Potter and continued to Mr. Robert Blake, and another written by Mr. Francis Barnett, to the first year of Mr. Jelliffs Majoralty, and another written by Mr. Abraham Astley, and continued to Mr. Sept. Bott, and another written by Mr. Abraham Boune to Humfrey Wrightwick, 1607." Wanley dates his list one year too late. In Dugdale's *Warwickshire* (1656) there is also a list of Mayors of Coventry; in the second edition, revised by William Thomas (1730), pp. 147–54, it appears with the following heading, the parts in square brackets being by Thomas : "I will here subjoin a catalogue (Ex Catal. Majorum penes praefat. *Joh. Hales*) of the Mayors thereof [which I have carefully compared with another Manuscript Catalogue of them which is wrought in a brown leather cover, *penes*, and with that lately published by Mr. *Hearne* at the End of his Edition of Fordun's Scotichronicon which was printed from a Manuscript communicated to him by Mr. *Tho. Jesson*, A. M. et Aed. Christi apud Oxon. Cap]." Sharp quotes *MS. Annals* and *Codex Hales*, and there was at least one copy of annals in the Birmingham Free Reference Library at the time of the fire, so that Sharp may represent an original. In Poole's *Coventry* (London, 1870) there is a list of mayors without annals. Many of the annals are contradictory in date; in the following list the dates are from Dugdale, who seems to be fairly correct :—

S. p. 8: *MS. Ann., Anno* 1416 4. Hen. V. The Pageants and Hox tuesday invented, wherein the King and Nobles took great delight.

Harl. 6388: Sir Robert Onley, merchant, Mayor, 1485[4]. At Whitsontide King Richard the 3d came to Kenilworth and at Corpus Christi came to Coventre to see the plaies.

Cov. Corp. MS., A. 26 : Thos. Bailey, Mayor, 1486. The King [Henry VII.] came to Coventry to see our plays, and lodged at Rob. Onely's house in Smithford Street before the conduit.[1]

Corp. MS., A. 26 : John Wigston, Mayor, 1490. This year was the play of St. Katharine in the Little Park.

Corp. MS., A. 26 : Thomas Churchman, bucklemaker, Mayor, 1492.[2] This year the King and Queen came to Kenilworth; from thence they came to Coventry to see our plays at Corpus Christitide and gave them great commendation.[3] Harl. 6388 : The King and Queen came to see the playes at the greyfriers and much commended them. Dugdale : In his Mayoralty K. H. 7. came to see the plays acted by the *Grey Friers*, and much commended them.[4]

Corp. MS., A. 26 : John Dadsbury, Mayor, 1504. In his year was the play of St. Christian[5] played in the Little Park.

Harl. 6388 : Richard Smith, merchant, Mayor, 1508[7]. He made the bakers pay to the smiths 13s. 4d. towards prest and pageants.

Corp. MS., A. 26 : John Strong, mercer, Mayor, 1510[1]. In this year King Henry [VIII.] and the Queen came to Coventry. . . . Then were 3 pageants set forth, one at Jordan Well with 9 orders of Angells, another at Broad gate with divers beautifull damsells, another at the Cross Cheeping with a goodly stage play.[6]

S. p. 11 : *MS. Ann.*, 1519. New Plays at Corpus xpityde which were greatly commended. S. p. 11 : *id. Codex Hales*, 1519–20. In that year was new playes at Corpus Christityd which playes were greatly commended.[7]

Corp. MS., A. 26 : Henry Wall, weaver, Mayor, 1526.[8] The Princess Mary came to Coventry and was presented with an 100 marks and a kercher, and see the mercers pageant play being finely drest in the Cross Cheeping and lay at the Priory.[9]

S. p. 11 : *MS. Annals*, 1561. This year was Hox tuesday put down.

Corp. MS., A. 26 : Edmund Brownell, Mayor, 1567. The Queen came to this city. The tanners pageant stood at St. Johns Church,

---

[1] In Harl. 6388 and A. 43.         [2] *Qy*. 1493.
[3] So A. 43.                         [4] So 11364 Plut. CXLII. A.
[5] S. St. Crytyan.  Both evidently mistakes for St. Katharine.
[6] All sources have this entry.
[7] S. says that he found nothing in the accounts to corroborate this.  The entries probably refer to the same year.         [8] Dugdale, 1525.
[9] 11364, Plut. CXLII. A. agrees with this.  Harl. 6388 has, *the Mercers* (*majors*) *Pageant was gallantly trimmed*, etc.  S. agrees with Harl. 6388.

the Drapers pageant at the cross, the smiths pageant at Little Park Street end, and the Weavers pageant at Much Park Street.[1]

Harl. 6388: Henry Kerwin, mercer, Mayor, 1568[7]. The Pageants and Hox Tewsday played.

S. p. 12: *MS. Annals*, 1575. This year the Pageants or Hox tuesday that had been laid down 8 years were played again.

Harl. 6388: Thomas Saunders, butcher, Mayor, 1580[79]. The pageants laid down.[2]

The item for the year 1492 gave rise to the impression in Sharp's mind, and in Dugdale's too in all probability, that there were plays in Coventry acted by the grey friars. The idea of plays acted by a religious brotherhood at so late a time, if ever, would probably have to be given up upon other grounds ; but in this case it is easy to see that we have to do with a misunderstanding. " By the grey-friers " need not mean agency ; but may mean " at the Grey-friers' Church," *the grey-friers* being the common way of indicating the church. At any rate Wanley says, in Harl. 6388, "to see the playes at the grey-friers," which, seeing the list of manuscripts from which he compiled, is more apt to be an ancient reading than the other which Sharp speaks of as a "solitary mention in one MS. (not older than the beginning of Cha. I.'s reign)." Dugdale probably had this entry to start him wrong, and the manuscript of *Ludus Coventriae* to confirm the error, the information gathered from " old people " being too vague to be definite as to who the actors were. Dugdale, writing of the *Gray Friers* of Coventry, says :[3] " Before the suppression of the Monasteries, this City was very famous for the *Pageants* that were played therein, upon *Corpus Christi* day ; which occasioning very great confluence of people thither from far and near, was of no small benefit thereto ; which *Pageants* being acted with mighty state and reverence by the Friers of this House, had Theaters for the severall Scenes, very large and high, placed upon wheels, and drawn to all the eminent parts of the City, for the better advantage of Spectators : And contain'd the story of the [Old and][4] New Testament, composed into old English Rithme, as appeareth by an antient *MS.* (In Bibl.

---

[1] So A. 43 ; quoted also in *S.* and in Fordun's *Scotichronicon*. *S.* mentions a charge in the books of the Smiths' Company for painting and gilding many pageant vehicles on the occasion of the Queen's visit.

[2] So 11364 Plut. CXLII. A. *S.* has, *again laid down*.

[3] *Antiq. of Warwickshire*, by Sir William Dugdale, 2nd *Ed.* rev. *etc.* by William Thomas, D.D. London : 1730, vol. i. p. 183.

[4] Not bracketed in first edition (1656). The passages do not differ otherwise in 1st and 2nd eds.

*Cotton.* sub effigie Vesp. D. 9 (8).) intituled *Ludus Corporis Christi*, or *Ludus Coventriae.*

" I have been told by some old people, who in their younger years were eye witnesses of these *Pageants* so acted, that the yearly confluence of people to see that show was extraordinary great, and yielded no small advantage to this City."

There would certainly have been a station where the pageants were acted at the Grey Friars Church, and there King Henry VII. and his Queen saw the pageants, just as Queen Margaret had seen them at a station in Earl Street. Reference has already been made to the performance of " the Mercers pageant play " in honour of Princess Mary, and the only other important entry is the one about the reception of Queen Elizabeth in 1567. It seems possible that the pageants put forth then had their own plays, or something connected with them, since no mention is made of any special pageant.

### THE NATIVITY, THE THREE KINGS OF COLOGNE, AND THE PRESENTATION IN THE TEMPLE.

The Shearmen and Taylors' pageant is made up of two very well developed plays. The subject of the first is the Annunciation, the Nativity, and the Shepherds; it ends with line 331. Then comes a dialogue between three Prophets which belongs rather to the succeeding play than to the one before, if one may judge by the very similar dialogue prefixed to the Weavers' pageant; since there the dialogue rehearses the events of the Visit of the Kings which immediately precedes it in the cycle just as this reviews the Shepherds' play which it follows here. The second play, which begins at line 475, treats of the Visit of the Kings, the Flight into Egypt, and the Slaughter of the Innocents. The second is longer and more elaborately developed than the first, a thing no doubt resulting from the evident popularity of its subject at Coventry. Two crafts have apparently been united and their pageants acted one after another. There is no direct evidence for such a union in any of the records; but at the very first there may be a trace of it. The Shearmen and Taylors' Guild, the Guild of the Nativity, called also St. George's Guild, was established by licence in the reign of Richard II. In 1392 there is a mention of the "tailour pageant howse", and before the formation of the Shearmen and Taylors' Guild, the tailors and the shearmen, whose occupation was not at that time separate from that of the fullers, may each have had a pageant of their own. More than this, there is reason to connect the shearmen (and fullers), but not the tailors, in particular with the visit of the Kings; for when fulling had become a separate occupation from cloth-shearing, and the fullers had formed a company of their own, the fullers were granted in 1439 the privilege of using a common seal with the shearmen.[1] This seal before referred to may perhaps be taken to be the original property of the shearmen.[2] It represented the Virgin Mary seated and crowned with the infant Christ in her lap, receiving gifts from the Magi. The inscription in capital letters round the margin, according to Fretton,[3] is, *sigillu' co'e scissor*[4] *fullonii' frat'nitat' gilde nati'utat' d'ni de Coventre*.

The Shearmen and Taylors' pageant was probably very old at Coventry, and in its earlier stages was of course very much shorter and simpler than it is now. Its variety of metres and its mixed character generally are due to many additions and revisions, made during the two hundred years or more preceding the final " correction" by Robert Croo in 1534. It is possible to see in it a very much earlier stage in the development of pageants than at first sight it would seem to represent. The substance of the pageant (most of what is essential to the story and, presumably, oldest) is contained in the octosyllabic quatrains scattered throughout the play; these quatrains, it will also be noticed, contain a great many archaic words. Some of the quatrains are doubtless late, and some of the parts of the original story are now told in other metres, but in general this is not the case. The Presentation in the Temple (Weavers' Pageant (WCo), ll. 1–721), which may not have been an original Coventry play, shows also the bare outline of a story in quatrains, a fact which bears further testimony to the existence of an early cycle, or part of a cycle, in this form.

The Nativity (Shearmen and Taylors' Pageant (STCo), ll. 2–331) has the following passages in quatrains: ll. 47–54, 55–8 (?), 68–99, 168–203, 278–81, 293–6, 303–6, 321–4.

---

[1] W. G. Fretton, *Memorials of Fullers' Guild, Coventry*, Birm. and Midl. Inst. Transactions, 1877.

[2] The arms of the Shearmen and Taylors' Company, which would be appropriate, though they may or may not be the original tailors' arms, are, as given by Reader: Argent tent royal, between two parliament robes gules, lined ermine, on a chief azure a lion of England. Crest a holy lamb in glory proper holding a flag. Supporters, two camels or. Motto: *Concordia parvae res crescunt*.

[3] *Loc. cit.* p. 44.

[4] *Scissor* seems to have meant shearman, cp. Du Cange, *Glos. Med. et Inf. Lat.* sub *scissor*.

The Three Kings of Cologne (STCo, ll. 475–900) : 521–4, 529–32, 540–7, 548–51 (?), 558–73, 582–9, 632–43, 652–5, 670–3, 680–4, 699–704 (?), 705–24, 733–44, 793–800, 802–13, 818–21 (?), 826–46, 884–91.

The Presentation in the Temple (WCo, ll. 177–721) : 314–7 (?), 367–70,[1] 383–6, 387–90 (?), 459–462, 479–82, 506–21,[2] 546–9, 557–64, 581–84, 593–602 (?), 611–4, 615–8 (?), 621–40, 641–4 (?), 657–60, 661–4, 670–3 (?), 695–7, 705–8, 709–12 (?).

The next most significant metre in these plays, though not necessarily older than the seven-line strophe of the longer speeches spoken of later, is a more or less successful attempt to conform to the riming scheme of the familiar eight-line stanza much used in the Chester Whitsun Plays.[3] It rimes *aaabaaab*, or *aaabcccb*, and has four accents to the line, except the fourth and eighth, which have three. Throughout the plays the passages written in Chester metre offer in general clear readings, and although this metrical scheme is used to corrupt every other variety of metre used, the passages written in it seem to be frequently uninterrupted. Moreover it is interesting to note that many of the most humorous parts of the plays, including most of the Shepherds' play, some of the Visit of the Kings, and nearly all of the dove episode in the Presentation in the Temple, besides a majority of the excrescences of story, the incidents and inessential speeches, are either in pure or approximate Chester metre. The natural inference is that one of the most thorough redactions these plays have ever had, and it must be added the only one of any spirit or excellence, was characterized by the use of the eight-line stanza, or an approximation to it in the use of the linking rimes. The passages which are written in this metre, or which show the influence of it, are :

The Nativity : ll. 17–36, 100–55, 160–7, 204–77, 297–302 (?), 325–31 (?).

The Three Kings of Cologne : ll. 574–81, 603–9, 611–21 (?), 622–31, 656–704, 725–32, 750–92, 818–25 (?), 847–69, 892–900 (?).

The Presentation in the Temple : ll. 314–34, 342–66, 371–82, 397–478, 481–505, 522–45, 565–80, 585–610,[2] 641–56, 661–94, 698–721.

The third metrical form is a seven-line stanza riming *ababbcc*.[4]

---

[1] Borrowed from STCo, 47–50.
[2] Manifestly new.
[3] Schipper, *Eng. Met.* I., § 154.
[4] Schipper, *loc. cit.*, § 171.

This is of two sorts. The first, *rime royal*, has five beats to the line, and is used for the opening speeches of Isaiah (STCo, ll. 1–14), Herod (*id.*, ll. 486–520), Simeon (WCo, ll. 177–204, 205–18 (?)) and Anna (*id.*, ll. 219–32).[1] The other seven-line stanza has the same riming scheme, but has usually only four beats to the line. In both, the rime of the final couplet is continued in the first and third lines of the succeeding strophe; three riming lines are thus thrown together, a circumstance which has no doubt rendered the metre liable to misunderstanding and corruption. The second variety of seven-line stanza has been very extensively used in the Presentation in the Temple and in the Doctors' Play which succeeds it, and rather scantily in STCo. It seems to have been corrupted in places by the Chester metre, which may indicate that it is older in the cycle than the passages in the Chester form.[2] It is noticeable that the Chester metre seems to make its appearance in the fragments of another probably earlier version of WCo.[3] The parts of the plays remaining in the seven-line stanza of four beats, though traces of it no doubt appear at other places, are :

The Nativity : ll. 307–20.

The Three Kings of Cologne : ll. 533–9, 870–83.

The Presentation in the Temple : ll. 233–60, 272–313, 335–41, 550–6.

### THE PROPHET PLAYS AND THE DOCTORS' PLAY.

It is impossible to make out anything like a consistent scheme in the metre of the Prophet play in STCo (ll. 332–474). Prof. Manly has broken up the long lines in Sharp, doubtless copied from Croo, since Sharp follows Croo very closely in transcribing WCo, into the short doggerel lines in which it was probably composed. The octosyllabic seven-line stanza was the original form of the Prophet play in WCo (ll. 1–176); but it is doubtful if some of the speeches of the second prophet (ll. 15–18, 46–9 (?), 75–8, 106–9), who is at first a sort of interlocutor, were ever in the regular strophe. The corruption which appears at ll. 46–50 is perhaps an attempt to conform to the Chester strophe. This metre makes its unmistakable appearance in ll. 110–76; the passage is evidently newer matter, telling as it does about the wonderful star upon the hill of Wawse,[4]

---

[1] The fragments show more of it; see below.
[2] See below.    [3] See Appendix IV., ll. 46–53.
[4] See *The Three Kings of Cologne*, E.E.T.S., Orig. Ser. No. 85, pp. 6 ff, 213 ff.

and rehearsing the events of the Visit of the Kings which it followed in the cycle.   This passage, besides being a parallel to the Prophet play in STCo, which tells the events of its preceding Shepherds' play, is also very irregular in metre and falls into the same doggerel which characterizes the Prophet play in STCo.[1]   This part and that play I should take to be from the same hand.

The Doctors' play (WCo, ll. 722–1192) also shows a mixture of metres.   The first three stanzas (ll. 722–45) are double quatrains perhaps composed in imitation of the first eight lines of the York twelve-line strophe in which the body of the play was composed, if not originally a part of the parent play.   Then comes one suspiciously modern sounding seven-line strophe (ll. 747–53), followed by a characteristic comic passage in Chester metre extending to line 815, where the parallel with the other Doctors' plays begins.[2]   From this point the play is in octosyllabic alternately riming stanzas of four to eight lines, based upon the northern twelve-line strophe, the hexasyllabic *caudae* having been lengthened throughout to four feet, except line 964.   The discourse of the doctors (ll. 857–84) is in the seven-line strophe and is similar in kind to the Prophet play and other passages earlier in the plays.   There are some metrical irregularities in the recital of the commandments, but its basis seems to be the northern strophe as is the case with the body of the play.   This is interesting because the other versions of the Doctors' play show still greater irregularity at this point.   The expanded leave-taking scene (ll. 1089–1145) is in Chester metre, which also appears in the final dialogue of the doctors (ll. 1146–92) probably originally composed in the seven-line form.   The importation of the Doctors' play cannot have been a very recent thing since both metres, the Chester metre and the seven-line strophe, appear in it.

The fact that the Chester metre seems always to be the disrupting, interpolating element has led me to think that the passages written in it are probably more recent than those written in the seven-line strophe, a conclusion somewhat strengthened by the fact that the parts in the latter variety are more dignified, conventional and pedantic, and therefore probably older.   Both metres were, however, in common use in the fifteenth century, and the statement that the seven-line stanza is the older would probably be true only of the bulk of the matter in each form.[3]

[1] See ll. 128–46.          [2] See below.
[3] Note the use of the seven-line stanza and the conventional style in the Pageants on Special Occasions published in Appendix III.

## THE FOUR PARALLEL VERSIONS OF THE DOCTORS' PLAY.

The Disputation in the Temple (WCo), which begins with line 722, is particularly interesting because the same play occurs with variations in the York Corpus Christi Cycle[1] XX (Y), in the Towneley Plays[2] XVIII (T), and in the Chester Whitsun Cycle[3] XI (Ch).

This agreement is mentioned by ten Brink,[4] and is the subject of a letter by Dr. Chas. Davidson to *Modern Language Notes,*[5] and of a chapter in his *Studies in the English Mystery Plays.*[6]

Dr. A. R. Hohlfeld,[7] Dr. Charles Davidson,[8] and A. W. Pollard, Esq.,[9] agree with ten Brink that the original doctors' play was of Northumberland origin, and probably grew up at York. It is evident for many reasons, corruptions, dialect, *etc.,* that neither Ch nor WCo could have been the original for Y and T. Moreover, Y in its present form cannot have been copied; for in many cases T and one of the other plays preserve better readings than those of Y. On the other hand, Y is often nearer the original than T is; hence an earlier play than either Y or T, as they now exist, must have been copied by Ch and WCo. Dr. Hohlfeld[10] found the facts derived from a comparison of Y, T and Ch insufficient to indicate definitely the source of Ch; but he saw, other agreements between the cycles taken into consideration, probability of closer kinship between Ch and T than between Ch and Y. Davidson,[11] whose study was of all four of the texts, was of the opinion that Ch was borrowed from the Coventry cycle. The questions, then, which a further study may help to solve are: Is WCo more closely related to Y or to T? and are, as Dr. Davidson stated, Ch and WCo interdependent?

The Disputation in the Temple in WCo is much longer and more detailed in story than is any other version of the play. It begins (l. 722) with the preparation by Joseph and Mary for the trip to Jerusalem and not with Mary's discovery that Jesus is

---

[1] *York Mystery Plays,* ed. Lucy Toulmin Smith, Oxford, 1885.
[2] *The Towneley Plays,* pub. E.E.T.S., Lond. 1897.
[3] *The Chester Plays,* Pt. I., pub. E.E.T.S., Lond. 1892; *Chester Mysteries,* ed. Thos. Wright for Shak. Soc., 1843-7.
[4] *Hist. Eng. Lit.* Eng. Ed. vol. ii. p. 281.
[5] Vol. vii. p. 92-3. See also *id.* (A. R. Hohlfeld), pp. 154-5.
[6] Doct. Diss. Yale, 1892.
[7] *Die altenglischen Kollektiv-misterien, etc.,* Anglia, vol. xi. pp. 219-310.
[8] *Loc. cit.* p. 281.    [9] *Towneley Plays,* Introduction, pp. xv.-xxi.
[10] *Kollektiv-mist.* loc. cit. pp. 260-7.    [11] *Loc. cit.* p. 167.

missing, as do Y and Ch.[1] After the preparation for the trip to
Jerusalem and the journey itself (722–814) have been represented
in the play, the parallel with Y and Ch begins with a speech of
Joseph (l. 815); the agreement, however, is almost never word for
word. In the following list of correspondences the comment refers
in each case to the agreement last cited:

WCo 817–18, Y 3–4, Ch 219–20.

Y reads, *Of solempne sightis that we haue sene | In that cite were
we come froo;* WCo in substantial agreement has, *With these solam
syghtys thatt we haue seyne | In yondur tempull that we cam froo;*
Ch perhaps introduces the first of its references to experiences and
dangers of travel in the words, *of fearly sightes that we have sene, |
sith we came the Citie froe.*

WCo 819,     Y 5,     Ch 221.
„     820,     „  6.
„     821–2,  „  7–8.
„     823,     „  9,     Ch 223, 228.

Ch 221–8, which corresponds to Y 5–12 and WCo 819–26, is very
much confused as to order, *etc.* On this and similar instances, see
Hohlfeld, *Kollektiv-mist.* loc. cit. pp. 264–5. Y 9, *Hamward I rede we
hye* becomes in WCo 823, *Then homwarde, Mare, lett vs goo.* *Goo* is
substituted for the northern word *hye*, which the rime *cumpany* (l. 825)
shows was original. Ch repeats this line, on which see Hohlfeld as
above, where the repetition is accounted for by oral borrowing.

WCo 824–8, Y 10–4, Ch 225–7.

Ch here shows a decided divergence in story. WCo has
expanded the idea in Y that company upon the journey is
desirable, but Ch has gone far in the other direction. Instead of
having Joseph urge Mary to make haste in order that the way
may be shortened with good company, as he does in Y and
WCo, Ch has (ll. 225–8), [MARIA.] *In all the might euer we
may | for dread of wicked company | lest anie us mete upon the
way, | Homeward therefore, I red we hye.*

WCo 830–6,     Y 20–6.
„     837,     „  37.
„     840–2,     „  30–2.
„     844–8,     „  40–4.
„     852,     „  39.
„     857–84,     „  49–72,     T 1–48.

[1] On the defect in T, see Holhfeld, *Kollektiv-mist.* loc. cit. p. 258, and
subsequent references in that article.

It is here simply to be observed that the discourse of the doctors occupies similar places in WCo, Y, and T, and that in Ch a colloquy of the doctors is implied; for *Primus* Doctor says before Jesus has spoken, *Heare our reason right on a row, | you clarkes that be of great coning ; | me thinke this childe learne our law, | he taketh great tent to our talking.* In these passages the other texts show slight agreements with Y: Ch with confusion in speeches preserves practically one whole line and parts of others (Y 50, Ch 222 ; Y 49, 65–6, Ch 233–4, 236) ; WCo bears resemblance to Y all through this passage, but is in a different metre (WCo 857–8, Y 48, 63 ; WCo 870, Y 53 ; WCo 875–6, Y 63–5 ; WCo 878, Y 69 ; WCo 882, Y 59–60) ; even in the part of the colloquy preserved in T there is at least one slight agreement (Y 61–2, T 9–10).

| | | | |
|---|---|---|---|
| WCo 885–94, | Y 73–82, | T 49–57. | |
| WCo 890, and | Y 78, warne; | T 54, tell. | |
| (WCo 899, | Y 91, | T 65, | Ch 243.) |
| WCo 900–1, | Y 87–8, | T 61–2, | Ch 233–40. |
| WCo 902–5, | Y 89–92, | T 63–66, | Ch 241–4. |

Y 90, *He wenes he kens more than we knawes ;* T 64, *he wenys he kens more than he knawys ;* Ch 242, *he wenes he kennes more than he knowes ;* WCo 903, *All secrettis surely he thynkith he knois.* T, Ch and WCo here represent evidently the same reading, one which makes sense too; but in Y the sense seems somewhat more original and *knawes* is perhaps a northern plural.[1] WCo 905 *clere,* Y 92 *yitt,* T 66 *yit,* Ch 244 *cleane.* *Clargy clere* (Y 54, WCo 870) is indicated by alliteration.

| | | | |
|---|---|---|---|
| WCo 911–7, | Y 94–100, | T 67–72. | |
| „  918–21, | Y 101–4, | „ 73–6, | Ch 253–6. |
| „  922–34 | „ 105–16, | „ 77–88. | |

WCo 932 and T after 86 have the Latin quotation, *Ex ore infancium, etc. ;* it does not occur in Y. In WCo 922–34 the paraphrase is exceedingly free.

| | | | |
|---|---|---|---|
| WCo 937–56, | Y 117–36, | T 89–108.[2] | |
| WCo 957–64, | Y 137–44, | T 109–16, | Ch 273–6. |

In Ch it is Jesus who asks for the first commandment; in Y and T, the third doctor ; in WCo, the first doctor. Ch 140, which is a part of the first doctor's answer, agrees with Y 140, T 112, WCo 960, where it is the second line of the question.

---

[1] See, however, *York Mist. Plays,* p. lxxii.     [2] See also Ch 268, 271–2.

WCo 965-68,    Y 145-8,    T 117-20,    Ch 277-80.

„    969-70,    „ 155-6,    „ 127-8.
„    971-2,    „ 151-2,    „ 123-4.
„    973-4,    „ 159-60,    „ 132-3.
„    975-6,    „ 169-70,    „ 141-2.
„    977-84,    „ 143-52.

Before considering this important correspondence of WCo and
T, the following minor agreements might be pointed out : Y 171-2,
T 143-4 ; WCo 985-6, Y 175-6 ; WCo 989-90, Y 181-2.    The
corresponding passages are : WCo 977-84.    *The thryd beddith the,
in any wey, | Thatt of thy labur thow schuldyst reste, | And truly
kepe thy Sabett day, | Thy-selfe, thi servande and thy best. | The
forthe bydithe the do thy best | Thy fathur and mothur for to
honowre; | And when ther goodis are decrest, | With all thy myght
thow shuldist them succure.*    T 143-52, *The thyrd bydys, " where
so ye go, | That he shall halow the holy day; || ffrom bodely wark
ye take youre rest; | youre household, look the same thay do, | Both
wyfe, chyld, seruande, and beest," || The fourt is then in weyll and
wo || " Thi fader, thi moder, thou shall honowre, || not only with
thi reuerence, || Bot in thare nede thou thaym socoure, | And kepe ay
good obedyence.''*    The writer or reviser of WCo was perhaps trying
to make an eight-line strophe which would have prevented a closer
agreement than exists, or, as is more likely, the difference has been
increased by the rewriting of T.    In any case, the diversity among
the plays in their recitals of the commandments, and the metrical
regularity and almost entire independence of Y being taken into
consideration, the conclusion is almost unavoidable that WCo and
T preserve here parts of the same original.

WCo 1001-10,    Y 193-202,    T 181-90,    Ch 257-66.

The placing of these speeches in Ch before the recital of the
commandments was certainly accidental, the result of unskilful
borrowing.

WCo 1011-26,    Y 203-18,    T 191-206.

WCo 1022 and T 202, *amend;* Y 214 mende.

WCo 1027-40,    Y 219-32,    T 207-20,    Ch 305-16.

The order in which lines of Y and T are reproduced in Ch is :
223, 224, 221 and 219, 222 ; 225 and 226 ; 231, 230, 229, 232.
Ch omits the idea of hurrying home on account of the lateness of the
hour (Y 227-8) and puts in (Ch 311-2), *thatt sitteth with yonder
Doctors gay; | for we haue had of hym great care.*    WCo follows

Y and T closely in sense and order of lines except in ll. 1037–40, where the arrangement is that of Ch. This is the most important of the resemblances between Ch and WCo; it can be easily seen how it came about. The passages are: Ch 313–6, *Mary, wife, thou wottes right well | that I must all my travayle teene, | With men of might I can not mell, | that sittes so gay in furres fyne.* WCo 1037–40, Ey! *Mare, wyff, ye kno ryght well, | Asse I haue tolde you many a tyme, | With men of myght durst I neyu*er mell. *| Loo! dame, how the sytt in there furis fyn!* Y 229–32, *With men of myght can I not mell, | Than all my trayvale mon I tyne, | I can noght with them, this wate thou wele, | They are so gay in furres fyne.* T follows Y. Ch differs from Y and T in its displacement of genuine lines; but WCo differs from them only because of the exigencies of paraphrasing the archaic words in Y 230 (Ch 314).

WCo 1041–64,    Y 233–56,    T 221–44,    (Ch 317–20).

WCo 1043 *haue reygardid you,* Y 235 *will take rewarde to you,* T 223 *will take hede to you.* WCo 1044 *this wott I well,* Y 236 *this wate ye wele,* T 224 *this wote I weyll.* Mary's speech to Jesus, Ch 317–20, follows Y and T in the use of the word *deare* and in the idea of the search for Jesus, but differs from them in having no reference to the distress of Joseph and Mary; it expresses their joy at having found him. WCo, on the contrary, uses the word *swete,* omits all reference to the search and dwells upon the grief which Joseph and Mary have felt during the three days of Jesus's absence.

WCo 1065–72,    Y 257–64,    T 245–52,    Ch 221–8.

Y 257 (T 245, WCo 1065) *Wherto shulde ye seke me soo?* does not appear in Ch, where the stanza begins with (321), *Mother, full oft I tould you till* (Y 258), and ends with (324), *that must I needes doe, or I goe,* which is a special line composed to go with the three which had been borrowed. Ch 328, *and found to do that they commaund,* diverges slightly from Y 264 (T 252), *To ffonde what is folowand;* WCo 1072, *Ys were glade I haue the fonde,* uses instead of the northern word found, *attempt,* the past participle of find, *discover,* which may have been suggested by the former word.

In connection with this passage arises also the question of the supposed interchange of speeches between Joseph and Mary. Dr. Chas. Davidson[1] says (referring to WCo 1057–64, Y 249–56, T 237–44, Ch 317–28): "Mary addresses Jesus.—Agreement of Y

[1] *Loc. cit.* p. 177. See also Review by Ungemach, *Anglia Beiblatt,* iv., pp. 258–9.

and W (T).  Immaterial changes in W of Co, speech reduced to
four verses of free paraphrase in Ch . . . Jesus replies.—Agreement
among W of Co, Ch, and Y.  W (T) adds verses after the manner
of W (T) in the ' Harrowing of Hell.'  Joseph addresses Jesus in Y
and W (T), but Mary addresses Jesus in W of Co and Ch.  This is
a significant difference.''  Further on, "Ch . . . because of agreement with W of Co in Mary's speech, when Joseph speaks in the
other plays, is without much doubt a borrowing from Coventry before
the days of Robert Croo, i. e. before 15—.''  This conclusion rests
upon a mistake, as will be seen by an examination of the texts.
T 249-52 is the only case where there is any material difference in
the plays as to speakers.  In Y 261-4, Mary, and not Joseph as
asserted by Dr. Davidson, addresses Jesus.  Moreover, Mary's speech
occurs in T in an exactly similar place to the one it has in the other
plays.  The mistake was due to the fact that Mary's speech is given
in T to Jesus, who speaks immediately before her.[1]  The Towneley
editor points out that the speech must have belonged to Mary by
referring to Luke ii. (misprinted iii.), 51.  These verses are not
extraneous as Dr. Davidson implies, but hold their proper place as
the conclusion of a twelve-line stanza.  In WCo Joseph makes his
own speech, but not until ll. 1122–4.

Ch ends at this point[2] and WCo expands into an extensive
leave-taking scene ; some correspondences can be discovered :

| WCo 1073–4, | Y 273–4, | T 261–2. |
|---|---|---|
| ,,  1081–2, | ,,  269–70, | ,,  257–8. |
| ,,  1085–88, | ,,  271–2, 279–80 ; | ,,  259–60, 267–8. |
| ,,  1113–4, | ,,  275–6, | ,,  263–4. |
| ,,  1222–4, | ,,  267–8, | ,,  255–6. |

There is no parallel in any play for the dialogue of the doctors
with which WCo comes to an end.

Except for T 1–48 and Y 1–73, and T 145–78 and Y 173–90,
Y and T are practically the same throughout.  Ch and WCo are
related to them in very different ways.  Ch usually corresponds
closely in language and rime, when it agrees at all ; strophes and
verses are often out of their original order ; parts of lines are pieced
together ; and the story, where it is deficient, is filled out with matter
in many cases peculiar to Ch.  It is an imperfect version, just such

---

[1] It must have been spoken by Jesus when the present version of T was
written, for *not* has been changed to *well.*

[2] See Hohlfeld, *loc. cit.* p. 260.

as would have resulted from oral transmission.    WCo is also corrupt
but in a different way.    In story it seldom departs from Y and T
except to interpolate and expand or to paraphrase into later English.
As we have seen, WCo and Ch never coincide in their deviations in
story.    The few cases in which WCo and Ch have in common readings which differ from Y and T are insufficient to indicate inter-
dependence.    Indeed, from agreements in text of WCo with any
other play, very little can usually be told; so much has WCo been
altered in revision and transmission.    This applies also to the relation
of WCo to Y and T, as concerns its derivation from one or the other.
The best piece of evidence, the agreement in the third and fourth
commandments, is in favour of its derivation from T.    Several
smaller agreements point in the same direction.[1]

A fact, which adds to the presumption in favour of T as the
original of WCo, is that in the Towneley cycle the Doctors' play
stands next after the Purification; but in the York Cycle the corresponding play came between the Massacre of the Innocents and the
Baptism of Jesus.[2]    The order of plays in the lost Beverley Cycle
was virtually the same as in York: . . . Fyshers, Symeon.    Cowpers,
fleynge to Egippe.    Shomakers, children of Israel.    Scryvners, dis-
putacion in the temple.    Barbours, sent John baptyste, *etc.*[3]

In light of the whole matter, therefore, it seems probable that
some Northumbrian nucleus of craft or church plays[4] was in possession of this Doctors' play, and, since the subject was unusually
attractive, the play spread to the south and west.    On its way to
Coventry it perhaps fell under the influence of T, or under influence
which also affected T.    This was probably also the case in its
journey to Chester; but there is no reason whatever to think that
the Play of the Doctors passed from Coventry to Chester or that
Ch and WCo in any way interdepend.

[1] Hohlfeld, *loc. cit.* pp. 265–7; and *Intro.* Towneley Plays, pp. xix–xx.
[2] If Towneley XVII and XVIII had possibly been combined into one, as in
Ch and WCo, the play would not have been inordinately long.    There is a
gap in the MS. between the plays; see *Towneley Plays,* p. 185.
[3] *Lansdown MS.* 896, fos. 133, 139–40; *Scaum's Beverlac,* by Geo. Poulson,
Esq., Lond. 1829, p. 272 : the list, taken from *Beverlac,* has been corrected
from Leach ; see below, note 4.
[4] See "Fragments of Liturgical Plays" and the editor's headnote in
*Specimens of Pre-Shak. Drama,* ed. Dr J. M. Manly, Boston, 1897, vol. i.
pp. xxvii–xxxvii; Davidson, *loc. cit.* pp. 83 ff.; ten Brink, *loc. cit.,* pp. 281–2.
See also article on the Beverley play by Arthur Leach, Esq., in *An Eng.
Miscellany, Presented to Dr. Furnivall in Honour of his Seventy-fifth Birthday*
(Oxford, 1901), pp. 205–304.

## NOTES ON THE FRAGMENTS OF ANOTHER VERSION OF THE WEAVERS' PLAY.[1]

Fragment I. is a variant of WCo ll. 1–58 ; Abbotsford Club print, pp. 31–4. The following are the significant variations and readings. MS. indicates the principal manuscript, MS. b. the fragments, S. the Abbotsford Club print, H. the edition of Prof. F. Holthausen, Anglia, N. F. XIII., 209–50.

1. *Ye gret*, MS. *E! grett* (cp. WCo, l. 864), S. *grett.*—2. *With youre*, S. *Youre*, H. *ye.*—3. *aspect*, MS. *reyspecte.*—4. *fracis*, MS. *seyng.*—7. MS. *Apon the hyll of Wawse.* This seems to me to indicate a later origin of MS. than of MS. b. Croo was probably familiar with the play, and repeated in line 7 the reference to the Hill of Wawse from line 115, where it belongs. In that place is an account, derived from the Legend of the Three Kings, of the appearance of the star of prophecy upon the Hill of Vaus. See *The Three Kings of Coloyne*, E.E.T.S., Orig. Ser. No. 85, pp. 6 ff., and the Latin version by John of Hildesheim in the same volume, pp. 213 ff.—9. *makis*, MS. *makyth*, S. *in wyth.* No other instance of the plural in s. occurs.— 10. *For*, in MS., is at the beginning of l. 9 ; MS. b. has the better reading.—15. *further-more*, MS. *Yet further, I pra you for my larning.*—15–8. In MS. there is a request; in MS. b., a mere proposition.—19. *demonstracion*, MS. *aftur a strange deformacion.* This is a characteristic mistake on the part of Croo.—25. Orreetur . . . Jacob . . . exurge, etc., MS. Orietur . . . Jacobo . . . exsurget, etc.— 32–4. MS. *Of this nobull prince of soo hi degree, / The wyche of all men, shall haue demeneon, / Vndur what maner borne he schuld be.* MS. b. has the better and more metrical reading.—35. *Worthele*, MS. *wonderfulle*, S. wonderfull, corr. emend. by H. ; MS. b. has the better reading.—39. MS. *Before prognostefide this to be done.*—41. . . . consepith aparet, fillium, MS. . . . . concipiet pariet filium ; the Latin is much more correct in MS.—43. *schuld be reysed*, MS. *spryng ;* MS. b. is nearer the original.—45. MS. vocabitur, better than vocatur of MS. b.—46–9. MS. *Yett haue I grett marvell, / How that men schuld tell / Off such strangis before the fell, / And man beyng here but a mortall creature.* Note that here and in the neighbouring strophes, which are very obscure in MS., MS. b., though slightly more archaic, is entirely clear and is metrical. 52. *espret*, MS. *sprete.*

Fragment II. offers a variant of WCo, ll. 182–233 *circa*, S.

[1] See Appendix IV.

pp. 39–41. It is a portion of the Presentation in the Temple, beginning with the sixth line of Simeon's opening soliloquy and including everything to the entrance and first speech of Anna. The reply of Simeon is broken off after the fourth line. This is probably the fourth page of the original:

MS. b. 183, *Under man . . . there*, MS. *Vndur hus . . . the.* —184. *anceant*, MS. *formere.*—186, *abowndant blis*, MS. *From the hy pales and.*—187. *Dovn . . . mundall*, MS. *Downe into this wale and meserabull mvndall.* MS. b. has the better reading, whatever *mvndall* may mean; it probably refers to the world.—188–90. MS. *For the wyche transgression all we ar now mortall, | Thatt before wasse infynite for eyuer to remayne | And now schall take yend be deyth and cruell payne.* The passages are much at variance; MS. is a paraphrase of MS. b.—191. *ded most dolorus*, MS. *Wyche grevoise sorro.*—192. *bytturle*, MS. *byttur teyris.*—195. MS. *syence;* this probably indicates that *sencis* is written for *siencis.*—196. MS. *In there awturs aperith to hus right manefestly.*—197. *Sebbelis*, MS. *Sebbellam*, a mistake of Croo's which would not have been corrected when once made.—198. MS. *In hart beseke I the.*—202. This line omitted in MS.—203–4. MS. *The wyche be reydemcion schall hus all reyles, | At whose cumyng the tru ovncion of Juda schall seyse.* MS. b. has here the more literal translation of the Latin words usually given to Daniel in the *Processus Propheterum*; [1] these words also occur in STCo, ll. 6 and 7.—206. MS. *For age draith me fast apon.* 208. *from*, MS. *fro.*—209–25. MS. 209–18 shows a curious abridgment:

> Now, Lorde, ase thow are iij in won,
> Grant me grace, yff thatt thy wyl be,
> In my nold age that syght for to see!
>
> Then at thy wyll, Lorde, fayne wold I be,
>  Yff thow soche grace woldist me sende,
> To loove the, Lorde, with all vmelyte,
>  And soo of my lyff then to make an ende!
>  Yett, Lorde, thi grace to me now extende,
> Suffer me rathur yett to lyve in peyne
> Then to dy, or thatt I thatt solam syght haue seyne!

How to account for this is not very easy. At first sight it looks as if lines 209–18 had been overlooked by Croo in his redaction. He may simply have composed lines 209–11 from the ordinary

---

[1] See *Towneley Plays*, VII, 216 f.

jargon of the first part of the play to complete the stanza, taking
up the earlier version again at lines 219–25 (MS. b.), which agree
fairly well with 212–8 (MS.) above. It might have been
accidental, as omissions of lines and even stanzas often occur in
this way. It seems, however, much more probable that Croo was
rewriting the play with a rather free hand, and that he had already
put the substance of lines 209–17 (MS. b.) into the speech of the
first Prophet, lines 61–74 (MS.); and since he had used it there,
omitted it here. MS. 61–74 :

> *Wyche cawsid Isaee to cast up his iees*
> *Toward heyvin with all his inward syght,*
> *Seying, " Good Lord, afarming thy promes,*
> *Send downe to hus this wonly sun off myght,*
> *Huse to reystore vnto owre right !*
> *Owt of deserte, from the hard stone,*
> *Reycomfordying thi doghtur dwylling in Sion ! "*　　　　67
>
> *Also Jaramo, thatt wholle mon,*
> *Seyd in heyvin God schuld make seede,*
> *A greyne off Davith, thatt now ys cum,*
> *Wyche eyuer in gracys shall spring and speyde*
> *And kepe Juda owt of drede*
> *And also Isaraell sett in surenes,*
> *And he schall make jugementis of rightwesenes.*　　　　74

These lines are probably in place in the prophet play for two
very slight reasons : Because of the use of the names of Isaiah and
Jeremiah, and because of the number of lines. Of the original
manuscript b., we have probably pages 1 and 4. Page 1 has 58
lines, page 4 has 61 lines. The lacuna, judging by MS. a., is about
120 lines. On the other hand, these speeches of Isaiah and Jeremiah
are very puzzling. It is difficult to find a source for them ; there is
nothing in the original *Processus Prophetarum* from which they
may be derived. The supposition that Croo substituted parts of the
original speech of Simeon for earlier and more customary speeches of
Isaiah and Jeremiah would clear up the difficulty. All of this
is on the supposition that MS. b. is earlier than MS. It must be
admitted, however, that almost nothing can be determined for or
against the idea of a greater age for MS. b. from the handwritings.
But it should be remembered that after the preparation of Robert
Croo's codex there would have been no necessity for another
" original " ; and MS. b. is to be regarded as the fragments of
a complete version and not as players' copies. Sharp seems to

have found no entries in the account-book which pointed to the making of another play-book after Croo's or even parts of another.

The agreement of the versions practically ends with the first strophe of Anna's speech (l. 226), and is not very close there. MS. b. represents a considerably earlier form of the pageant; but it seems to be somewhat nearer the source (*S. Luke* ii. 22–39) in these speeches of Simeon and Anna, than is MS.; see ll. 224–5, 233–6. It may be too much to suppose that ll. 233–43 show any evidence of having been once in the form of quatrains, in which I am disposed to think the body of the play was originally composed. They are, at any rate, simpler and more essential to the play of the Presentation in the Temple than the corresponding lines in MS.

In all respects, except the correctness of the Latin quotations, MS. b. is better than MS.—spelling, readings, metrical regularity, strophe-form, sense, and style. It is probably the version which Robert Croo " translated ".

-----

## KEY TO MAP.

THIS section of Bradford's map shows intramural Coventry in 1750.

Stations of pageants, some known, some conjectural [*v.* Introd. xiii–xiv], are, one in each of the ten wards of the city, beginning from the east of the central thoroughfare. (1) In Gosford Street. (2) In Jordan Well, a continuation of the thoroughfare; or possibly at the junction of New Street and Mill Lane, as a prolongation of New Street, not marked in this map, was anciently called Corpus Christi Lane. To the south of the thoroughfare in Much Park Street on the London Road is (3) New Gate. (4) Little Park Street ends in Earl Street. To the north of the thoroughfare in Bayley Lane ward is (5) S. Michael's Churchyard [picture of church in map]. In the centre of the city in Cross Cheaping ward is (6) The Cross [picture in map]. Further north, near Bishop Street, is (7) S. John's Hospital [Free School and Library in map]. To the south of the thoroughfare again in Broad Gate ward is (8) Grey Friars' Church [picture of steeple in map]. Continuing the thoroughfare along Smithford Street we arrive at (9) The Conduit [just legible in map opposite the "Bull" and "Green Dragon" inns]. Further on, close to Spon Street Gate is (10) S. John's or Bablake Church [picture in map].

Pageant houses were in Hill Street by Bablake Church, and in Mill Lane, which runs at right angles to Jordan Well.

# SUPPLEMENT TO THE INTRODUCTION.

In looking over the Introduction preparatory to a re-issue of
my *Two Corpus Christi Plays*, I found only two things that it
seemed well to supply.  To correct the text itself seemed hardly
necessary, since what I wrote more than fifty years ago was not
wrong in the light of what was then known about the subjects
treated.  As is not infrequently the case, what I then said was
merely imperfect.

The first of these matters has to do with the then current theory
of the origin of the Old Testament plays.  Marius Sepet's brilliant
discovery of the role played by the Pseudo-Augustinian *Sermo
contra Judaeos, Paganos et Arianos de Symbolo* [1] in the origin of
*Processus Prophetarum* was widely accepted and deserved to be.
But it has since been pointed out that, although Sepet was un-
questionably right in his account of the origin of the prophet-play
and manifestly right also in his contention that certain plays on
Old Testament subjects, such as the Balaam play, originated as
dramatic scenes from the prophet-play, he was wrong in his contention that the main body of Old Testament plays, those derived
from the Pentateuch, had, to use Chambers' figure, " budded off "
from the *Prophetae*.[2]  These originated in the normal course of the
derivation of dramatic offices from the services of the hours in the
*cursus* of the liturgical year.  The period from which they came
was the days after the Epiphany embracing *Dominicae in Septua-
gesima, Sexagesima*, extending into the lenten period of *Quadri-
gesima*.  This is borne out by an exact correspondence of the
*lectiones* and the antiphons, responses and other formularies that
accompany them with the original series of the plays of the
patriarchs.  Parallels in content and accompaniment are otherwise
unaccountable.  I did not know this when I wrote the original
Introduction.  I see no reason, however, to change my belief that

[1] M. Sepet, " Les prophètes du Christ," *Bibliothèque de l'École des Chartres*,
xxviii (1867), 1–27, 211–64; xxix (1868), 105–39, 261–93; xxxviii (1877),
397–443; also published separately in Paris in 1878; Sir E. K. Chambers, *The
Mediaeval Stage* (2 vols., Oxford, 1903), ii, 52–57; Karl Young, *The Drama of
the Medieval Church* (2 vols., Oxford, 1933), ii, 125–71.
[2] Hardin Craig, " The Origin of the Old Testament Plays," *Modern
Philology*, x (1912–13), 473–87, and the same author's *English Religious Drama
of the Middle Ages* (Oxford, 1955), 58–61, 63–74.

in the Coventry plays a *Prophetae* has been, so to speak, broken
up and distributed among other plays, mainly of the Nativity.

In the Introduction, believing that there was no evidence that
there were Old Testament plays at Coventry, I constructed a rather
elaborate argument that there were no such plays at Coventry. I
know of no tangible evidence now, but my further studies have convinced me that Old Testament plays were a necessary part of a
Corpus Christi play. I was and still am convinced that there were
only ten pageants in the cycle, and I did not think there was room
for Old Testament plays. I now see that there probably was.[1]
I was misled by an entry quoted in Sharp from a lost " rules and
orders of the company of pinners and needlers " of 1414, which
recited *inter alia* that the company were to bear the charges and
reparations of " her pagent callyd the takyng down of God fro the
Cros." The company was a large one with many contributors,
and, in view of the tendency of the Coventry plays to combine
many themes in a single pageant, it seems improbable that the
pageant of the pinners and needlers presented only the story of
the Burial. The record, which is early, probably represents an
earlier state of the cycle when the units were smaller and the
number of pageants greater. The smiths presented the Crucifixion,
and the cappers the Setting of the Watch, and there is hardly room
for the pinners and needlers between them. It may, with their
many subjects, have been taken over by the smiths. Certainly in
1435 the pinners and needlers were given joint responsibility with
the tilers for an unnamed pageant. This would indicate that at
least one new subject, possibly two, were added to the cycle, and,
if at that time the pinners and needlers were still playing the
Burial, there would have been no subjects to add, since that play
was a single episode between the Crucifixion and the Setting of the
Watch. If, for example, the tilers' play had occupied the whole
fraternity and had dealt with the Creation, then the original
wrights' play, which the tilers got into their possession in 1453,
might have dealt with Adam and Eve and probably with Cain and
Abel, a subject united in its earlier history with that of Adam and
Eve. In this case a play of characteristic scope would have been
provided. Since on the basis of only ten pageants we have four
guilds the subjects of whose plays are unknown, and since at
Coventry the pageants presented such large groups of subjects,

[1] Craig, *English Religious Drama*, pp. 287–91.

two or even three of the pageants may have been devoted to Old Testament subjects, although it must be admitted that the absence of plays dealing with Christ's ministry and with the conspiracy, trial and capture is most unlikely.   The mercers may have played the Ascension and Pentecost, since those plays are closely related to the Assumption of the Blessed Virgin Mary.   I now think, however, that such renowned subjects as the Creation, Cain and Abel, Noah and the Flood, and probably Abraham and Isaac must have been played at Coventry because of their popularity elsewhere and because the idea of a Corpus Christi play demands the fall of man as well as his redemption.

A subject treated in the Introduction that caused perplexity has been greatly clarified by another discovery.   The problem studied was the relation among the four versions of the play of *Christ before the Doctors* (Luke ii. 43–52)—York (xx), Wakefield (xviii), Chester (xi), and the Weavers' pageant of Coventry.   It was seen that the York and the Wakefield versions are almost identical, that that of Chester is an imperfect borrowing, possibly by ear, from the York–Wakefield text, and that the version in the Weavers' pageant has been much and rather ignorantly modified, but is nevertheless recognizable as originally the same text as that of York and Wakefield.   It was easy to conclude that some Yorkshire cycle was in possession of this Doctors' play, and that, since the subject was unusually attractive, the play spread to the south and west; but, since the Chester and the Coventry versions agreed sometimes with that of York and sometimes with that of Wakefield, it was not possible to determine whether the two derivative versions came from York or from Wakefield.

A later discovery has made the matter entirely clear.   Dr. Marie Lyle, in a Ph.D. dissertation done under my direction at the University of Minnesota, proved beyond any reasonable and intelligent doubt that the York and the Wakefield versions were originally one and the same play.[1]   Both the York and the Wakefield texts underwent some changes and corruptions after the date of their separation (before 1390).   Since the Chester and the Coventry versions agree now with one and now with the other in preserving original readings, it is obvious that they were both

[1] Marie C. Lyle, *The Original Identity of the York and Towneley Cycles* (Minneapolis, 1919); also, by the same author, " The Original Identity of the York and Towneley Cycles," *PMLA*, xliv (1929), 319–28.

borrowed from the original text before the separation. It is probable that, since York was a great ecclesiastical centre and Wakefield was not, Wakefield was the borrower and that the whole York Corpus Christi play, of course in a simpler and older form, was transferred to Wakefield and played there. Subsequently it underwent many independent alterations. After the separation the York plays were also greatly altered and amplified. *Christ before the Doctors* is one of the five plays of the original cycle that remained relatively unaltered in the two cycles, whereas other plays of the original cycle have been revised in either the York or the Wakefield cycle or in both. Dr. Lyle's textual studies make this clear, and the Doctors' play, having undergone no considerable revision, gives no trouble.

HARDIN CRAIG

# 𝕿𝖍𝖊 𝕻𝖆𝖌𝖊𝖆𝖓𝖙 𝖔𝖋 𝖙𝖍𝖊 𝕾𝖍𝖊𝖆𝖗𝖒𝖊𝖓 𝖆𝖓𝖉 𝕿𝖆𝖞𝖑𝖔𝖗𝖘.[1]

[DRAMATIS PERSONAE.

| | | | |
|---|---|---|---|
| *Isaiah* as Prologue (Ll. 1–46). | | *Nuncius* | |
| *Gabriel* | | *Herod* | |
| *Mary* | | *i. Rex* | |
| *Joseph* | In the Annuncia- | *ii. Rex* | |
| *i. Angel* | tion and the Na- | *iii. Rex* | In the Adoration of |
| *i. Pastor* | tivity (Ll. 47– | *Mary* | the Kings and |
| *ii. Pastor* | 331). | *Angelus* | the Slaughter of |
| *iii. Pastor* | | *i. Miles* | the Innocents (Ll. |
| *ii. Angel* | | *ii. Miles* | 475–900). ] |
| *i. Profeta* | Participants in a | *Joseph* | |
| *ii. Profeta* | learned dialogue | *i. Woman* | |
| *iii. Profeta* | (Ll. 332–474). | *ii. Woman* | |
| | | *iii. Woman* | |

[*Enter Isaiah as prologue.*]

ISAYE.  The Sofferent thatt seithe evere seycrette,  (83)

He saue you all and make you parfett *and* stronge,[2]

And geve us[3] grace wit*h* his marce forto mete !

For now in grett mesere mankynd ys bownd,

The sarpent hathe gevin vs soo mortall a wonde

That no creature ys abull vs forto reyles

Tyll thye right vncion of Jvda dothe seyse.  7

Then schall moche myrthe and joie in-cresse ;

And the right rote in Isaraell sprynge,

Thatt schall bryng forthe the greyne off whollenes ;

And owt of danger he schall vs bryng

In-to thatt reygeon where he ys kyng

Wyche abowe all othur far dothe a-bownde,

And thatt cruell Sathan he schall confownde.  14

*Isaiah prays God to release mankind from misery.*

*Dan.* ix. 24.

*Isa.* xi. 1.

*Then holiness shall flourish and Satan be confounded.*

---

[1] Reprinted from *A Dissertation on the Pageants or Dramatic Mysteries Anciently Performed at Coventry . . .* by Thomas Sharp. Coventry, 1825.  In most matters I have followed by permission the edition of Professor John Matthews Manly in his *Specimens of the Pre-Shakspearian Drama*, Boston, 1897, vol. i, pp. 120–52. His treatment of lines and strophes has not been altered ; stage-directions, punctuation, and text but seldom.  M. in the notes indicates this edition ; S., the edition of Thomas Sharp above referred to.  The *MS.* was destroyed in the burning of the Free Reference Library at Birmingham in 1879.  Numbers in parentheses are pp. in S.

[2] M. *Qy.* sounde.  *Cp. ll.* 222–4.  [3] S. geven*us*, *emend. by* M.

Where-fore I *cum* here apon this grownde          (84)
    To comforde eyue*re*[1] creature off birthe ;
For I, Isaye the pro*f*et, hathe fownde
    Many swete matt*er*s whereof we ma make myrth
        On this same wyse ;                                19
For, thogh that Adam be demid to deythe
*With* all his childur, asse Abell *and* Seythe,
Yett *Ecce virgo*[2] *consepeet*,—
    Loo, where a reymede schall ryse !                     23

Be-holde, a mayde schall conseyve a childe
    And gett vs more *grace* then eyu*er* men had,
And hir meydin-[h]od[3] nothing defylid.
    Sche ys deputyd to beare the Sun, Almyghte God.
    Loo ! sufferñtis, now ma you be glad,                  28
For of this meydin all we ma be fayne ;
    For Adam, *that* now lyis in sorrois full sade,
Hir gloreose birth schall reydeme hym ageyn
        From bondage and thrall.                           32
    Now be myrre eyu*ere* moñ
For th'is dede bryffly in Isaraell schalbe done,
    And before the Fathur in trone,
        Thatt schall glade vs all.                         36


More of this matt*er* fayne wolde I meve,
    But lengur tyme I haue not here for to dwell.
That Lorde *that* ys m*ar*cefull his m*ar*ce soo in vs ma
        preve
    For to sawe owre sollis from the darknes of hell ;  40
        And to his blys
            He vs bryng,
        Asse he ys
            Bothe lord *and* kyng,
            And schalbe[4] eyu*er*lastyng,
            *In secula seculo*rum, *amen* ![5]            46

[1] S. ey*er*ue, *corr. by* M.
[2] *The sign for* er *is used for* ir, ri, ar (marce), e (under), *as
well as for* er *and* re.          [3] *Correct. by* M.
[4] *So* S., M. shall be.
[5] *Lines* 41–46 *as two in* S., *the first ending with* kyng.

[*Exit Isaiah; enter Gabriel to Mary.*]

*Luke* i. 26-46.

GABERELL. Hayle, Mare, full of grace !

    Owre Lord God ys with the ;[1]

Aboue all wemeñ *that* eyuer wasse,

    Lade, blesside mote thow be !           50

*Salutation of Mary.*

MARE. All-myght Fathur and King of blys,

    From all dysses *tho*u saue me now !

For inwardely my spretis trubbuld ys,

    Thatt I am amacid *and* kno nott how.   (85)  54

*She is troubled.*

GABERELL. Dred the nothyng, meydin, of this ;

    From heyvin a-bowe hyddur am I sent

Of ambassage from that Kyng of blys

    Unto the, lade *and* virgin reyuerent !

Salutyng the here asse most exselent,

Whose virtu aboue all othur dothe abownde.

Wherefore in the grace schalbe fownde ;

For thow schalt conseyve apon *thi*s grownd   62

    The Second Persone of God in trone ;

    He wylbe borne of the alone ;

        With-owt sin *tho*u schalt hym see.[1]

    Thy grace *and* thi goodnes wyl neyuer be gone,

    But eyuer to lyve in virgenete.        67

*'Fear not;*

*thou shalt conceive the Second Person of the Trinity.*

MARE. I marvell soore how thatt mabe.

    Manis[2] cumpany knev I neyuer yett,

Nor neyuer to do, kast I me,

    Whyle thatt owre Lord sendith me my wytt.   71

*'How may this be ?'*

GABERELL. The Wholle Gost in the schall lyght,

    And schado thy soll soo with virtu

From the Fathur thatt ys on hyght.

    These wordis, turtill, the[3] be full tru.   75

*The Holy Ghost shall light in her.*

This chylde that of the schalbe borne

    Ys the Second Persone in Trenete ;

He schall saue that wase forlorne

    And the fyndis powar dystroie schall he.   79

*Her son a saviour.*

[1] *This and the preceding line as one in* S.

[2] *The contraction here is for* us, *and is used to represent the genitive and the plural throughout. It has been written* is, *the customary spelling in* S.   [3] M. *here and throughout prints* the[y].

These wordis, lade, full tru the bene,
    *And* furthur, lade, here in thy noone lenage

Her kins-
woman
Elizabeth.

Be-holde Eylesabeth, thy cosyn clene,
    The wyche wasse barren *and* past all age,      83

And now w*ith* chyld sche hath bene
Syx monethis and more, asse schalbe sene ;

Nothing
impossible
to God.

    Where-for, discomforde *the* not, Mare !
    For to God onpossibull nothyng mabe.      87

MARE.   Now, and yt be thatt Lordis wyll    (86)
    Of my bodde to be borne *and* forto be,
Hys hy pleysuris forto full-fyll

His hand-
maid.

    Asse his one hande-mayde I submyt me.      91

Gabriel's
blessing

GABERELL.   Now blessid be *th*e tyme sett
    That *th*ou wast borne in thy degre !
For now ys the knott surely knytt,
    And God conseyvide in Trenete.      95

and farewell.

Now fare-well, lade off myghtis most !
    Vnto the God-hed I the be-teyche.
MARE.   Thatt Lorde the gyde in eyu*er*e cost,
    And looly he leyde me *and* be my leyche !      99

*Matt.* i. 18-
25.
*Pseudo-
Matth.* x, xi.

*Here the angell dep*art*yth*, and *Joseff cum*y*th in* and *seyth :*

JOSOFF.   Mare, my wyff soo dere,
How doo ye, dame, and whatt chere
    Ys w*ith* you this tyde ?
MARE.   Truly, husebonde, I am here
    Owre Lordis wyll forto abyde.      104

JOSOFF.   Whatt ! I troo thatt we be all schent !

'Who hath
been with
thee ?'

Sey, womoñ ; who hath byn here sith I went,
    To rage wyth thee ?
MARE.   Syr, here was nothur mañ nor mans eyvin,

The messen-
ger of God.'

But only the sond of owre Lorde God in heyvin.    109
    JOSOFF.   Sey not soo, womoñ ; for schame, ley be !

He dis-
believes.

Ye be w*ith* chyld soo wondurs grett,
Ye nede no more *th*erof to tret
    Agense all right.

For-sothe, this chylde, dame, ys not myne.
Alas, that eyue*r* wit*h* my nynee
   I suld see t*hi*s syght !                    116

Tell me, womoñ ; whose ys this chyld ?          (87)     'Whose is
this child ?'
MARE.  Non but youris, husebond soo myld,
  And thatt schalbe seyne, [ywis].[1]
JOSOFF.  But myne ? allas ! alas ! why sey ye soo ?
Wele-awey ! womon, now may I goo,
   Be-gyld as many a-nothur ys.             122

MARE.  Na, truly, sir, ye be not be-gylde,     She declares
Nor yet wit*h* spott of syn I am not defylde ;          her inno-
   Trust yt well, huse-bonde.                cence.
JOSOFF.  Huse-bond, in feythe ! *and tha*t acold !     She is false in
A ! weylle-awey, Josoff, as thow ar olde !               spite of his
   Lyke a fole now ma I stand       128       kindness to
      And truse.[2]                her and her
  But, in feyth, Mare, *tho*u art in syn ;        kin.
  Soo moche ase I haue cheyrischyd t*h*e, dame, *and*
     all t*h*i kyn,
   Be-hynd my bake to s*e*rve me thus !        132

All olde men, insampull take be me,—              Let all old
How I am be-gylid here may you see !—              men take
   To wed soo yong a chyld.               example
Now fare-well, Mare, I leyve the here alone,—      from him.
[Wo][1] worthe the, dam, and thy warkis ycheone !—   He leaves
   For I woll noo-more be be-gylid [3]     138    her.
     For frynd nor fooe.[2]
Now of this ded I am soo dull,
And off my lyff I am soo full,
   No farthur ma I goo.[2]                142

    [*Lies down to sleep ; to him enters an angel.*]

I. ANGELL.[4]  Aryse up, Josoff, *and* goo whom ageyne     'Arise, go
   Vnto Mare, thy wyff, that ys soo[5] fre.   home again
To comford hir loke *that* thow be fayne,             unto thy
   For, Josoff, a cleyne meydin ys schee :   146    wife.

[1] *Emend. by* M.    [2] *This and the preceding line as one in* S.
[3] S. be gylid be, *emend. by* M.
[4] S. ANGELL J ; *so below for angels, shepherds, kings, knights,
and women, alteration by* M.    [5] M. so.

Sche hath conseyvid w*ith*-owt any trayne

**The child is Jesus.'**
  The Seycond P*er*son in Trenete ;

Je*su*s[1] schalbe hys name, sarten,

  And all thys world sawe schall he ;  (88) 150

  Be not agast.[2]

**He will go home in haste.**
JOSOFF.  Now, Lorde, I thanke the w*ith* hart full sad,

For of these tythyngis I am soo glad

  Thatt[3] all my care awey ys cast ;

  Wherefore to Mare I woll in hast.   155

    *[Returns to Mare.]*

**He begs forgiveness ;**
A ! Mare, Mare, I knele full loo ;

  Forgeve me, swete wyff, here in *thi*s lond !

Marce, Mare ! for now I kno

  Of youre good gou*er*nance and how yt doth stond. 159

**he has misnamed her.**
  Thogh[4] thatt I dyd the mys-name,

Marce, Mare ! Whyle I leve

Wyll I neyu*er*, swet wyff, the greve

  In ernyst nor in game.[2]   163

MARE.  Now, thatt[3] Lord in heyvin, sir, he you for-

  gyve !

  And I do for-geve yow in hys name

   For euer*more.[2]

JOSOFF.  Now truly, swete wyff, to you I sey the

  same.   167

**He must go to Bethlehem.**
But now to Bedlem must I wynde

  And scho my-self, soo full of care ;

And[5] I to leyve you, this grett, behynd,—

  God wott, the whyle, dame, how you schuld fare. 171

MARE.  Na, hardely, husebond, dred ye nothyng ;

**'I will walk with you.'**
  For I woll walke w*ith* you on the wey.

I trust in God, all-myghte kyng,

  To spede right well in owre jurney.  175

JOSOFF.  Now I thanke you, Mare, of youre[6] goodnes

  Thatt[3] ye my wordis woll nott blame ;

And syth *tha*t to Bedlem we schall vs dresse,

  Goo we to-gedur in Goddis wholle name.  179

---

[1] S. Jhu *here and throughout.*
[2] *This and the preceding line as one in* S.  [3] M. That.
[4] *So* M., S. *has* Thoght.  [5] *Qy.* Am.  [6] M. your.

[*They set out and travel a while.*]     *Luke* ii. 4-7.

Now to Bedlem haue we leygis three;     Three leagues
       The day ys ny spent, yt drawyth toward nyght;    to Bethlehem.
Fayne at your es, dame, I wold *that* ye schulde be,
       For you groue[1] all werely, yt semyth in my syght.   183

MARE.   God haue marcy, Josoffe, my spowse soo dere;   (89)   The time
       All *pro*fettis herto dothe beyre wyttnes,                foretold
The were tyme now draith nere                              draws near.
       Thatt[2] my chyld wolbe borne, wyche ys Kyng
         of blis.                                   187

Vnto su*m* place, Josoff, hyndly me leyde,     'Lead me to
       Thatt I moght rest me w*ith* gr*a*ce in *thi*s tyde.    a place where
The lyght of the Fathur ou*er* hus both spreyde,    I may rest.'
       And the gr*a*ce of my sun w*ith* vs here a-byde!   191

JOSOFF.   Loo! blessid Mare, here schall ye lend,     'Stay here:
       Cheff chosyn of owre Lorde *and* cleynist in degre;
And I for help to towne woll I wende.              I go to the
       Ys nott this the best, dame? whatt sey ye?   195   town for
                                                       help.'

MARE.   God haue marce, Josoff, my huse-bond soo
       meke!
       *And* hartely I p*ra* you, goo now fro me.
JOSOFF.   Thatt schalbe done in hast, Mare soo[3] swete!
       The comford of the Wholle Gost leyve I w*ith*
       the.                                      199

Now to Bedlem streyght woll I wynd
       To gett som helpe for Mare soo free.
Su*m* helpe of we*m*en[4] God may me send,
       Thatt[2] Mare, full off gr*a*ce, pleysid ma be.     203

[*In another part of the place a shepherd begins to speak.*]    *Luke* ii. 8-20.

I. PASTOR.   Now God, that art in Trenete,     'My fellows
Thow sawe my fellois and me!                  and my sheep
For I kno nott wheyre my scheepe nor the be,    are lost.'
       Thys nyght yt ys soo colde.              207

---

[1] M. *changes to* grone, *but suggests that it may be for* growe.
[2] M. That.     [3] M. so.     [4] M. we*m*men.
    D

Now ys yt nygh the myddis of the nyght;
These wedurs ar darke and dym of lyght,
Thatt of them can hy haue noo syght,
    Standyng here on this wold.         211

*He will call them.*

But now to make there hartis lyght,
Now wyll I full right
    Stand apon this looe,[1]
And to them cry wi*th* all my myght,—
    Full well my voise the kno :
    W*h*a*t* hoo ! fellois ! hoo ! hooe ! hoo !    217

*[Two other shepherds appear (in the street).]*

*Another shepherd hears and recognizes his voice.*

II. PASTOR.   Hark, Sym, harke ! I here owre brother
      on the looe ;             (90)
This ys hys woise, right well I knoo ;
There-fore toward hym lett vs goo,
    And follo his woise a-right.       221
See, Sym, se, where he doth stond ?
I am ryght glad we haue hym fond !
Brothur, where hast thow byn soo long,
    And hit ys soo cold this nyght ?[2]    225

*The first shepherd explains.*

I. PASTOR.   E ! fryndis, *the*r cam a pyrie of wynd
      wi*th* a myst suddeñly,
Thatt[3] forth off my weyis went I
And grett heyvenes then [4] made I
    *And* wase full sore afryght.[5]    229
Then forto goo wyst I nott whyddur,
But trawellid on this loo hyddur *and* thyddur ;
I wasse so were of this cold weddur
    Thatt nere past wasse my might.    233

*' It is nearly day ;*

III. PASTOR.   Brethur, now we be past *tha*t fryght,
And hit ys far wi*th*in the nyght,
Full sone woll spryng the day-lyght,
    Hit drawith full nere the tyde.    237

---

[1] *This and the preceding line as one in* S.
[2] S. And this nyght hit ys soo cold, *corr. by* M.    [3] M. That.
[4] S. in, *corr. by* M.    [5] S. afrayde, *emend. by* M.

Here awhyle lett vs rest,

And repast owreself of the best ;

Tyll thatt the sun ryse in the est

 Let vs all here abyde.    241

*There the scheppardis drawys furth there meyte and doth*
*eyte and drynk ; and asse the drynk, the fynd the star,*
*and sey thus :*

III. PASTOR.   Brethur, loke vp and behold !

 Whatt thyng ys yondur thatt schynith soo
  bryght ?

Asse long ase eyu*er* I haue wachid my fold,

 Yett sawe I neyu*er* soche a syght

  In fyld.[1]    246

A ha ! now ys cu*m* the tyme *tha*t old fathurs hath
 told,

Thatt in the wynturs nyght soo cold

A chyld of meydyñ borne be he wold

 In whom all p*r*ofeciys schalbe fullfyld.   250

I. PASTOR.   Truth yt ys wi*th*-owt naye,    (91)

Soo seyd the p*r*ofett Isaye,

 Thatt a[2] chylde schuld be borne of a made soo
  bryght

In wentur ny the schortist dey

 Or elis in the myddis of the nyght.    255

II. PASTOR.   Loouid be God, most off myght,

That owre g*r*ace ys to see thatt syght ;

Pray we to hym, ase hit ys right,

 Yff thatt his wyll yt be,    259

Thatt[3] we ma haue knoleyge of this syngnefocacion

And why hit aperith on this fassion ;

And eyu*er* to hym lett vs geve lawdacion,

 In yerthe whyle thatt we be.    263

*There the angelis syng " Glorea in exselsis Deo."*

III. PASTOR.   Harke ! the syng abowe in the clowdis
 clere !

Hard I neyuer of soo myrre a quere.

----

[1] *This and the preceding line as one in* S.

[2] S. *has* I.   *Emend. by* M.    [3] M. That.

*Marginal notes:*

let us refresh ourselves.'

He sees a star, and at once guesses that it is the star of prophecy.

'Yes ; for it is nigh the shortest day.'

Thanksgiving.

A merry choir !

Now, gentyll brethur, draw we nere
        To here there armony.[1]                              267
    I. PASTOR.   Brothur, myrth and solas ys cum hus
        among;
For be the swettnes of ther songe,
Goddis Sun ys cum, whom we haue lokid for long,
        Asse syngnefyith thys star that we do see.            271

The shep-
herds recall
the song.
    II. PASTOR.   " Glore, glorea in exselsis," that wase
        ther songe;
How sey ye, fellois, seyd the not thus?                       273
    I. PASTOR.   Thatt ys wel seyd;[2] now goo we hence
To worschipe thatt chyld of hy manyffecence,
And that we ma syng in his presence
        " Et in tarra pax omynibus."                          277

*There the scheppardis syngis " Ase I owt Rodde,"[3] and   (92)
    Josoff seyth :*

JOSOFF.   Now, Lorde, this noise that I do here,
        With this grett solemnete,
Gretly amendid hath my chere;
        I trust hy nevis schortly wolbe.                      281

*There the angellis syng " Gloria in exsellsis" ageyne.*

Mary an-
nounces the
Saviour's
birth.
MARE.   A! Josoff, husebond, cum heddur anon;
        My chylde ys borne that ys Kyng of blys.
JOSOFFE.   Now welcum to me, the Makar of mon,
        With all the omage thatt I con;
        Thy swete mothe here woll I kys.                      286

MARE.   A! Josoff, husebond, my chyld waxith cold,
        And we haue noo fyre to warme hym with.
Warmed by
the breathing
of the beasts.
JOSOFF.   Now in my narmys I schall hym fold,
        Kyng of all kyngis be fyld and be fryth;
He myght haue had bettur, and hym-selfe[4] wold,
        Then the breythyng of these bestis to warme
        hym with.                                             292

[1] M. armonye.          [2] S. welseyd.
[3] *The song (I.) is at the end of the pageant.*
[4] M. hymselfe.

MARE.   Now, Josoff, my husbond, fet heddur my
    chyld,
    The Maker off man and hy Kyng of blys.
JOSOFF.   That schalbe done anon, Mare soo myld,
    For the brethyng of these bestis hath warmyd
    [hym]¹ well, i-wys.                      296

        [*Angels appear to the shepherds.*]

I. ANGELL.   Hyrd-meñ hynd,              'Fear no-
Drede ye nothyng ²                       thing,
    Off thys star thatt ye do se ;
For thys same morne
Godis Sun ys borne ²
    In Bedlem of a meydin fre.          302

II. ANGELL.   Hy you thyddur in hast ;    (93)    but hasten to
    Yt ys hys wyll ye schall hym see          see him.'
Lyinge in a crybbe ³ of pore reypaste,
    Yett of Davithis lyne cumoñ ys hee.    306

    [*The shepherds approach and worship the Babe.*]

I. PASTOR.   Hayle, mayde-modur ⁴ *and* wyff soo myld !    A greeting
    Asse the angell seyd, soo haue we fonde.    to Mary,
I haue nothyng to present w*ith th*i chylde    and a present
    But my pype ; hold, hold, take yt in thy hond ;    to Jesus ;
    Where-in moche pleysure *tha*t I haue fond ;    he gives his
And now, to oonowre thy gloreose byrthe,    pipe.
Thow schallt yt haue to make the myrthe.    313

II. PASTOR.   Now, hayle be thow, chyld, *and* thy
    dame !
    For in a pore⁵ loggyn here art thow leyde,
Soo the angell seyde *and* tolde vs thy name ;
    Holde, take thow here my hat on thy hedde !    'Take my
    And now off won thyng thow art well sped,    hat on thy
For weddur thow hast noo nede to complayne,    head !'
For wynd, ne sun, hayle, snoo and rayne.    320

¹ *Suppl. by* M.    ² *This and the preceding line as one in* S.
³ M. cribbe.    ⁴ M. mothur.    ⁵ S. apore, *corr. by* M.

III. PASTOR.   Hayle be thow, Lorde ouer watur *and*
            landis !
        For thy cumyng all we ma make myrthe.

*'Here are*
*my mittens*
*to put on thy* Haue here my myttens to pytt on *th*i hondis,
*hands!'*        Othur treysure haue I non to present the w*ith*.   324

MARE.   Now, herdmeñ hynd,
        For youre comyng [1]
*She will pray*            To my chyld schall I p*ra*e,                327
*for them.*
        Asse he ys heyvin kyng,
        To grant you his blessyng,[1]
        And to hys blys *that* ye may wynd
            At your last day.[1]                         331

> *There the scheppardis syngith [2] ageyne and goth forthe*
> *of the place ; and the ij profettis cumyth in and seyth*
> *thus :*

*Wonderful*   I. PROFETA.   Novellis, novellis
*tidings !*  Of wonderfull m*a*rvellys,[1]
        Were hy *and* defuce vnto the heryng !
        Asse scripture tellis,
        These strange novellis
            To you I bryng.[3]                           337

II. PROFETA.   Now hartely, sir, I desyre to knoo, (94)
        Yff hytt wolde pleyse you forto schoo,
            Of whatt maner a thyng.
*The nativity*        I. PROFETA.   Were mystecall vnto youre her-
*of a king,*            yng,—
            Of the natevete off a kyng.                  342

II. PROFETA.   Of a kyng ?  Whence schuld he cu*m* ?
        I. PROFETA.   From  thatt  reygend  ryall  *and*
            mighty mancion,
        The sede seylesteall and heyvinly vysedome,
            The Seycond[4] Person *and* Godis one Sun,
        For owre sake now ys man be-cuñ.                  347

        This godly spere,
        Desendid here [1]

---

[1] *This and the preceding line as one in* S.
[2] *The song* (III.) *is at the end of the pageant.*
[3] *Lines 335-7 as one in* S.     [4] M. Second.

In-to a virgin clere,[1]                              born of a
    Sche on-defyld; [2]                            virgin un-
                                                      defiled.
Be whose warke obskevre
Owre frayle nature
    Ys now begilde.[2]

II. PROFETA.   Why, hath sche a chyld?         355


I. PROFETA.   E! trust hyt well;
    And neuer the las [2]
    Yet ys sche a mayde evin asse sche wasse,
And hir sun the king of Isaraell.              359


II. PROFETA.   A wondur-full marvell            Truly mar-
    How thatt ma be,[2]                          vellous!
And far dothe exsell
    All owre capasete : [2]                      363
    How thatt the Trenete,
        Of soo hy regallete,[2]
    Schuld jonyd be [3]
        Vnto owre mortallete ! [2]                367


I. PROFETA.   Of his one grett marce,          Adam's
    As ye shall se the exposyssion,[2]           progeny shall
                                                      be redeemed.
Throgh whose vmanyte
All Adamis progene [2]
    Reydemyd schalbe owt of perdyssion.        372


Syth mañ did offend,                            Man must
Who schuld amend [2]                             redeem man.
    But the seyd moñ and no nothur?
For the wyche cawse he
Incarnate wold be [2]
    And lyve in mesere asse manis one brothur.  378


II. PROFETA.   Syr, vnto the Deyite,        (95)
I beleve parfettle,[2]
    Onpossibull to be there ys nothyng;

---

[1] M. puts a period here and a comma after Sche ; he suggests that
a line is omitted after 351.
[2] This and the preceding line as one in S.
[3] S. be jonyd, emend. by M.

How be yt this warke
Vnto me ys darke [1]
 In the opperacion or wyrkyng.   384

The folly of
doubting.
I. Profeta. Whatt more reypriff
Ys vnto belyff
 Then to be dowtyng ? [2]   387

II. Profeta. Yet dowtis oftym*is* hathe derevacion.
I. Profeta. Thatt ys be *th*e meynes of comenecacion
Of trawthis to haue a dev *pro*bacion
 Be *th*e same dowts reysoning.
  II. Profeta. Then to you this won thyng :
Of whatt nobull *and* hy lenage ys schee
Thatt myght *thi*s verabull [3] *pri*ncis modur be ? 394

The lineage
of Mary.
I. Profeta. Ondowtid sche ys cu*m* of hy parrage,
Of the howse of Davith *and* Salamon the sage ;
And won off the same lyne joynid to hir be mareage ;
  Of whose trybe
   We do subscrybe [4]
This chy[l]dis [5] lenage. [6]   400

II. Profeta. And why in thatt wysse ?
I. Profeta. For yt wasse the gysse
 To conte the parant on the manys lyne,
 And nott on the feymyne, [7]
  Amonst vs here in Isaraell.  405
II. Profeta. Yett can I nott aspy be noo wysse
How thys chylde borne schuldbe w*ith*-ow[t] [5] naturis
 *pre*judyse.
God may act
contrary
to nature ;
I. Profeta. Nay, no prejvdyse vnto nature, I dare
  well sey ;
For the kyng of nature may
  Hawe all at his one wyll. [1]  410
consider
Aaron's rod.
 Dyd not *th*e powar of God
 Make Aronis rod
Beyre frute in on day ? [8]   413

---

[1] *This and the preceding line as one in* S.
[2] *Lines 385-7 as one in* S.
[3] M. *Qy.* renable. [4] S. subscryve, *corr. by* M.
[5] *Corr. by* S.   [6] *Lines 398-400 as one in* S.
[7] M. *prints* feymy[ny]ne. [8] *Lines 411-3 as one in* S.

II. PROFETA.   Truth yt ys in-ded.

I. PROFETA.   Then loke you and rede.          (96)

II. PROFETA.   A ! I perseyve the sede
Where apon thatt you spake.[1]                    417
Yt wasse for owre nede
   *That* he frayle nature did take,[1]
And his blod he schuld schede
   Amens forto make[1]
     For owre transegression ;          422
   Ase yt ys seyd in *pro*fece
   *That* of the lyne of Jude[1]
Schuld spryng a right Messe,
   Be whom all wee
     Schall[2] haue reydemcion.[1]          427

*(The second prophet now understands the plan of redemption.)*

I. PROFETA.   S*i*r, now ys the tyme cu*m*,
*And* the date there-of ruñ,
   Off his Natevete.
   II. PROFETA.   Yett I beseke you hartele
   *That* ye wold schoo me how[1]
Thatt this strange nowelte
   Were broght vnto you.                    434

*(The time is come.)*

I. PROFETA.   This othur nyght soo cold
Hereby apon a wolde
Schep*par*dis wachyng there fold,
   In the nyght soo far
   To them aperid a star,
   *And*[3] eyu*er* yt drev them nar ;          440
Wyche star the did behold
Bryght*er*, *th*e sey, M folde
   Then the sun so clere
   In his mydday spere,
And the these tythyngis tolde.                  445

*(The shepherds have seen his star, 1000 times brighter than the noonday sun.)*

II. PROFETA.   Whatt, seycretly ?
I. PROFETA.   Na, na, hardely ;
   The made there-of no conseil ,

*(No secret.)*

[1] *This and the preceding line as one in* S.
[2] *So* M.; S. schalld ; *Qy.* schulld.     [3] M. And.

For the song ase lowde
Ase eyuer the cowde
   Presyng the kyng of Isaraell.     451

'In what palace was it?'

II. PROFETA.  Yett do I marvell    (97)
In whatt pyle¹ or castell
   These herdmeñ dyd hym see.    454

'In no such place;

I. PROFETA.  Nothur in hallis nor yett in bowris
   Born wold he not be,
Nother in castellis nor yet in tówris
   *That* semly were to se;    458

But att hys Fathurs wyll,
The *profeci* to full-fyll,

between two beasts according to prophecy.' *Hab.* iii. 2 (Sept.).

   Be-twyxt an ox and² an as
   *Jesus*, *this* kyng, borne he was.
Heyvin he bryng us tyll!    463

II. PROFETA.  Si*r*, a! but when these schepp*ardis*³
   had seyne hym there,
In-to whatt place did the repeyre?

The shepherds went forth rejoicing,

I. PROFETA.  Forthe the went and glad *the* were,
   Going *the* did syng;
W*ith* myrthe *and* solas *th*e made good chere
   For joie of *that* new tything;    469

And aftur, asse I hard the[m]⁴ tell,
He reywardid them full well:
He graunt them hevyn *ther*-in to dwell;
   In ar the gon w*ith* joie and myrthe,

singing a Christmas song.

And there songe hit ys " Neowell."    474

   *There the profettis gothe furthe* and *Erod cumyth in, and the messenger.*

A herald.

NONCEOSE.⁶  Faytes pais, dñyis,⁵ baronys de grande
   reynowne!

¹ 1817 *ed.* pallays.    ² *Repeated in* M.
³ M. shepp*ardis*.    ⁴ *So* M.
⁵ Sheldon *suggests that this is the* pl. *of* O.F. dame, damne, *influenced by the spelling of some form of* Lat. dominus.
⁶ *In his note Prof. Manly says:* " In reading this proclamation I have had the aid of both Prof. Kittredge and Prof. Sheldon. As this aid, however, was given a year or two ago in the form of a

Payis, seneoris, schevaleris de nooble posance ! [1]
Pays, gentis homos,[2] *companeonys petis egrance* ! [3]
Je vos com*m*and dugard treytus [4] sylance.
Payis, tanque vottur nooble Roie syre ese p*r*esance ! [5]  479  commands<br>everybody to<br>be silent,
Que nollis [6] *p*ersone ese non fawis *p*er*w*ynt [7] dedfffer-
    ance,
Nese [8] harde de frappas ; [9] mayis gardus to to [10]  patient and<br>reverential in<br>presence of<br>King Herod.
    paceance,—
Mayis gardus [11] voter seneor to cor [12] reyue*r*ance ;  (98)
Car elat vottur Roie to to puysance.[13]
Anon̄ de leo,[14] pase tos ! je vose cum*m*ande,
E lay Roie erott la grandeaboly vos vmport.[15]    485


ERODE.  *Qui statis* [16] in Jude et Rex Iseraell,
    And the myghttyst conquerowre [17] *that* eyue*r*  Herod made<br>heaven and<br>hell,
      walkid on grownd ; [17]
For I am evyn he thatt made bothe hevin *and* hell,
    And of my myghte powar holdith vp *thi*s world
      rownd.
    Magog *and* Madroke, bothe *th*e[m] [18] did I con-  defeated<br>Magog and<br>Madroke,
      fownde,
And wit*h* this bryght bronde there bonis I brak on-
    sund*er*,
Thatt all the wyde worlde on those rappis did wonder. 492

---

pretty lively oral discussion of the most perplexing of the difficulties,
and as I unfortunately neglected to take any notes at the time, I
find myself unable, except in one or two cases, to remember to
which of the two each suggestion belongs. Of course they are not
responsible for any mistakes that may appear here. I have printed
the text with no change except in punctuation." *All of the notes
upon this passage are taken directly from* M.

  [1] puissance.
  [2] *The second* o *is probably only a careless form of* e.
  [3] et grands.    [4] de garder trestous.
  [5] roi seit ici present.    [6] nulle.
  [7] Kittredge : ici non fasse point.    [8] Ne se.
  [9] frapper.   [10] gardez tote.
  [11] *A preposition before the indirect object seems unnecessary.*
  [12] tote.   [13] Sheldon : Car il est votre roi tout puissant.
  [14] A (=au) nom de lui (Sheldon *suggests* loi *instead of* lui).
  [15] Sheldon *suggests that the line properly ends with* grand (*modify-
ing* Erott *and rhyming with* 484),—diable vos emporte ! *being
merely an unattached pleasantry addressed to the audience.*
  [16] Qui statis *is in red in* S.
  [17—17] M. *that . . .* ground.    [18] *So* M.

the cause of
light and
thunder

I am the cawse of this grett lyght and thund*er*;
  Ytt ys throgh my fure *that* the soche noyse dothe
    make.

My feyrefull contenance *the* clowdis so doth incumbur
  *That* oftym*is* for drede *the*r-of the verre yerth

and earth-
quakes;

    doth quake.
  Loke, when I w*ith* males this bryght brond doth
    schake,
All the whole world from the north to *the* sowthe
I ma them dystroie w*ith* won worde of my mowthe !  499

To reycownt vnto you myn innevmerabull substance,—
  Thatt were to moche for any tong to tell;

he is prince
of purgatory
and captain
of hell,

For all the whole Orent ys und*er* myn obbeydeance,
  *And* prynce am I of purgatorre *and* cheff capten
    of hell;
  And those tyraneos trayturs be force ma I co*m*pell

and could
annihilate his
enemies by
batting his
eye.

Myne eñmyis to vanquese *and* evyn to dust them
    dryve,
*And* w*ith* a twynke of myn iee not won to be lafte
    alyve.                                            506

Behold my contenance and my colur,
  Bryghtur then the sun in the meddis of *the* dey.

To look at
him is better
than meat or
drink.

Where can you haue a more grettur succur
  Then to behold my p*er*son that ys soo gaye ?
  My fawcun *and* my fassion, w*ith* my gorgis araye,—
He thatt had the gr*ace* all-wey *the*r-on to thynke,
Lyve the[1] myght all-wey w*ith*-owt othur meyte or
    drynke.                                           513

*And* thys my tryomfande fame most hylist dothe a-
    bownde
  Throgh-owt this world in all reygeons abrod,

He resembles
Mahomet, is
descended
from Jupiter
and is a
cousin to
the Deity.

Reysemelyng the fau*er* of thatt most myght Mahownd;
  From Jubytor be desent *and* cosyn to the grett
    God,                                             (99)
  And namyd the most reydowndid kyng[2] Eyrodde,
Wyche thatt all pryncis hath und*er* subjeccion
And all there whole powar vndur my p*ro*teccion.     520

_____

[1] M. *emends to* he.   *Cp. ll.* 685–8.      [2] M. king.

And therefore, my hareode here, callid Calcas,
  Warne thow eyue*ere*[1] porte thatt noo schyppis
   a-ryve,
Nor also aleond stranger throg my realme pas,
  But the for there truage do pay markis fyve. 524
   Now spede the forth hastele,
   For the thatt wyll the contrare
   Apon a galowse hangid schalbe,
*And*, be Mahownde, of me the gett noo *grace*! 528

*His herald Calchas must announce a tax of five marks on foreigneıs.*

NONCIOS. Now, lord and mastur, in all the hast
  Thy worethe wyll ytt schall be wroght,
*And* thy ryall cuntreyis schalbe past
  In asse schort tyme ase can be thoght. 532

*Calchas will do it.*

ERODE. Now schall owre regeons throgh-owt be soght
  In eyue*ere*[1] place bothe est *and* west;
Yff any katyffis to me be broght,
  Yt schalbe nothyng for there best.
  And the whyle thatt I do resst,
Trompettis, viallis, and othur armone
Schall bles the wakyng of my maieste. 539

*A search for aliens ordered.*

  *Here Erod goth awey* and *the iij kyngis speykyth in* the
  strete.

*Matt.* ii. 1-12.

I. REX. Now blessid be God of his swet sonde,
  For yondur a feyre bryght star I do see!
Now ys he co͞mon, vs a-monge,
  Asse the *p*rofet[2] seyd thatt yt schuld be. 543

*The first king sees the star*

A seyd[3] there schuld a babe be borne,
  Comyng of the rote of Jesse,
To sawe mankynd that wasse for-lorne;
  And truly come*n* now ys he. 547

*and remem-bers the prophecy, Isa.* ix. 1.

Reyue*rence and* worschip to hym woll I do  (100)
  Asse God and man, thatt all made of noght.
All the *p*rofettis acordid and seyd evyn soo,
  That wit*h* hys *p*resseos blod mankynd schuld be
   boght. 551

---

[1] *Contraction for* er.  [2] S. profettis, *emend. by* M.
[3] S. Aseyd, *corr. by* M. *Qy.* A seyd = they said.

He grant me *grace*,
  Be yonder star *tha*t I see,[1]
And in-to thatt place
  Bryng me [1]
    Thatt I ma hym worschipe w*ith* umellete
And se hys gloreose face.                                   557

*The second King has lost his way,*

II. REX.    Owt of my wey I deme thatt I am,
    For toocuns of thys cuntrey can I non see ;
Now, God, thatt on yorth madist man,
    Send me su*m* knoleyge where thatt I be !        561

*sees the star of prophecy,*

Yondur, me thynke, a feyre, bryght star I see,
    The wyche be-tocunyth the byrth of a chyld
Thatt hedur ys cu*m* to make man fre ;
    He borne of a mayde,[2] and sche nothyng defyld.  565

*will worship the child.*

To worschip thatt chyld ys myn in-tent ;
    Forth now wyll I take my wey.
I trust su*m* cu*m*pany God hathe me sent,
    For yonde*r* I se a kyng labur on the wey ;      569

*He sees the other King.*

To-warde hym now woll I ryde.
    Harke ! cu*m*ly kyng, I you pray,
In-to whatt cost wyll ye thys tyde,
    Or weddur lyis youre jurney ?                     573

*They converse.*

I. REX.    To seke a chylde ys myne in-tent
Of whom the p*r*ofetis hathe ment ;
The tyme ys cu*m*, now ys he sent,
    Be yondur star here ma [you][3] see.               577
II. REX.    Sir, I prey you, w*ith* your lysence,
To ryde w*i*th you vnto his presence ;
To hym wyll I offur frank-in-sence,
    For the hed of all Whole Churche schall he be.  581

*The third King is also lost,*

III. REX.    I ryde wanderyng in veyis wyde,    (101)
        Ou*er* montens and dalis ; I wot not where I am.
Now, Kyng off all kyngis, send me soche gyde
        Thatt I myght haue knoleyge of thys cuntreys
            name.                                          585

---

[1] *This and the preceding line as one in* S.
[2] S. *amayde, corr. by* M.        [3] *Supplied by* S.

A! yondur I se a syght, be-semyng all afar,
    The wyche be-tocuns sum nevis, ase I troo;
Asse me thynke, a chyld peryng in a stare.
    I trust he be cum *that* schall defend vs from woo. 589

*(margin: and also sees the star.)*

To kyngis yondur I see,
    And to them woll I ryde[1]
Forto haue there cumpane;
    I trust *th*e wyll me abyde.[1]      593

*(margin: The Kings meet,)*

Hayle, cumly kyngis augent![2]
Good surs, I pray you, whedder ar ye ment?
I. Rex.   To seke a chylde ys owre in-tent,
    Wyche be-tocuns yonder star, asse ye ma see.    597
II. Rex.   To hym I purpose thys present.
    III. Rex.   Surs, I pray you, and thatt ryght
             vmblee,
    With you thatt I ma ryde in cumpane.
    [? All.][3]   To all-myghte God now prey we
    Thatt hys pressiose persone we ma se.      602

*(margin: and ride in company.)*

    *Here Erode cumyth in ageyne* and *the messengere seyth:*

Nuncios.   Hayle, lorde most off myght!
Thy commandement ys right;
In-to thy land ys comyn *thi*s nyght
    iij kyngis and *with* them a grett cumpany.    606
Erod.   Whatt make those kyngis in this cuntrey?
Noncios.   To seke a kyng and a chyld, the sey.
    Erode.   Of whatt age schuld he bee?
    Noncios.   Skant twellve deyis old fulle.      610

*(margin: Herod learns of the kings and their mission.)*

Erod.   And wasse he soo late borne?      (102)
Noncios.   E! syr, soo the schode me, thys same dey
    in the morne.
Erod.   Now, in payne of deyth, bryng them me
    beforne;
    And there-fore, harrode, now hy the in hast,    614
In all spede thatt thow[4] were dyght
    Or thatt those kyngis the cuntrey be past;
Loke thow bryng them all iij before my syght;    617

*(margin: 'Bring them before me on pain of death.)*

---

[1] *This and the preceding line as one in* S.
[2] M. *Qy.* and gent.     [3] *Suggested by* M.     [4] M. thou.

And in Jerusalem[1] inquere more of that chyld.

But I warne the that thy wordis be mylde,
For there must[2] thow hede and crafte wey[lde][3]
How to for-do his powere ; and those iij kyngis shalbe
   begild.         621

NONCIOS. Lorde, I am redde att youre byddyng
To sarve the ase my lord and kyng ;
For joye there-of, loo, how I spryng
With lyght hart and fresche gamboldyng
   Alofte here on this molde !    626
ERODE. Then sped the forthe hastely,
And loke that thow beyre the eyvinly ;
And also I pray the hartely
Thatt thow doo comand me
   Bothe to yong and olde.[4]    631

    [*The messenger goes to the kings.*]

NUNCIOS. Hayle, syr kyngis, in youre degre ;
  Erood, kyng of these cuntreyis wyde,
Desyrith to speyke with you all thre,
   And for youre comyng he dothe abyde. 635

I. REX. Syr, att his wyll we be ryght bayne.
  Hy us, brethur, vnto thatt lordis place ;
To speyke with hym we wold be fayne ;
   Thatt chyld thatt we seke, he grant us of his
    grace !         639
    [*They go to Herod.*]

NUNCIOS. Hayle, lorde with-owt pere !
  These iij kyngis here have we broght.

ERODE. Now welcum, syr kyngis, all in fere ; (103)
  But of my bryght ble, surs, bassche ye noght ! 643

Sir kyngis, ase I vndurstand,
A star hathe gydid you into my land,
Where-in grett harie[5] ye haue fonde
   Be reysun of hir beymis bryght.   647

---

[1] S. Jerusalen, *corr. by* M.
[2] S. mast, *corr. by* M.  [3] *Emend. by* M.
[4] *Lines* 629–631 *as two in* S., *the first ending with doo.*
[5] M. *changes to* harting.

u································································································································································································································

Wherefore I pray you hartely
The vere truthe thatt ye wold *sertefy*,
How long yt ys surely
    Syn of that star you had furst syght.     651

*He inquires about the star.*

i. REX. Sir kynge, the vere truthe to sey
    And forto schoo you ase hit ys best,
This same ys evin the xij^th dey
    Syth yt aperid to vs to be west.[1]     655

ERODE. Brethur, then ys there no more to sey,
But *with* hart and wyll kepe ye your jurney
And cum whom by me this same wey,
    Of your nevis thatt I myght knoo.     659
You schall tryomfe in this cuntre
And *with* grett conquorde bankett *with* me,
And thatt chyld myself then woll I see
    And honor hym also.     663

*'Come home this way and banquet with me.'*

ii. REX. Sir, youre commandement we woll fullfyll
And humbly abaye owreself there-tyll.[2]
He thatt weldith all thyng at wyll
    The redde way hus teyche,[3]
Sir kyng, thatt we ma passe your land in pes!
ERODE. Yes, and walke softely eyvin at your one es; 669

*They agree,*

Youre pase-porte for a C deyis
    Here schall you haue of clere cummand,
Owre reme to labur any weyis
    Here schall you haue be spesschall grante.     673

*and receive a passport.*

iii. REX. Now fare-well, kyng of hy degre,   (104)
    Humbly of you owre leyve we take.
ERODE. Then adev, sir kyngis all thre;
And whyle I lyve, be bold of me!
There ys nothyng in this cuntre
    But for youre one ye schall yt take.     679

[1] 1817 Ed. *has* to us be west, *which is probably the original reading.*
[2] M. *Qy.* there-to.   [3] M. *Qy.* show.

E

*[Exeunt the three kings.]*

Herod will
put them to
death when
they return.

Now these iij kyngis are gon on the*r* wey ;
    On-wysely *and* on-wyttely haue the all wroghte.
When the cum[1] ageyne, the schall dy *tha*t same dey,
    And thus these vyle wreychis to deyth *the* schalbe
        broght,—
        Soche ys my lykyng.                             684
He that agenst my lawis wyll hold,
Be he kyng or keysar neyu*er* soo bold,
I schall them cast in-to caris cold
        And to deyth I schall them bryng.               688

    *There Erode goth his weyis and the iij kyngis cum in
    agcyne.*

The kings
pray for
guidance and
behold the
star.

I. Rex.   O blessid God, moche ys thy myght !
Where ys this star thatt gawe vs lyght?                       690

II. Rex.   Now knele we downe here in this presence,
Be-sekyng that Lord of hy mangnefecens [2]
That we ma see his hy exsellence
    Yff thatt his swet wyll be ?[3]                         694

III. Rex.   Yondur, brothur, I see the star,
Where-by I kno he ys nott far ;
Therefore, lordis, goo we nar
    Into *thi*s pore place.                                  698

    *There the iij kyngis gois in-to the jesen, to Mare and hir
    child.*

The first
brings gold;

I. Rex.   Hayle, Lorde thatt all this worlde hathe
        wroght !
    Hale, God and man to-gedur in fere !    (105)
For thow hast made all thyng of noght,
    Albe-yt thatt thow lyist porely here ;
A cupe-full [of] [4] golde here I haue the broght,

the second,
incense ;

    In toconyng thow art w*ith*-out pere.                   704
II. Rex.   Hayle be thow, Lorde of hy mangnyffecens![5]
    In toconyng of preste[h]od[6] *and* dyngnete of
        offece,

---

[1] M. cum.    [2] S. maugnefecens, *corr. by* M.
[3] S. wylbe, *corr. by* M.    [4] *Corr. by* S.
[5] S. maugnyffecens, *corr. by* M.    [6] *So* M.

To the I offur a cupe-full off in-sence,
　　For yt be-hovith the to haue soche sacrefyce.　　708

III. REX.　Hayle be thow, Lorde longe lokid fore !
　　I haue broght the myre for mortalete,　　*the third, myrrh.*
In to-cunyng thow schalt mankynd restore
　　To lyff be thy deyth apoñ a tre.　　712

MARE.　God haue marce, kyngis, of yowre goodnes ;　　*Mary blesses them.*
　　Be the gydyng of the godhed hidder ar ye sent ;
The provyssion[1] off my swete sun your weyis whoñ
　　　　reydres,
And gostely reywarde you for youre present !　　716

*[As the kings go away, they say :]*

I. REX.　Syr kyngis, aftur owre promes　　*They are going home by way of Herod, but decide to rest.*
　　Whome be Erode I mvst nedis goo.
II. REX.　Now truly, brethur,[2] we can noo las,
　　But I am soo for-wachid[3] I wott not wat to do.　720

III. REX.　Right soo am I ; where-fore I you pray,
　　Lett all vs rest vs awhyle upon *this* grownd.
I. REX.　Brethur, your[4] seying ys right well vnto my
　　　　pay.
　　The grace of thatt swet chylde saue vs all sownde ! 724

*[They lie down, and while they sleep, an angel appears.]*

ANGELLUS.　Kyng of Tawrus, Sir Jespar,　　*An angel greets them and warns them.*
Kyng of Arraby, Sir Balthasar,
Melchor, Kyng of Aginare,
　　To you now am I sent.　　(106) 728
For drede of Eyrode, goo you west whom ;
In-to those parties when ye cum downe,
Ye schalbe byrrid with gret reynowne ;
　　The Wholle Gost thys[5] knoleyge hath sent. *[Exit.]* 732

I. REX.　Awake, sir kyngis, I you praye,　　*They talk it over.*
　　For the voise of an angell I hard in my dreyme.
II. REX.　Thatt ys full tru thatt ye do sey,
　　For he reyherssid owre names playne.　　736

---

[1] 1817 Ed. puyssion.　　[2] S. berthur, *corr. by* M.
[3] S. far wachid, *corr. by* M.　　[4] *Contr. for* er.　　[5] S., M. thus.

III. REX.   He bad thatt we schuld goo downe be west
       For drede of Eyrodis fawls be-traye.

I. REX.   Soo forto do, yt ys the best;
       The Child that we haue soght, gyde vs the wey !   740

Now fare-well, the feyrist of schapp so swete !
     And thankid be Jesus of his sonde,
Thatt[1] we iij to-geder soo suddenly schuld mete,
     Thatt dwell soo wyde and in straunge lond,      744

And here make owre presentacion
     Vnto this kyngis son clensid soo cleyne
And to his moder for ovre saluacion ;
     Of moche myrth now ma we meyne,
Thatt we soo well hath done this obblacion.      749

II. REX.   Now farewell, Sir Jaspar, brothur, to yoeu,
       Kyng of Tawrus the most worthe ;
Sir Balthasar, also to you I bow ;
     And I thanke you bothe of youre good cumpany
        Thatt we togeddur haue had.      754
     He thatt made vs to mete on hyll,
     I thanke hym now and eyuer I wyll ,
     For now may we goo with-owt yll,
        And off owre offerynge be full glad.[2]      758

III. REX.   Now syth thatt we mvst nedly goo    (107)
       For drede of Erode thatt ys soo wrothe,
Now fare-well brothur, and brothur also,
     I take my leve here at you bothe
        This dey on fete.[3]      763
     Now he thatt made vs to mete on playne
     And offur[4] to Mare in hir jeseyne,
     He geve vs grace in heyvin a-gayne
        All to-geyder to mete !      767

*[They go out, and Herod and his train occupy the pageant.]*

NUNCIOS.   Hayle, kynge,[5] most worthist in wede !
       Hayle, manteinar of curtese throgh all this world
       wyde !

---

[1] M. That.     [2] S. fayne, *corr. by* M.     [3] S. fote, *corr. by* M.
[4] S. offurde, *corr. by* M.     [5] M. kyng.

Hayle, the most myghtyst that eyu*er* bestrod a stede!
Ha[y]ll,[1] most monfullist moñ in armor man to
    abyde!
      Hayle, in thyne hoonowre!      772
Thesse iij kyngis *tha*t forthe were sent
And schuld haue cu*m* ageyne before *th*e here
  p*r*esent,
Anothur wey, lorde, whom the went,
    Contrare to thyn honowre.      776

*The three kings went home another way.'*

ERODE.  A-nothur wey? owt! owt! owtt!
  Hath those fawls traytvrs done me *thi*s ded?
I stampe! I stare! I loke all abowtt!
  Myght I them take, I schuld them bren at a glede!
I rent! I rawe! *and* now run I wode!
A! thatt these velen trayturs hath mard *thi*s my mode!
    The schalbe hangid yf I ma cu*m* them to!  783

*Herod rages.*

*Here Erode ragis in* the *pagond* and *in the strete also.*

    E! and thatt kerne of Bedlem, he schalbe ded
    And thus schall I for-do his profece.[2]    785

*He will slay the Child. Matt.ii.16-18.*

How sey you, s*i*r knyghtis? ys not this the best red,
Thatt all yong chyldur for this schuld be dede,
    Wyth swor*d*e to be slayne?    (108) 788
  Then schall I, Erod, lyve in lede,
  And all folke me dowt and drede,
  And offur to me bothe gold, rychesse, *and* mede;
    Thereto wyll the be full fayne.    792

I. MYLES.  My lorde, kyng Erode be name,
  Thy wordis agenst my wyll schalbe;
To see soo ma*n*y yong chyld*e*r dy ys schame,
  Therefore consell *the*r-to gettis *tho*u non of me.  796

*The soldiers would rather not.*

II. MYLES.  Well seyd, fello, my trawth I plyght.
  S*i*r kyng, p*er*seyve right well you may,
Soo grett a morder to see of yong frute
  Wyll make a rysyng in *th*i noone cuntrey.  800

ERODE.  A rysyng! Owt! owt! owt!    801

---

[1] *Corr. by* S.    [2] *Qy.* his profece for-do.

*There Erode ragis ageyne and then seyth thus:*

Herod threat-
ens to hang
them.

Owt! velen wrychis, har apon you I cry!
    My wyll vtturly loke *that* yt be wroght,
Or apon a gallowse bothe you schall dy,
        Be Mahownde most myghtyste, *that* me dere
            hath boght!                                        805

I. MYLES.    Now, cruell Erode, syth we schall do this
        dede!
    Your wyll nedefully in this realme mvste be wroght;
All the chylder of *that* age dy the mvst nede;
    Now w*ith* all my myght the schall be vpsoght.      809

They swear
obedience.

II. MYLES.    And I woll sweyre here apon your bryght
        sworde,[1]
    All the chylder thatt I fynd, sclayne *the* schalbe;
Thatt make many a mod*er* to wepe and be full sore
        aferde[2]
    In owre armor bryght when the hus see.    (109) 813

ERODE.    Now you have sworne, forth *that* ye goo,
    And my wyll thatt ye wyrke bothe be dey *and*
        nyght,

He trips like
a doe.

And then wyll I for fayne trypp lyke a doo.
    But whan the be ded I warne you bryng ham[3]
        be-fore my syght.                                    817

*Matt.* ii. 13-15.

[*Herod and his train go away, and Joseph and Mary are,*
    *while asleep, addressed by an angel.*]

ANGELL*US*.    Mare and Josoff, to you I sey,
    Swete word from the Fathur I bryng you full
        ryght:

'Go forth
into Egypt!'

Owt of Bedlem in-to Eygype forth goo ye *the* wey
    And w*ith* you take the King, full of myght,
        ·For drede of Eroddis red*e*!                       822

JOSOFF.    A-ryse up, Mare, hastely and sone;
    Owre Lordis wyll nedys mvst be done,
        Lyke ase the angell vs bad.                         825

───────────

[1] M. *changes to* swerde.
[2] *This line as two in* S., *the first ending with* wepe.
[3] M. *prints* [t]ham.

MARE.  Mekely, Josoff, my none spowse,                      'Meekly let
    Towarde that cuntrey let vs reypeyre;                us go!'
Att Eygyp [1]to sum cun off[1] howse,
    God grant hus grace saff to cum there !        829

    *Here the wemen[2] cum in wythe there chyldur, syngyng[3]*
    *them; and Mare and Josoff goth awey cleyne.*

I. WOMON.  I lolle my chylde wondursly swete,             The mothers
And in my narmis I do hyt kepe,                           hush their
    Be-cawse thatt yt schuld not crye.               babes.

II. WOMAN.  Thatt babe thatt ys borne in Bedlem,
      so meke,
    He saue my chyld and me from velany !          834

III. WOMAN.  Be styll, be styll, my lyttull chylde!
    That Lorde of lordis saue bothe the *and* me! (110)
For Erode hath sworne with wordis wyld
    Thatt all yong chyldur sclayne the schalbe.    838

I. MYLES.  Sey ye, wyddurde wyvis, whydder ar ye         The soldiers
    a-wey?                                           will obey
    What beyre you in youre armis nedis mvst we se.  Herod's
Yff the be mañ-chyldur, dy the mvst this dey,            commands.
    For at Eroddis wyll all thyng mvst be.         842

II. MYLES.  And I in handis wonys them hent,
    Them forto sley noght woll I spare ;
We mvst full-fyll Erodis commandement,
    Elis be we asse trayturs *and* cast all in care.   846

I. WOMAN.  Sir knyghtis, of youre curtessee,             'Desist, for
Thys dey schame not youre chevaldre,                     shame!' says
But on my child[4] haue pytte                             the first.
      For my sake in this styde ;                850
For a sympull sclaghtur yt were to sloo
Or to wyrke soche a chyld[5] woo,
That can noder speyke nor goo,
      Nor neuer harme did.                       854

---

[1]—[1] M. *introduces this emend. by* Kittredge; S. *sum tocun off.*
[2] M. *wemen.*      [3] *The song* (II.) *is at the end of the pageant.*
[4] M. *chyld.*      [5] M. *chylde.*

The second
will defend
her child.
II. WOMON.[1]  He thatt sleyis my chyld in syght,
Yff thatt my strokis on hym ma lyght,
Be he skwyar or knyght,
   I hold hym but lost.       858
Se, thow fawls losyngere,
A stroke schalt thow beyre me here[2]
   And spare for no cost.      861

A third will
lay on with
a pot ladle.
III. WOMAN.  Sytt he neyuer soo hy in saddull,
But I schall make his braynis addull,
*And* here w*ith* my pott-ladull
   W*ith* hym woll I fyght.    (111) 865
I schall ley on hym, a[s] thogh[3] I wode were,
W*ith* thys same womanly geyre ;
There schall noo man steyre,
   Wheddur thatt he be kyng or knyght.    869

*[Here they kill the children.]*

' Did you
ever hear
such a cry ? '
I. MYLES.  Who hard eyuer soche a cry
   Of wemen thatt there chyldur haue lost,
And grettly reybukyng chewaldry
   Throgh-owt this reme in eyuere[4] cost,
   Wyche many a mans lyff ys lyke to cost ?
For thys grett wreyche *tha*t here ys done
I feyre moche wengance *the*r-off woll cu*m*.    876

II. MYLES.  E ! brothur, soche talis may we not tell ;
   Where-fore to the kyng lett vs goo,
The King
must bear
the blame.
For he ys lyke to beyre the perell,
   Wyche wasse the cawser that we did soo.
Yett must the all be broght hym to
W*ith* waynis and waggyns fully fryght ;
I tro there wolbe a carefull syght.   *[They go to Herod.]* 883

They report.
I. MYLES.  Loo ! Eyrode, kyng, here mast thow see
   How many M' thatt we haue slayne.
II. MYLES.  And nedis thy wyll full-fyllid must be ;
   There ma no mon sey there-ageyne.    887

[1] M. WOMAN.    [2] *Contr. for* er.
[3] S. athog, *corr. by* M.    [4] *So* M., S. eyueer.

[*Enter Nuntius.*]

Nuncios.   Eyrode, kyng, I schall the tell,
   All thy dedis ys cum to noght;
This chyld ys gone in-to Eygipte to dwell.
     Loo! sir, in thy none land what wondurs byn
       wroght!                   891

*The flight into Egypt made known.*

Erod.   Into Eygipte? alas, for woo!     (112)
   Lengur in lande here I canot abyde;
Saddull my palfrey, for in hast wyll I goo,
     Aftur yondur trayturs now wyll I ryde,
       Them for to sloo.              896
     Now all men hy fast
     In-to Eygipte in hast!
     All thatt cuntrey woll I tast,
       Tyll I ma cum them to.        900

*Herod rides after the fugitives.*

## Fynes lude de taylars and scharmen.

Tys[1] matter / nevly correcte be Robart Croo / the xiiij[th] dey of marche / fenysschid in the yere of owre Lorde God / M CCCCC & xxxiiij[te]. / then beyng mayre mastur Palmar / also mastris of the seyd fellyschipp Hev Corbett / Randull Pynkard and / John Baggeley.

---

*Theise songes* (113) / *belonge to / the Taylors* and *Shearemens Pagant. / The first and the laste the shepheards singe / and the second or middlemost the women singe.*

### Thomas Mawdycke

Die decimo tertio Maij anno domini millessimo quingentesimo nonagesimo primo. / Praetor fuit ciuitatis Couentriæ D. Mathaeus[2] Richardson, tunc Consules / Johanes Whitehead *et* Thomas Grauener.[3]

---

### Song I.

As I out rode this enderes night,
Of thre ioli sheppardes I saw a sight,
And all a-bowte there fold a star shone bright;
    *They sange terli terlow;*
    *So mereli the sheppards ther pipes can blow.*   5

[1] S. T[h]ys.    [2] S. Mathaens, *corr. by* M.    [3] M. Crauener.

## Song II.

*Lully, lulla, thow littell tine child,*
*By by, lully lullay, thow littell tyne child,*
*By by, lully lullay !*

O sisters too,
How may we do[1]
    For to preserve *th*is day
This pore yongling
For whom we do singe[1]
    By by, lully lullay ?              6

Herod, the king,                  (114)
In his raging,[1]
    Chargid he hath this day
His men of might
In his owne sight[1]
        All yonge children to slay,—      12

That wo is me,
Pore child, for thee,[1]
    And ever morne and may[2]
For thi parting
Nether say nor singe,[1]
    By by, lully lullay.            18

## Song III.

Doune from heave*n*, from heave*n* so hie,
Of angeles *th*er came a great co͞mpanie,
Wi*th* mirthe and ioy and great solemnitye,
    *The sange terly terlow ;*
    *So mereli the sheppards ther pipes can blow.*    5

[1] *This and the preceding line as one in* S.
[2] S. say; M. *attrib. corr. to* Kittredge.

# The Pageant of the Weavers.

[DRAMATIS PERSONÆ.

*i. Profeta*
*ii. Profeta*  } In the Prophet Play (Ll. 1–176).
*iii. Profeta*
*Simeon*
*Anna*
*i. Angel*
*ii. Angel*
*Clarecus*  } In the Purification (Ll. 177–721).
*Gabriel*
*Mary*
*Joseph*
*Joseph*
*Mary*
*Jesus*      In the Disputation in the Temple
*i. Doctor*      (Ll. 722–1191).]
*ii. Doctor*
*iii. Doctor*

PROFETA *PRIMUS.*   Ye grett[2] astronemars[3] now awake, (31)   'Strange news! A star has appeared in the east.'
   W*ith* youre[4] fam*us* fatheres of felosefy
And in-to the oreient reyspecte[5] ye take,
   Where nevis *and* strangis be c*um* of lately,
   Affermyng the seyng of old p*ro*fecie,
Thatt a star[6] schuld apere
Apon the hyll of Wawse among hus here!                    7

II. PROFETA.[7]   Ye brethur all, then be of good chere,   'It is the star of prophecy.'
   For those tythings makyth[8] my hart ful lyght!
We haue desirid many a yere
   Of thatt star to haue a syght,
   And spesschalli of that kyng of myght

[1] Reprinted from *The Presentation in the Temple, A Pageant,* *as originally represented by the Corporation of Weavers in Coventry.* Edinburgh : Printed for the Abbotsford Club, 1836.   The editor of this was Thomas Sharp.   In the footnotes, S. indicates this edition. H. indicates the edition by Professor F. Holthausen in *Anglia,* N. F. XIII., 209–50.   The MS., with which this text has been collated, belongs to the Clothiers and Broad Weavers' Company of Coventry, and is to be placed among the Corp. MSS.   MS. b refers to the fragments of another version printed for the first time in Appendix IV.
[2] MS. b. Ye gret, MS. E! grett (?), S. Grett.
[3] H. *emends to* astronomars, *many similar changes below.*
[4] S. youre, H. ye.   [5] MS. b. aspecte.   [6] H. *inserts* [of Jacob].
[7] S. PROFETA II ; *so below for prophets, angels, and doctors.*
[8] S. in wyth, *corr. emend. by* H.

Of whose cum*yng* we haue playne warnyng
Be this same star aftur *pro*fettis desernyng.[1]   (32)      14

The second
prophet
wishes to
know more
of it.

Yet furthur, I p*ra*[2] you for my larnyng,
Lett hus hawe[3] *sum* comenecacion
Of this star be oldd prog*no*stefying[4]
How hit aperid[5] *and* under whatt fassion.                18

I. PROFETA.   Sir, aftur a strange deformacion[6]
As be atorite reyherse I can ;

It signifies
the Nativity,

For this same star be int*er*pretacion
Syngnefyth[7] the natevete of a man ;                        22

according to
the prophet
Balaam.'
*Num.* xxiv.
17.

As the p*ro*fett Balam
    In his text afarmyth right well,
        Seying : " *Orietur stella ex Jacobo, et exsurget*
            *homo de Israel.*"                               25

He seyd of Iacobe a star schuld springe,
Wyche syngnefyith only this same kynge
    Thatt amongist vs now ys *cum.*
And as towchyng the letter folloyng :
    *Et ip*s*e dominabitur omni gene*ra*cione.*             30

the manner
of his birth.

II. PROFETA.   Sir, here ma be movid a questeon
    Of this nobull prince of soo hi degree,
The wyche of all men schall haue domeneon,
    Vndur what maner borne he schuld be.

I. PROFETA.   Ase ye schall here right wonder-
    fulle[8]
Be devine powar of a virgene pure,
Afarmyng the p*ro*feci agenst all nature.        (33)      37

II. PROFETA.   Where fynde you *that* in wholle scrip-
    ture
    Before prog*no*stefide[4] this to be done ?

Isaiah the
authority.
*Isa.* vii. 14.

I. PROFETA.   Isaee the p*ro*fett wrytith full sure,
    *Ecce virgo concipiet,*[9] *pariet filium !*      [f. 1 *a*]
    Balam seyng of the heyvinly wyssedome[10]

---

[1] H. *changes to* desarnyng ; *many similar alterations throughout.*
[2] H. *writes* pra[y], *similarly below in numerous other cases.*
[3] H. *changes* w *to* v ; *so below in other similar words.*
[4] *Contraction for* pro.      [5] S. aperie.      [6] MS. b. demonstracion.
[7] S. Syngnefyn, MS. *illegible,* MS. b. singnefith.      [8] S. wonderfull.
[9] H. *inserts* [et].      [10] H. *puts this line in the foot-notes.*

A man schuld spryng here in Isaraell,
  The [1] seyd Isayee answeyring to *that* questeon : [2]
*Et vocabit*ur *nomen eius Emanvel.*    45

II. PROFETA.  Yett haue I grett marvell,    *' How could such a pro-phecy be made ? '*
How thatt men schuld tell [3]
Off such strangis before the fell,
  And man beyng here but a mortall creature.[2]    49
    I. PROFETA.  Be devine powar, I make you sure,
The sprete of profece to them was sent,
  Soo to subscrybe in wholle scripture,[2]
And yett them-selfe wyst not watt yt ment.    53

II. PROFETA.  Now laude be vnto hym *that* soche
    knoleyge sent
Vnto hus wreychis of pore symplecete.
Where[4] he ys Lord *and* God om*n*ipotent,    (34)
  In this hys wyll to make hus preve !
    I. PROFETA.  Did nott *that* profett man Malache    *The prophecy of Malachi. Mal.* iv. 2.
Resite vnto hus on this same wyse
Thatt the sun of lyff schall spring *and* arise?    60

Wyche cawsid Isaee to cast up his iees    *Isaiah's prayer.*
  Toward heyvin w*ith* all his inward syght,
Seying, " Good Lord, afarmyng thy promes,
  Send downe to hus this wonly sun off myght,
  Huse to reystore vnto owre right !
Owt of deserte, from the hard stone,    *Isa.* li. 3.
Reycomfordyng th*i* doghtur dwyllyng in Sion ! "    67

Also Jaramo,[5] thatt wholle mõn,    *Jeremiah's prophecy.*
  Seyd in heyvin God schuld make seede,
A greyne off Davith, thatt now ys cu*m*,    *Jer.* xxxiii. 22. (?)
  Wyche eyu*er* in gracys shall spring and spreyde
  And kepe Juda owt off drede
And also Isaraell sett in surenes,
And he schall make jugementis of rightwesenes.    74

---

[1] H. *emends* The[n].
[2] *This and the preceding line inverted in* H.
[3] *This and the preceding line as one in* H.
[4] H. *h*is Where[as].   [5] H. *alters to* Jareme.

The second
Prophet is
astonished.

II. Profeta.   I wondre to here you this expres,
    Be actoris hi, this worthe mystere,
And spesschalle of this virtu rightwessenes,
    Where hit schalbe vsid and in whatt parte.      78

More about
the coming of
the Messiah.

I. Profeta.   Apon the yarthe bothe with hy and loo
    degre ;
And rightwessenes men schall hym call,    (35)
When he schall cum to sit in the see    [f. 2]
    Of King Davit, that most riall stall ; [1]
    And ther schall he before the pristis all
Of Juda and Leyve be his powar device,
    With nev [2] insence to do sacrefyce.      85

To God aboue for the grett offence
    Of the peple and for [3] yngnorance,[4]
With there offeringe to make reycompence
    For the lenage of Adamis progeny.
    This schall this childe by theym free
From all the offencis thatt the haue done
Be cruell deyth and bytter passion.      92

Further
question
about the
star.

II. Profeta.   Good [5] sir, yett under produstacion [6]
    Owre feyth thereby for to incresse,
Of this star lett hus haue reylacion,
How hit aperid and vndur whatt fassion,
    Yff hit wold pleyse you for to expresse.[7]

Description
of the vision.

I. Profeta.   With diuers streymis of grett
    brightnes,      98

A child therin of flagrant swetnes,
    Wyche apon his bake a crosse did beyre,
And of an eygull hit bare the lykenes,
    Beytyng his wyngis into the eyre ;
    A woise there-in off lange feyre [8]
Thatt wasse hard throgh-owt the cuntrey,

Luke ii. 11.

Seyinge : " Natus est nobis oddie rex Judeorum—et
    sethere." [9]    (36)  105

---

[1] S. of all.  H. omits of all.
[2] H. changes v to w ; so below in similar words.
[3] H. inserts [their].    [4] H. inserts [hi]
[5] H. God.    [6] H. changes to protestacion.
[7] H. inverts this and the preceding line.    [8] S. lange feyfe ;
H. has lang[ag]e feyre.    [9] H. corr. [h]odie . . . cetera.

ii. Profeta.  Of a farthur declaracion I wold you praye,    *Further*
    Whatt trybus the were *and* in whatt p*a*rte,    *question.*
The were date, *and* whatt maner a wey
    They haue made p*ro*bate of this p*ro*fece.    109

i. Profeta.  And thatt schall I scho you right    *Twelve lords*
    eyvedently.    *of Chaldea*
The grett lordis of the land of Caldy    *kept watch*
    *900 years for*
Fowndid twelve masturs of asestronemy    *the star,*
    For to se this star apere ;
And when these masturs were eylecte,
On the hill of Wawse *ther* wache the kepte
And the all togedder neu*er* sclepte
    Abowe ix$^c$ yere.    117

ii. Profeta.  And dide the soo longe wache[1] *that*
    hill ?    [f. 2 a]
i. Profeta.  Ye truly, tyll *th*at hit was this kyngis    *which was a*
    will    *guide for the*
    *three Kings.*
This seyd p*ro*fece for to fullfyll,
Thatt strange star to send them till,[2]
    Whereof the had intellegence ;    122
That aftur the darkenes of the nyght
In the day hit schone soo bright,
Thatt when the sun *and* the stare
In the yeyre togeythur warre,    (37)
    Betwyxt them wasse lyttull or non indyfference.  127

And soo this stare wasse a s*er*veture    *Matt.* ii. 9.
And vnto iij kyngis a playn cundeture
Vnto the mancion of a v*ir*gin pure.    130

ii. Profeta.  But ar you sure for whatt intent ?
i. Profeta.  Forsothe to Bedlem streyght the went,    *The offerings*
Whereasse the offurd to this childe reu*er*ent    *of the Kings.*
W*ith* grett omage a fam*us* present.    134

The furst wasse gold, as most myghte kyng ;
The seycond wasse myr, asse prist of pristis beyng ;
The thryd wasse insence, in tokyning of byrring.[3]    137

[1] H. *inserts* [on].    [2] H. *changes to* there.
[3] H. *changes to* byriing.

II. PROFETA.   Yet wold I kno the cawse spesschally,
Whatt movid these kyngis to cum so hastely,
And whedur the cam oopun or prevy.                    140

I. PROFETA.   The star broght them throgh eyu*ere* cuntre ;
And eyu*er* as the cam oopunly,
    The dide inquere of those nevis ;

*'Where is*
*He that is*
*born King of*
*the Jews?'*
*Matt.* ii. 2.

Eyu*er* the axid, " Where ys he
Thatt ys borne for to be
    The kyng of Juys?" [1]                        146

*'Let us*
*depart to pay*
*our devotion*
*to the child.'*

Therefore lett hus w*ith* all delegence
Vnto *that* chyld geve honowre *and* reyu*er*ence,    (38)
And thatt we ma cum vnto his presence
    To haue fruyssion of his hi deyit[e].            150
And, brothur, I thanke you of youre pacyence ;
    For now att thys tyme dep*arte* wyll wee.

        *Exceat.* [2]

II. PROFETA.   Now, brothur, for youre swete sentence,
Att all tym*is* welcum to me—                         154

*They praise*
*God for their*
*particular*
*enlighten-*
*ment,*

Loo ! fryndis,[3] there may you see
    How God in man workith alwey.
Now all we *that* his servandis be                    [f. 3]
    Hathe grett cawse in hym to joie,
    Wyche sendyth hus knoleyge the truth to sey ;
And he soo meraculosly wyrkyng the*r*w*ith*
Thatt of all seycrettis we wryte[4] *the* were pyth ;  161

Wherefore moche cawse haue we to make myrth,
When we reyme*m*bur the gloreose birthe
    Of this v*i*rgyns sun.
He the Seconde P*er*son in the Trenete
Eyquall w*ith* his Fathur in deyite
And[5] under the curteyne of owre vmanete,
    For hus wold man becu*m*.                        168

*and exhort*
*all here*

Wherefore, here I exsorte you all,
    That in this place here asembulde be,
Vnto this chylde for me*r*ce cawll,

---

[1] *This and preceding line as one in* S., *corr. by* H.
[2] *Stage-direction omitted in* S.   *Speech of second prophet begins at*
*line* 155 *in* S.         [3] H. *inserts* [dere].
[4] H. *changes to* wyte.       [5] H. *omits* And.

Wyche schall reydeme vs apon a tre.    172   to pray for redemption.
And thatt gloreose blys thatt we ma see,
    Wyche he hathe ordenide for all men
In his selesteall place to be    (39)
    *In secula seculo*rum, *amen !*    176

*Here Semeon intrythe* and *the last profett gothe owtt.*   *Luke* ii. 25-35.

SEMEON.  The seylesteall Soferent, owre hy Gode   Simeon's prayer.
    eternall !
Wyche of this mervelus world ys *the* fowndatur,
And create[1] the hy heyvins his one see emp*er*ell
    W*ith* sun, mone *and* staris, yorthe,[2] sky and
        wattur[3]—
    And al for the sustenance of owre vmayne
        nature—
W*ith* fysche, fowle, best, *and* eyu*er*e othur thyng,
Vndur hus to haue *the* naturall cowrs *and* beyng.    183

Yett owre form*er*e parence at the begynnyng   Adam's fall and man's mortality.
    Throgh dyssobeydence had a grevose fawll
From the hy pales *and* blys eyu*er*lastyng
    Downe into this[4] wale[5] off[6] meserabull mvndall ;
    For the wyche transgression all we ar now
        mortall,
Thatt before wasse infynite for eyu*er* to remayne
And now schall take yend[7] be deyth *and* cruell
    payne.    190

Wyche grevoise sorro ofte dothe me constrayne   Simeon's sighs and tears.
    Inwardly to syghe *and* byttur teyris to wepe,
Tyll thatt I reyme*m*bur the grett comforde ageyne
    Of anceant p*r*ofettis w*ith* *the*r sentens swete,  [f. 3a]
    Whose fructu*us* syence of p*r*ofownde larnyng
        depe
In there awturs aperith to hus right manefestly,
Of Isaee, Sebbellam,[8] Balam, *and* Malache.    197

O Lorde of lordis !  In hart beseke I the,
    Of this infinite worke to send me the tru lyght,   He prays

---

[1] H. *omits* And *and writes* Create[d].
[2] S. *th*orthe.  H. *chanṣes to* for the.   [3] S. matter.
[4] *Omitted in* S.  [5] H. *changes to* vile.  [6] *So* MS. b., MS. *and.*
[7] S. *th*end.    [8] MS. b. *has* the Sebellis.

F

for a sight
of the Re-
deemer,

Truly to expownde this seyde wholle profece;
　　　And also of that kyng that I ma haue a syght, (40) 201
　　　And that we ma walke in his weyis uppright,[1]
The wyche be reydemcion schall hus all reyles,
At whose cumyng the tru ovncion of Juda schall
　　　seyse.                                          204

for he is
growing old.

Now, Lord, fullfyll thatt hy tyme of pes !
　　　For age draith me fast apon.
Fayne wold I see thatt wholle of whollenes,
　　　Or this mortall lyff fro me were gone.
　　　Now, Lorde, ase thow art iij in won,
Grant me grace, yff thatt thy wyl[2] be,
In my nold age that syght for to see !              211

He would
then depart
in peace.

Then at thy wyll, Lorde, fayne wolde I be,
　　　Yff thow soche grace woldist me sende,
To loove the, Lorde, with all vmelyte,
　　　And soo of my lyff then to make an ende !
　　　Yett, Lorde, thi grace to me now extende,
Suffur me rathur yett to lyve in peyne
Then to dy, or thatt I thatt solam syght haue seyne ! 218

Luke ii. 36-38.

*Here Ane cumyth in to Semeon and seythe :*

Anna asks
to be remem-
bered in his
prayer.

ANE.   O sufferent Semeon !   With all solemnete,
　　　Thatt of owre gloreose tempull hath the gouern-
　　　ance,
With all dev reuerance here beseke I the
　　　Thi[3] olde frynde in Gode to haue in reymembur-
　　　ance,
　　　The wyche hathe tarrid be a long contenvance
For the comyng of the right Messee,
Wyche hathe byn promysid vnto hus be profece.        225

O Lorde ! thogh that I be nothynge worthe
　　　To see the fassion of thi most presseose pyctore,
Yett, Lorde, acsepte me of thi grett marce,      (41)

---

[1] *This line supplied from MS. b.*
[2] H. *inserts* [hit].     [3] H. *writes* thi[n].

Asse thy pore ser̄wand *and* feythfull creature.
 To se the, Lorde, yff *that* I myght be sure,
No lenger on grownd wold I reyquere
In this mortall lyff to contenev here.  [f. 4] 232

She would also die gladly if she could see the Lord.

SIMEON. O feythefull frynde and louer dere!
 To you this text ofte haue I tolde,
That the lyght of Leyve amonge vs here
 In Isaraell schuld be boght *and* sold;
 Asse avnceant *pro*fettis hereof hathe told,
That in this lande here he schuld make surenes,
And he to be cawlid the Kyng of Pes.  239

He quotes prophecy.

Asse Isaee hymselfe herein to wyttnes,
 " *In facie populo*rum," this did he sey,
"*Cum venerit sanctus sancto*rum *cessabit unctio vestra.*"
And soo when owre ryght blod schall seyse,
Moche v*ir*tu and g*ra*ce then schall incresse
W*ith* hy jugeme*n*tis of rightwessenes
 Amongest hus evyn here in Isaraell.  246

*Dan.* ix. 24.

ANE. Yff thatt I myght abyde *that* dey,
 Thatt wholle off wholleis for to see
Wyche thatt I haue desyrid allwey,
 In this worlde[1] well were me.
 Now, Lord, *and* yff thy wyll hit be,
Grant me my hoope, longe lokid fore;
Then joie nor welthe kepe I no more. (42) 253

Anna prays that she may abide until the coming.

SIMEON. Now, Ane, systur and dere frynde,
 Lett hus bothe w*ith* a whole intent
In thys tru feyth owre lyvis yend,
 Lawdyng thatt Lorde wyche ys *om*nipotent;
 Wherefore I thynke hyt full expeydente[2]
In conteniall preyar for to indure,
To kno *ther*by his graceose plesure.  260

They must endure in continual prayer.

ANE. O sofferent Semeon! Thi fam*us* consell
 Inwardely gladyth me in my hart.
No-thyng contentyth my mynd soo well,
 Wherefore at *thi*s tyme woll we dep*ar*te.  264

Anna is encouraged.

[1] H. *inserts* [so].
[2] S. expeydent. H. *changes to* expedyent; *so other similar words.*

'The Lord be thy guide!' SIMEON.   Now, Ane, syth *that* ye wol hence nede[1]
Vnto the tempull wi*th* all spede                    [f. 4a]
   Owre Lordis wyll for to abyde,
   That Lord of lordis be thy gyde
      And sende the *that* wyche thow lovist most;
   Bothe heyle[2] *and* bote for the provide,
      Where-eyu*er* thow goo in any cost!          271

*Ane goes out.*

Simeon always prays before he goes to rest. Fryndis, now ys hit tyme to prey.
   Before that I my rest do take,
My custome hathe yt byn alwey,
   Asse long ase eyu*er* I am awake,            (43)
   Intersession vnto that Lorde to make
Of hym to obteyne all my reyquest,
And then full peysable to take my rest.[3]          278

His prayer. Now, Lorde, that madist all thyng of noght,
   Both hevyn *and* hell and eyu*er*e creature,
Asse thow knoist myn inwarde thoght,
   Reycomforde [me][4] when hit ys thy plesure;
   For I do covett no more treysure
Then the tyme of thy natevete
Wi*th* my mortall yeeis thatt I myght se.          285

But asse thow wolt, Lorde, all thyng mvst be,
   And reysun hit ys thatt hit be soo;
My wyll *ther*to schall eyu*er* agre.
   My wholle desyre now dost *tho*u kno.
   Or thatt I vnto slepe do goo,
I commytt my warkis wi*th* all the si*r*cum*s*tance
Wholly vnto thy lawis *and* ordonance.             292

*There Semeon settys hym doune to rest, ase hit were, and*
*the Angell seythe to hym:*

An angel announces I. ANGELL.   Semeon, of thy rest awake;
   Owre Lorde in heyvin he sendyth[5] the gretyng
Of my message, wi*th* the for to make,

---

[1] S. yede.   H. *changes to* rede *and inserts* [I] *before it.*
[2] *Changed by a later hand to* heylth.        [3] *Omitted in* S.
[4] *Supplied by* H.        [5] *So* H., S. sendyght.

W*ith* the, hys frind, a solame metyng;    [f. 5]    that Christ is
shortly to
be brought to
the temple.
    Hys blessid bode vnto thi kepyng
W*ith*in schort tyme schal be broght,
And here in thy tempull thow schalte be soght.    299


SEMEON.   Lorde, whence cam this solam noyse  (44)
    That awoke me here soo suddenly ?
My spretis *therwith* did soo reyjoyse,
    Thatt no lenger slepe cowlde I.
    Me-thoght he seyde right p*er*fettly,
Thatt solam Sufferent thatt I schulde see
And haue hym here in my custode.    306


II. ANGELL.   Semeon, thatt Lorde in Trenete    'Speed that
thy temple be
in order.'
    Whom thow hast desirid to see alwey
At thy tempull offurde schal be
    Vnto thy honde this same day ;
    *Ther*fore spede in all thatt thow may,
That the tempull in ordur be
This prynce to reyseyve w*ith* all vmelete.    313


        [*Exeunt the two angels.*]


SIMEON.   Now, Lorde of lordis, thankis be to the!    Simeon
rejoices,
    These gloreose tythyngis *tha*t here be tolde
In my hart soo gladith me
    Thatt I am lyghtar a M folde
        Then eyu*er* I wasse before.    318
    Therefore wyll I[1] w*ith* al my myght
To se my tempull soo presseoosly pyght
    In gorgis araye thatt hyt be dyght
        This prynce for to ownowre.[2]    322


    *There Semeon gothe to his Clarks and seyth:*


Now, fryndis all, be of good chere,    (45)    and informs
his clerks.
And to owre tempull draw we nere ;
Soche solam nevis now I here,
    Thatt all my spretis dothe glade.    326
Thatt babe ys borne of dyngnete
Thatt we soo long hathe desirid to see,


   [1] H. *inserts* [spede].    [2] H. *has* [h]onowre, *similarly below.*

Oure Lord *and* Kyng[1] most myghte,
  Thatt all this world[2] made.     330
CLARECUS. Now blessid mot that lorde[3] be,
Thatt dey *and* owre thatt we schall see
His gloreose bodde in Trenete,
  Thatt flowre that neu*er* schall fade !   334

He bids them<br>prepare to<br>receive the<br>Lord.SEMEON. No lenger, Surs, lett vs abyde,
  But to the tempull w*ith* all spede
To reyseve the Saueowre of this world wyde  [f. 5 a]
  And hym to se*r*ve w*ith* lowe and drede !
  Now, Sirs, loke thatt ye take good hede
To wayte *and* serve w*ith* all delegence,
His g*r*ace to ownowre w*ith* humble reu*er*ence !  341

A clerk asks<br>for instruc-<br>tions about<br>the sacrifice.CLARECUS. To se*r*ue a prynce of soche magneffecens,
  S*ir*, I wasse neu*er* wont there-to.
Sythe ye *ther*in hathe more intellegence,
  Instructe me, S*ir*, how *that* I schuld do,
   Lest thatt I do offende ;   (46) 346
  For rathur then I wolde hym greive,
  Thatt Lord on whom I do beleve,—
  Yett had I leyu*er* my-self reymeve
   Vnto the worldis yende.   350

How it is to<br>be performed.SEMEON. Sith thatt ye for knoleyge dothe make sute,
Your wyttis the bettur do I reypute.
   W*ith* humble hartis and[4] meke,  353
  Won of hus must holde the lyght
Ande the othur the sacrefyce ;
And I on kneis, asse hyt ys right,
  The offece to exsersyse
   Vnto thatt babe soo swette.  358

CLARECUS. Then hast we this alter to araye
And clothis off onowre *ther*on to laye
Ande the grownde straw we w*ith* flowris gay
  Thatt of oddur swetely smellis.  362

---

[1] H. *inserts* [*th*at].   [2] H. *inserts* [hath].
[3] H. *has* lord[ing]e.   [4] H. *inserts* [ful].

SEMEON.   And when he aprochis nere this place,

Syng then wi*th* me thatt conyng hasse                    They sing.

And the othur the meyne space

    For joie rynge ye the bellis.          *Cantant.*[1]   366

> *There Semeon and his Clarks gothe vp to the tempull and*
> *Gaberell cumyth to the tempull dore and seyth : [Mary*          Luke ii. 22-25.
> *and Joseph with the child have occupied the front part*
> *of the pageant.*]

GABEREEL.   Hayle, Mare, meke and myld !          (47)          Gabriel greets
                                                                 Mary and the
    The vi*r*tu in the schall neyu*e*r fade.                     Child.

Hayle, meydyn, and thy chylde,

    Thatt all this world [2] made !                    370

Thy seylesteall Fadur wyche ys om*n*ipotent          He bids her
                                                     make offering
Of his [3] ambassaye hethur hathe me sent            in the temple.

Vnto the, lade and vi*r*gyn reyu*e*rent,

    Wi*th* thy sun, owre heyviñ Kynge !               374

Vnto the tempull thatt *th*ou schuldist goo,          [f. 6]

And to whyt turtuls wi*th* the also,

And present the chyld and them to,

    All iij of them in offeryng.                       378

Spede you forth thatt ye were gone !

But leyve nott ye [4] wold Josoff at whome ;          Joseph must
                                                     accompany
For nedely, lade, he mvste be won                    her.

    In this sacrefyce doyng.                           382

MARE.   Wi*th* hart and wyll hit schal be done          Mary will
                                                        obey.
    In pleysing of that fathur of myght.

Thyddur wyll I bothe hastely *and* sone

    And take [with] [5] me my child soo bryght.        386

GABERELL.   Then to Josoff goo ye full right,          Gabriel de-
                                                       parts.
    And make hym preve of this case.

Byd hym hast *that* he were dyght

    To gyd you theddur into that place.

    Now rest well, Mare, wi*th* moche solas !     (48)

        For I mvst thiddur asse I cam froo.            392

        [*Gabriel goes out.*]

---

[1] *This song* (I.) *is at the end of the pageant.*   [2] H. *inserts* [hath].
[3] S. this.   [4] H. *changes to the.*   [5] *So* H.

MARE.   He thatt ys ande eyu*er* wasse
  Be thy gyde where-eu*er* thow goo,
  And send hus all[1] of his grace !
   I pray here knelynge hit ma be soo.    396

*[Addresses Jesus.]*

*She addresses Jesus,* Now, cu*m* heddur to me, my darlyng dere,
  My myrthe, my joie, and al my chere !
  Swetter then eyu*er* wasse blossu*m*[2] on brere !
   Thy swete mowthe now wyll I kis.    400
  Now, Lorde of lordis, be owre gide,
  Where-eyu*er* we walke in cuntreyis wyde,
  And these to turtuls for hus *p*rovide
   Off them thatt we do nott mys !    404

*Here Mare goth to Josoff and seyis :*

*and tells Joseph of the command.* Rest well, Josoff, my spouse soo free !
JOSOFF.  Now welcu*m*, Mare !  Dame, whatt sey yee ?
MARE.   Swet nevis, husebond, I bring to thee ;
  The angell of God wi*th* me hath be
   To geve hus bothe warnyng,    409
  Thatt you *and* I wi*th* a wholle intent,
  Aftur the law thatt here ys ment,
  Schuld in the tempull owre chyld present
   In Jerusalem, *ther* to make offeryng.   (49)   413

*He is ready to go.* JOSOFF.   Now, Mare, thatt woll I neu*er* deny ; [f. 6 a]
  But aftur my powar for to apply
  And thatt you kno, dame, asse well asse [I][3] ;
   You neu*er* cawll but I am reddy.    417
  MARE.   Now, husebond, ye speyke full gentylle ;
  *Ther*fore loke, Josoff, *and* ye cold spy
*Will he pro-cure two doves ?* To turtyll dowis, how thatt we myght cu*m* ny :
   For nedely turtullis offer mvst we ;
   Thatt offeryng fawlyth for owre degre.    422

JOSOFF.   Nay, nay, Mare, thatt wol not be.
*Indeed he will not.* Myne age ys soche, I ma not well see ;
  There schall noo duffu*s*[4] be soght for me,    425
   Also God me saue ![5]

---

[1] H. *inserts* [the gift].
 MS. (?) blassom.  *It is often difficult to differentiate the scribe's*
e's *and* o's, *and* o's *and* a's.    [3] *Supplied by* S.
 [4] *Contraction for* us.    [5] H. *adds* [so fre].

MARE.  Swette Josoff, fullfyll ye owre Lordis hestes.

JOSOFF.  Why *and* woldist th[o]u haue me to hunt

    bridis nestis?

I pray the hartely, dame, leve thosse jestis

    And talke of thatt wol be.              430

*He cannot be hunting birds' nests.*

For, dame, woll I neu*er* vast my wyttis,

To wayte or pry whe*re* the wodkoce syttis;   (50)

Nor to jubbard among the m*er*le pyttis,

    For thatt wasse neyu*er* my gyse.        434

Now am I wold *and* ma not well goo:

A small twyge wold me ou*er*throo;

And yche were wons lyggyd aloo,

    Full yll then schulde I ryse.         438

MARE.  Ye hardely, Josoff, do nott drede!

Owre Lorde wyll quyte right well youre mede,

And att all tym*is* be youre spede,

    And further you in youre viage.       442

*The Lord will help him.*

JOSOFF.  Ey! dame, ey!  God helpe hus all!

Me-thynke youre meymorre were[1] small,

On me soo whomly eyu*er* to call:

    You mynde nothynge myne age       446

But the weykist gothe eyu*er* to the walle:

Therefore go thyself, dame; for me thow schall,[2]

    Ye, or ellis get the a nev page.      449

*She imposes on age and weakness.*

MARE.  Husebande, these be no womens dedis;

Therefore, Josoff, ye must forthe nedis;

    For surely there ys no reymedy.      452

JOSOFF.  Noo remedy then but I mvst goo?   [f. 7]

Now be my trowthe,[3] I ma tell you,   (51)

    Thosse tythingis ar but cold.       455

Then nedis mvste thatt nedis schall;

And now he thatt ma worst of all

    The candyll ys lyke to holde.       458

*He submits ungraciously,*

MARE.  Now, gentyll Josoff, when wyll ye goo

    To make an ende of this owre jurney?

---

[1] H. *writes* veré.    [2] H. *supposes that a line is here omitted.*

[3] *See note on line* 399.

JOSOFF.   *That* shal be or I have any lust thereto[1]
  And thatt dare I boldely sey.                                462

How sey ye all this cumpany
Thatt be weddid asse well asse I?
  I wene *that* ye suffur moche woo;                           465
For he thatt weddyth a yonge thyng
Mvst fullfyll all hir byddyng,
Or els ma he his handis wryng,
Or watur his iis when he wold syng;
  And thatt all you do knoo.                                   470

MARE.   Why sey ye soo, sir?   Ye be to blame.
JOSOFF.   Dame, all this cumpany wyll sey the same.
Ys itt not soo?   Speyke, men, for schame!
  Tell you the trothe ase you well con!                        474
For the *that* woll nott there wyffis plese          (52)
Ofte-tym*is* schall suffur moche dysees;
Therefore I holde hym well at es
  Thatt hathe to doo w*ith* non.                               478

MARE.   Leyve of these gawdis for my lowe;
  And goo for these fowlys, S*ir*, I you pray.
The Fadur of heyvin thatt ys abowe
  Wyll spede you well in youre jurney.                         482

JOSOFF.   No reymede but I mvst forthe nede.
Now owre Lord grant me well for to spede!
Loo! feyre wordis full[2] ofte doth leyde
  Men cleyne agen there mynd.                                  486
Now, Lorde God, thow sende me feyre weddur,
And thatt I ma fynd those fowlis togeddur,
Whytt or blake, I care nott wheddur,
  So thatt I ma them[3] fynde!                                 490

MARE.   Full well schall you spede hardely,
Yff thatt ye goo abowt hytt wyllyngly.
JOSOFF.   Then I woll goo by *and* by,          [f. 7a]
Thogh[4] hit be not full hastely.
W*ith* all my hart I wol goo spy,                              495

complaining of his lot in having married a young thing.

All the company know that you have to mind your wife.

The Lord send him fair weather and those birds, black or white!

[1] *So* H., S. thereta.     [2] MS. *and* S. ffull.     [3] MS. then.
[4] S. Thoght.

Yff any be in my wey,          (53)
I wyll them fynd *and* I may,[1]
    Or thatt I make an ende.       498

*He will find any that come in his way.*

MARE.   Now that Lorde, thatt best[2] may,
He be your spede in youre jurney,
    Ande good tythyngis of you me send !     501

JOSOFF.   Yea, he thatt hatth soche on on hym to crawe
He schal be sure, asse God me sawe,
Eyu*er* the worse yend of the staff to haue,[3]
    Att the lattur yend.       505

*Here Josoff gothe from Mare[4] and seyth :*

I wandur abowt myself alone,
    Turtulis or dowis can I non see.
Now, Kyng of heyvin, thow amend my mone ;
    For I tro I seke nott where the be !     509

*He wanders about,*

My myght, my strenth ys worne fro me ;[5]
    For age I am waxun almost blynd.
Those fowlys the ar full far fro me
    And werie yvill for me to fynde.     513

*the fowls are evil to find,*

I loke fast and neu*er* the nere ;
    My wynd for feynt ys allmost gone.
Lord, *benedissete !* Whatt make I here
    Among these heggis myself alone ?     517

For-were I ma no lengur stond ;
    These buskis the teyre me on eyu*er*e syde.
Here woll I sytt apon this londe,
    Oure Lordis wyll for to abyde.     521

*and he is weary.*

I. ANGELL.   Aryse vp, Josoff, *and* take no thoght (54)
For these to fowlys thatt thow hast soght.
Evyn to thy hond I haue them broght,
    And therefore be off good chere.     525
Take them here bothe to
And ageyne to Mare thy wyff thow goo
Yn all the hast thatt hit be doo ;
    Thow tarre noo lengur here !     529

*An angel brings them to him.*

---

[1] *This and the preceding line as one in* S. *and* MS.
[2] H. *inserts* [so].     [3] H. *prints* to have *with the following line.*
[4] *Qy.* into the street.     [5] *So* H., S. [me] frome.

He rejoices  
and returns.

JOSOFF.   O! lawde be vnto thatt Lorde soo exsellent  
For those to fowlis thatt I haue soght!  
Fullfyllid now ys myn intent;                    [f. 8]  
My hart ys evyn asse yt oght,[1]  
All care fro me ys past,                    534  
Now thatt Mare my wyff these birddis had![2]  
For to make hir hart asse glad[3]  
To hir wyll I in hast.   [*Returns to Mary.*]   537

He delivers  
the doves to  
Mary.

Now rest well, Mare, my none darlyng!  
Loo! dame, I haue done thy byddyng  
And broght these dowis for oure offeryng;  
Here be the bothe alyve.                    541  
Womon, haue them in thy honde,  
I am full glade I haue them[4] fond.  
Am nott I a good husbonde?  
Ye! dame, soo mot I thryve!                    545

MARE.   Now, the Fathur of heyvin that ys abowe,  
He quyt you, Josoff, for this dede;        (55)

'Let us make  
speed to the  
temple!'

And furthur I pray you for my lowe,  
Vnto the tempull lett vs make spede!        549

Joseph would  
like to 'blow  
awhile.'

JOSOFF.   Ey! bloo a whyle, dame, I the pray!  
For soft *and* essele men goo far.  
I haue laburde all this dey;  
Yett am I vere lyttull the nar.  
I tro thatt I schall neyu*er* be war.  
Soo full of feyre wordis these wemen be,  
Thatt men thereto must nedis agre;        556

And therefore, dame, alsoo mote I the.  
Aftur my labur fayne wolde I rest;

'Go thyself!'

Therefore goo thyselfe thow schalt for me,  
Or tarre att whome wheddur *tho*u thynkist beste. 560

She cannot  
go alone.

MARE.   Na, swet husebond, ye do well kno  
To goo alone ys not for me;  
Wherefore, good *sir*, I pray you soo  
Thatt I ma haue your cu*m*pany.        564

---

[1] Manly's *suggestion.* S. *and* MS. *have* wold be; H. *has* wold be [thoght].  
[2] *As two lines in* H., *first ending with* wyff; *he adds the words* [as fast].        [3] H. *substitutes* blith.        [4] *Bracketed in* H.

JOSOFF.   Loo! fryndis,[1] here ma you knoo
Thatt *with* hyr nedis mvst I goo,
    Wheddur I wyll or nyll.                        568
Now ys nott this a cumburs[2] lyff?
Loo! sirs, whatt ytt ys to haue a wyff!        (56)
Yett had I[3] leyu*er*, nor to live in stryff,
    Apply evyn to hir wyll.                          572

For syth *that* here ys no remede,
Take vp youre chylde, I sey, Mare,
And walke we togedur feyre *and* essele
    And soo to stynt all strywe;
And[4] I woll trusse vp thys gere,            [f. 8 *a*]
For I se well I mvst hit beyre.
At Jerusalem I wold all ye[5] were,
    Also[6] mote I thryve.[7]                          580

MARE.   There schall we be when God wyll,
    For at his plesure all thyng mvst be.
JOSOFF.   Dame, and thatt ys bothe reysun and skill;
    Sett forward then and lett me see.               584

    [*They continue in the front part of the pageant as if making
    a journey.   An angel appears in the temple.*]

II. ANGELL.   Awake, Semeon, and drede the noght!
And reyseyve that Lord thatt all hathe wroght,
    *With* hym his modur Mare.                        588
Make spede, Semeon, *th*at thow **were** dyght
To reyseyve thatt chyld w*ith* all thy myght
Now schalt thow see the blessidist syght
    Thatt eyu*er* thow didist see.                    592

SEMEON.   O Lord of lordis! this solam noyse   (57)
    From the Maker of heyvin *and* hell,
My hart therew*ith* soo dide reyjoise,
    Thatt the myrthe *ther*off can noo tong tell,
        Nor hand w*ith* pen subscrybe.

---

[1] H. *inserts* [dere].   [2] H. *writes* cumbrus; *so similar words below.*
[3] S. *omits;* H. *writes* [I].      [4] H. *omits* And.
[5] H. *changes to* we.      [6] S. Alse.
[7] *Line in later hand,* Also well that ye thrive; *line as printed by*
S. *canceled but legible.*

and thanks God.

I thanke *th*at Lorde *and* Kyng of myght,
   Thogh all my lust throgh age be worne,
Thatt I schall see this gloreose syght.
   Blessid be the owre thatt thow wast borne,
     This dey *that* eyu*er* I do abide.     602

Now to reyseve this Kyng of pes
Thatt owt of dangyr schall hus reles.
Owre hy merrettis schall he incres
   In joiye abundantly ;     606
For here kepe I no more blis,
But thatt he m*a*rke me[1] for won of his,
And then whan his swete wyll[2] ys,
   Am I evyn redde to dy.     610

He calls upon his clerks.

Now, Clarkis, cu*m* forth *and* do your offes,
   And this awter hastely *th*at ye aray ;
For here schal be the solamyst sacrefyce
   Thatt eyu*er* wasse seyne in Juda.     614

Make sure, fryndis, *and*[3] all thatt ye may
   Thatt ordur be hade in eyu*er*e place.
CLARECUS.   Now *that* Lord of lordis thatt best may
   To do oure devties he grant vs gr*a*ce !
And for to plese hym to his paye     (58)
   Sey al you *Deo gracias.*     620

'All is ready.'

Loo ! mastur,[4] bothe man *and* place     [f. 9]
   Be all redde at your byddyng.

'Ring the bells !'

SEMEON.   Then, surs, cu*m* forthe[5] apase
   And myrrele the bellis ryng.     624

Ane, systur, goo ye[6] wi*th* me
   For to reyseyve that p*r*ince of onowre
And hym to welcu*m* reu*er*ently,
   Ase of this world lorde *and* gouernowr*e*.     628

Anna comes with him.

ANE.   Now, fathur Semeon, I am obeydentt,
   Youre gr*a*ceose pleysure for to obbey.
To s*er*ve thatt Lorde wyche ys omn*i*potent,
   Lett vs goo mete hym on the wey.     632

---

[1] H. *brackets* me *and puts it before* m*a*rke.    [2] H. *inserts* [hit].
[3] H. *changes to* in.    [4] H. *inserts* [now].
[5] H. *inserts* [with me`.    [6] H. *inserts* [alse].

CLAREOUS. Mastur, now ar the bellis rong
 And redde att hond ys eyu*er*e thyng.
SEMEON. Then lett me see w*ith* hart *and* tonge.
How myrrely thatt ye can syng.   *Cantant.* 636

 *Here the cum downe with pressession*[1] *to mete them:*

MARE. Heyle, suffurent Semeon so good!     Mary greets
 My semely sun here I bryng to the   (59)   Simeon.
To offur hym vp in flesche and blode,
 Ase be the law he oght to be.       640

SEMEON. Now, wholle Mare *and* Josoff also,   He bids them
 Ye be ryght welcu*m* vnto this place;    welcome.
For off God ar ye blessid bothe to
 Thatt hath you grondid in soche gr*a*ce:
  And ye, Josoff, of soo grett age    645
 Thatt soche a babe forth can bryng,
 In whom all owre reydemcion dothe hyng,
 And off this worlde ys lorde *and* kyng;
  This[2] wase a graceose mareage.    649

JOSOFF. Now gentill bysschope, I the pray,   Joseph
Evyn the verre truth thow woldist me sey,   praises the
Ys nott this a prette bewey      Child.
 Asse eyu*er* thow hast knone?    653
Now, be hym th*a*t made both heyvin *and* hell,
This lyttull myte I lowe as well,
 Asse thogh he were myn oone!    656

MARE. Reyseyve [him],[3] Semeon, w*ith* good chere;   Mary brings
 The law[4] wyll hit schall so be,     him accord-
For wyche cawse I bryng hym here;     ing to the
 Here in thi hondis take hym the.   [f. 9 a] 660   law.

SEMEON. Now welcu*m*, Lord [5] of honowr![5]  (60)   Simeon's
 Now welcu*m*, Prince, vnto this place![6]   welcome.
Welcu*m*, owre sufferent Saweowre![7]

---

[1] H. *writes* prossession.   [2] S. *and* MS. Thus.   [3] *So* H.
[4] H. *inserts* [hit].
[5]—[5] S. *prints* vnto my hand, *which is written on an erasure; a smudged and obliterated termination of the line has what looks like* of honowr.
[6] S. *omits* of honowr *from end of this line; it is in different ink and above.*   [7] H. *inverts* sufferent *and* Saweowre.

Welcum, the Growndr of owre grace !
                Welcum, owre joie ! welcum,[1] owre myrthe ! 665
Welcum, owre graceose Gouernowre !
Welcum to huse, thatt heyvinly flowre !
Now, blessid be the dey and owre
                [2] Of thy gloreose byrthe !                        669

Anna's wel-
come.
ANE.  Now welcum, Kyng of kingis all !
        Now welcum, Maker of all mankynd !
Welcum to hus, bothe grett and small !
        Good Lord, thy sarvandis now haue in mynd
                Thatt longe hath levid here,                        674
        In clenes pure withowt offence,
        With grett desyris for to be hence ;
        But now the syght of thy presence
                Hath amendid all owre chere.                        678

The clerk's
welcome.
CLARECUS.   Now welcum, Lord, vnto all hus,
Thi none tru servandis, as reysun ys ![3]
Welcum, owre God and Kyng of blys,
        Owre Lorde, longe lokid fore !                        682
All the profettis thatt of the spake
Seyd thow schuldist, for owre sake,
Fleysche and blod of a meydyn take          (61)
        Owre joys to reystore.                        686

Simeon re-
ceives the
Child and
begins his
prayer.
SEMEON.   On, on with me, my fryndis dere,
With this chylde thatt we haue here,
Of this worlde the lanterne clere
        Of whom all lyght schall spryng !                        690
With hoole hartis, now lett hus praee !
Thatt owre and tyme now blesse we may
That eyuer we abode the dey
        Of this chyldis comynge.          Cantant.[4]          694

        Here Semeon goth to the awtere with the chyld in hys
          armis and seyth:
[5] Now art thow cum, Lorde, to my honde,
        Thogh thatt I onworthe were ;
Yett, Lorde, forgeve thi pore serwande[6]—                        697
. . . . . . . . . . . . .

---

[1] MS. velcum ; H. omits this word.          [2] H. here inserts [Child],.
[3] H. supposes that a line is omitted here.          [4] Qy. [Song II.]
[5] MS. repeats SEMEON.          [6] Folio 10 is missing.

[MARE.]  Whyle[1] the weddur ys soo feyre ; [f. 11]

Mary and<br>Joseph<br>journey<br>homewards.<br>*Luke* ii. 39.

And I woll cum aftur asse I may,

For now att whome I wolde we weyre.  700

JOSOFFE.  To[1] goo before now I woll asaye,

Thogh thatt my fetemanscipe[2] be not full gaye.

I pray God spede vs in oure jurney ;  (62)

For I schall be were or thatt I cum there.  704

*There Mare and Josoff departis owt of the vpper parte of*
*the pagand.*

SEMEON.  Loo ! fryndis, how God for vs hathe wroght,

And schode hymself here at this tyde !

Blessid mot he be in word *and* thoght,

[3]Myghtefull Maker of thy[s][4] world wyde !  708

Simeon<br>thanks the<br>Lord;

I wasse lame of fote *and* hand,

And now am whole ase ye ma see.

he was lame<br>in foot and<br>hand and is<br>now whole.

I thanke thatt[5] Lord of his sond,

And eyuer his servande wyll I be,

Thatt Lorde soo moche of myght.  713

Now, Lorde of lordis that hath no pere,

Wyche att this tyme wase offurd here,

Sende you all the fruysson clere

Of his heyvinly mancion soo bryght !  717

CLARECUS.  And of owre mys he amend vs,

And from owre foys[6] defend vs,

And[7] his hy trone he send vs,

*In secula seculorum, amen !*  721

*Here gothe Semeon and his Clarkis out of the tempull.*[8]

*Luke* ii. 40-42.

\* \* \* \* \* \* \* \* \*

[*Mary and Joseph enter the lower front-part of the*
*pageant.*]

JOSOFF.  Now, Mare, my wyff here present,

Vnto [God][9] myche bondon, dame, ar we  (63)

Thatt soo goodly a childe here hath vs sent ;

In this world a feyrear *ther* canott be.  725

MARE.  I thanke *that* Lord omnipotent,

For yt dothe me good hym for to see ;

Joseph and<br>Mary decide

[1] *Repeated in* MS.  [2] H. *changes to* fote-.
[3] H. *inserts* [The].  [4] *Emend. by* S.  [5] H. *inserts* [hi].
[6] H. *inserts* [he].  [7] H. *inserts* [to].
[8] Presentation in the Temple *ends and* Doctors' Play *begins.*
[9] *Emend. by* H.

G

to take Jesus
to Jerusalem.

Wherefore, Josoff, I wold he went
Vnto Jerusalem with you and me.                          729

He is twelve
years old.

For now he ys xij yere of age,
Full well reyconid yt ma be,
Of lymys he waxith feyre and large,
And moche he desyrith cumpane.                           733
JOSOFF.   Now, dame, he ys a prette page        [f. 11 a]
And, as ye sey, full well cum on.
I kno non soche on of hys age ;
I pra God make hym a right good mon.                     737

MARE.   Now, Jesus,[1] my son, with you whatt chere?
Whatt m[y]rthe[2] make ye, chyld, this dey?
Thow art he thatt I love most dere,
My joie, my myrthe and all my pley ![3]                 741

Jesus is will-
ing to go.

IESUS.   I thanke you, my modur, in all thatt I may ;
And at youre hand, I am here
To do you serves, bothe nyght and dey,          (64)
And redde alwey to make you chere.                      745

Now, Gods blyssyng haue you and myne ![4]               746

Joseph tells
the company
how obedient
Jesus has
always been.

JOSOFF.   Loo ! fryndis,[5] here doth apere,
Yt ys eyrly scharp thatt wol be thorne.
How glad he ys his modr to pleyse !
And eyuer hathe byn syth he wasse borne.
Thogh thatt my vthe frome me be worne,
Yet in his dedis I have moche joie ;
For, in feythe, he woll preve evin[6] a prette bwey.    753

Cum, my sun, well mot thou thee ![7]
Thow schalt to Jerusalem with thi modur and me,
Sum goodly syghtis, sun, for to see
Apon this owre festefawll dey.                          757

Mary wishes
for company.

MARE.   Now truly, Josoff, as ye sey,
And merely for to pase forthe the wey,
Sum vertuos cumpany I wold we had.

---

[1] S. Jhu here and below.      [2] Corr. by S.
[3] Deleted in MS. ; glee substituted in later hand, Mawdycke's (?).
[4] This line in parentheses in S.: in footnotes in H. ; in contemporaneous hand but different ink and in margin in MS.
[5] H. inserts [dere].            [6] H. omits evin.
[7] S. thriv thee ; H. changes to yee.

JOSOFF. Ye, dame, God shal be owre gyde.[1]     761

Dame, I kepe noo moo but evyn this lad ;
For you nor I canot be sade
    Thatt dey *that* we hym see.     764
Mary, you kno thatt I am olde,
And in cumpany canot be soo bolde,
    Asse I wasse wont to be ;    (65)   767

*'The lad is company enough for me.'*

Therefore, Mare, leyde ye the wey
    And essely lett vs togeddr goo ;
Thogh yt be far furth on the dey,
Yett all be owre fryndis I dare wel sey,
    And neuer a won owre foo.
MARE.   Now, God hold[2] thatt wyche best may ;[3]
    And, gentyll Josoff, lett vs goo !     774
Be the hand the chylde wyll I leyde ;
I trust the bettur for to spede,
    Ande ye,[4] Josoff, alsoo.

*Mary will lead Jesus by the hand,*

JOSOFF.   Ye dame, lett hym goo before ye and me,[5]
    And[6] be nothyng afrayde !     779
For the best foteman of hus thre,     [f. 12]
In good feyth, dame, thatt ys hee,
    Yff he were well asayde.     782

*but Joseph says Jesus is the best walker of the three.*

JESUS.   I am full redde w*ith* you to goo
At your bydding in weyle *and* woo,
And to do you s*er*ves bothe to,
    In hart w*ith* all mekenes.     786
Cum on, my mothur, and dred ye noght ;
And on your jurney, ase you oght,
The Fadur of heyvin *that* all hat[h][7] wroght,
    He kepe you from dystres !    (66)   790

JOSOFF.   Now, thys ys wyttele sayde *and* wyll ![8]     791

*Joseph speculates upon*

---

[1] *This line in parentheses in* S.; *in footnotes in* H.; *as* 746 *in* MS.
[2] H. *changes to* wold.    [3] H. *inserts* [rede].    [4] *So* H., S. yo.
[5] S. *ends line with* goo *and retains* hardely *after* Ye ; H. *adds*
[fre] ; MS. *has in margin as* 746 : Ye, dame, let hym goo before ye
*and* me.     [6] H. *inserts* [Mare].     [7] *Corr. by* S.
[8] H. *changes to* wall ; *line in margin as* 746.

the precocity
of children.

Now, Lord, when I to mynde do call
In vthe when I was werre small,
    Many wynturs agone,—
        Lord God, *benedicete!*
        Yong chyldur now more wyser be,
    Nor wase then an olde mon.         797

        *[They set out and travel a while.]*

The journey.

MARE.   Now welcum be owre Lordis sond!
Therefore cum on, gentyll husbond,
The sytte ys evyn at owre honde;
    Good cumpany there ma we fynd.         801
JOSOFF.   Ey! ey! dame, in feyth, I can noo more;
My leggis byn were, my fete be soore.
That man thatt canot goo before
    Nedis mvst cum behynd.         805

      *There the all goo vp to the awter* and *Iesus before.*   The
      *syng an antem.*

Now, Mare, my wyff, cum hethur to me!
    (Now, Mare, harke what I shall say!)[1]
All thyng ys done ase yt schuld be

Joseph
praises the
service.

And serves song full sollamle
    For this owre festefawll dey.         810
MARE.   Now, huseband, then lett vs iij     (67)
Make the hast *that*[2] ma be
Whom to goo with cumpane
    To bryng vs on the wey!         814

*Luke* ii. 43-51.

    *There the goo done into the for pagond and Iesus steylyth*
    *awey.*

They rejoice
in the solemn
sights and
that Jesus
has seen
them.

JOSOFF.   Mare, my spretis be ravisschid cleyne,
    And clerely cast owt off all woo
With these solam syghtys thatt we haue seyne
    In yondur tempull *that* we cam froo.         818
MARE.   Now, serten, Josoff, you wold not wene [f. 12]
    Whatt myrthe I make without[3] woo,
Thatt my chylde with hus hathe bene
    And those solam syghtis seyne alsoo.         822

    [1] *This line is entirely omitted in* H.; *in margin as* 746.
    [2] H. *inserts* [made].     [3] H. *writes* withowt[en].

JOSOFF.   Then whomwarde,[1] Mare, lett vs goo [2]
    Whyle thatt we haue the lyght off *the* day ;
For you haue eyu*er* lovid c*u*mpany,
    For yt dothe schorttun well youre wey.     826

Joseph
speaks of
company on
the way.

    Yett in good owre we ma bothe sey,
For othur did we neyu*er* fynde.
    MARE.   Alas ! Josoff, and well-awey !
Now haue we lefte owre chyld behynd.     (68)   830

Mary misses
Jesus.

JOSOFF.   Whatt ! Mare, I sey amend thy chere !
    Pa*r*dy ! dame, he dothe but as othur done ;
Chyldur togedur woll draw nere,
    He woll I warrand oue*r*take vs sone.     834

' He will
overtake us
soon.'

MARE.   Oue*r*take vs sone ? q*uotha* nay ! s*er*tes na !
    Whatt nede you me soche talis to tell ?
He ys gon su*m* othur wey,
    Or s*er*ten, Josoff, he ys not well.     838

JOSOFF.   Dame, he ys nott far awey.
    From vs no man wyll hym wyle.

MARE.   Hyt helpyth not, Josoff, soche wordis to sey ;
    My chylde ys gone, alas the whyle !     842

She is incon-
solable.

JOSOFF.   We schall haue [hym],[3] dame, or hit be longe,
    Yff we serche well yondur sytte ;
Su*m* chyldur there he ys amonge,
    Or elis surely whomwarde ys he.

MARE.   Off sorro now schal be my song*e*,
    My chylde ageyne tyll I ma see.     (69)   848

JOSOFF.   Dame, of his welfare I wold be glade,
    And of the othur I wolde be woo ;
Therefore, Mare, no more be sade,
    But agene to the sytte lett vs goo.     852

They will
return to the
city.

MARE.[4]   Make hast, Josoff, thatt we were there ;
    For had I neu*er* more lust thereto.
Bake agane lett vs reypeyre ;
    For thatt ys best for vs to do.     856

*Here Mare and Josoff goth downe into the tempull-warde.*   [f. 13]

---

[1] S. homwarde.      [2] H. *substitutes the original word* [hye].
[3] *Supplied by* S.      [4] *So* H., S. JOSOFF, *marg. in* MS.

<table>
<tr><td>A doctor<br>holds forth<br>upon the<br>penalties of<br>the law.</td><td>

I. DOCTOR..   Now, lordyngis, lystun to me a whyle,<br>
  Wyche hathe the lawis vndur honde,<br>
And thatt no man fawll in soche perell<br>
  Agenst any artyccull for to stand ;<br>
  For the comen statute of this lande<br>
Woll that all soche personys schulde be tane<br>
And in the face of[1] peple ooponly slayne.    863

</td></tr>
</table>

<table>
<tr><td>They are<br>holding dis-<br>putations.</td><td>

II. DOCTOR.   E ! and the othur wholle decryis ageyne,<br>
  Wyche vnto Moyses wonly wasse sent<br>
In tabulis of ston only to reymayne<br>
  Vndur an hy and streyte cummandement,<br>
  Wyche at thys tyme we thynke convenent  (70)<br>
There-apon to holde dyssepyssions[2] here<br>
Be polatike syence of clarge clere.    870

</td></tr>
</table>

<table>
<tr><td>Let every<br>one attend ;<br>for they are<br>doctors of<br>high degree.</td><td>

III. DOCTOR.   Wherefore, all peple, now draw nere<br>
  And in this place gewe your atendence.<br>
How ye schuld lyve, here ma you lere<br>
  Acordyng vnto your aleygence ;<br>
  For yt ys well knone vnto thys presence<br>
Thatt doctoris we ar and of hy degre,<br>
And haue the lawis in custode.    877

</td></tr>
</table>

<table>
<tr><td>The law of<br>Moses.</td><td>

I. DOCTOR.   Ley forth youre reysonis ; now lett me see<br>
  How lawe[3] of leygence oght to be lade,<br>
Wyche of the Ebruys subscribyd be<br>
  With othur of Moyses thatt now ys hade.<br>
  To contend herein I wold be glade<br>
Amonge the peple here manefestly,<br>
And the truthe expownd[4] to them oopinly.    884

</td></tr>
</table>

[Jesus comes in.]

<table>
<tr><td>' Peace be<br>among this<br>company !'<br><br>' Run away !'</td><td>

IESUS.   Lordis, moche lowe with you be lent,<br>
  And pes be amonge this cumpany !<br>
III. DOCTOR.   Sun, awe I wold thow went,<br>
  For othur haft[5] in hand haue we.    888

</td></tr>
</table>

---

[1] H. *inserts* [*the*].<br>
[2] H. *has* dyssepu[ta]ssions ; *similarly below.*   [3] H. *has* lawe[s].<br>
[4] S. expoundid, H. *emends* [were] expoundid.<br>
[5] *So* H., S. *and* MS. hast.

II. DOCTOR. Chylde, who-soo-eyu*er* the hyddur
    sent,                 (71)
The were not wyse thus warne I the ;
For we haue othur talis to tent,
    Then w*ith* chyldur bordyng to bee.         892

     *' We cannot be bothering with children.'*

I. DOCTOR. Good sun, thow art to yonge to larne
    The hy mystere of Mosees law ;
Thy reysun canot yt deserne,
    For thy wytt ys [1] not worthe a strawe ;
    And no marvell thogh thow schuldist be rawe,
In soche hy poyntis for to be reysonyng
For of age art thow a vere yonglyng.   [f. 13 a]  899

     *' Thou art too young to learn Moses' law.'*

IESUS. E! Surs, whatt-soo-eyu*er* to me you sey,
Me nedith not of you to lerne nothyng.        901

     *He does not need to learn of them ;*

II. DOCTOR. This besse bweye [2] of his tong
    All secrettis surely he thynkith he knois.
III. DOCTOR. Nay, serten, sun, thow art to yonge
    Be clarge clere to kno owre lawis.       905

IESUS. Ye doctoris all, thatt be present,
    Suffyce *and* mvse no more off me ;     (72)
For off your lawis the wholl intent,
    No-thyng *ther*off ys hyde froo me ;       909
    For in those placis haue I be
Where all owre lawis furst were wroght.

     *he knows their law already.*

    I. DOCTOR.[3] C*um*, sett the here *and* we schall
       see !
For sarten, sun, soo semys yt noght.       913

     *They invite him to sit among them.*

    *There the Doctoris settyth Cryst among them.*

Now were yt nott a wondurs thyng,
    Thys chylde owre reysuns *that* he schuld reyche ?
And yett he seyth he hath a felyng
    Owre lawis truly for to teyche.       917
IESUS. Suris,[4] the whoole goste in me hath lyght,
    Thatt my powar ys to preyche ;
And of the Godhed most of myght
    Most perfettly here ma I teyche.       921

---

[1] S. wyttys, H. *inserts* [ar].       [2] H. *inserts* [proud].
[3] H. [Doctor II.], S. [DOCTORS].     [4] S. Syris.

'Whence
came this
child?'

III. DOCTOR.   Whense cam thys chylde, I marvell
　　　soore,
　　Thatt speykyth to vs this mystecawlly?
IESUS.   Surs, I wasse all you before
　　And aftur you agen schal be.                        925

The first
doctor re-
members the
prophecy
about babes
and suck-
lings.
Ps. viii. 2.

I. DOCTOR.[1]   Surs, ys nott this a wondurs thyng, (73)
　　And also a moche more mervell?
How-be-yt, surely, in his workyng,
　　The actis thereof ma follo right well;
For ase Dauith in his salme dothe tell,
Be chyldur yong, seyng of them,
Ex ore infancium[2] et lactancium perfecisti laudem.      932
　　Of chyldurs mothis, ye kno right well,
God hath performyde[3] loving;
　　But of such on hard I neuer tell,
He beyng but soo yong a thyng.              [f. 14]   936

Yet Jesus
had spoken
too freely;

Yett, sun, sum-whatt thow schuldest haue let
　　In this place here to speyke so large;
Where nobull doctors togeddur are met,
　　There chyldurs wordis ar at no charge.               940

he cannot
know their
law.

For sure, yff thow woldist neuer so fayne,
　　Labur thi wyttis to lerne owre lawe;
Yett art thow nodur of myght nor mayne
　　To perseyve thatt ase a clark ma knoe.               944

Jesus will
not debar the
truth
by silence.

IESUS.   My wordis in noo wyse wole I reyfrayne,
　　The trawthe thereby for to debarre;
I woll them prove both platt and playne
　　Be youre one lawis, and neuer arre.                   948

Astonish-
ment.

II. DOCTOR.   Mastur[s][4] all, whatt ma this meyne?
　　I wondur soore how this can be;         (74)
Soo yong a chylde haue I nott seyne
　　With clarkis to talke soo conyngle.                   952

III. DOCTOR.   Ase wyde in wor[l]de asse eyuer I went,
　　Saw I neyuer non soche before;
But I troo amonst vs he be sent
　　To be the saluer of owre sore.                        956

---

[1] Later hand puts iij.          [2] MS. infanciom.
[3] H. inserts [him].             [4] Corr. by S.

Iesus.　Suris, I woll prove be actoris evedent
　　　Har mystereis than eyuer you red or saw.

i. Doctor.　Sey, sun, wyche wasse the furst com-　　　'Which is
　　　mandement　　　　　　　　　　　　　　　　　　the first com-
　　　　Thatt wasse subscribyd in Moses lawe ?　　960　mandment?'

Iesus.　Sythe all you masturs togethur be sett
　　　And youre bokys here leyde on breyde.
Ley forthe youre reysunis and do nott lett
　　　How right thatt ye can rede.　　　　　　964

ii. Doctor.　I rede this in¹ the furst byddyng,　　'Honour God
　　　Wyche Moses dyd rede² vs vntill,　　　　and love thy
　　　　　　　　　　　　　　　　　　　　　　　neighbour as
Furst honor God aboue all thyng　　　　　　　thyself.'
　　　With all thy hartt and all thy wyll,
And asse thy-self love thy neybur　　　　(75)
　　　And in noo wyse to do hym yll.　　　　970

Iesus.　Ye nede noo nodur bokis to bryng;
　　　But these to pwyntis for to insev,
In whome the whole afecte³ doth hynge
　　　Of all owre⁴ lawis bothe olde and nev.　974

iii. Doctor.　Syth he these to, son, hath the schoide,
　　　Tell me the othur, chylde, I the pra.
　　　Iesus.　The thryd beddith the, in any wey,　[f. 14 a]　Jesus recites
Thatt of thy labur thow schuldyst reste,　　　　the other
　　　　　　　　　　　　　　　　　　　　　　commandments.
　　　And truly kepe thy Sabett day,
Thy-selfe, thi serwande, and thy best.　　　980

The forthe bydithe the do thy best⁵
　　　Thy fathur and mothur for to honowre ;
And when ther goodis are decrest,
　　　With all thy myght thow schuldist them succure.　984

The fyfte cummandythe for any reygur
　　　Man nor woman that thou schuldist kyll.
To fle advltre ys anothure,⁶
　　　And all thatt towchis any yll.　　　　988

¹ H. changes to is.　　² H. changes to teche.　　³ H. has ef[f]ecte.
⁴ H. has [y]owre.　　⁵ H. has [The fourthe beddith, the alderbest].
⁶ S. another.

The vij[th] seyis thow schuldyst nott steyle
    Thy neyburis goodis, more nor les.
The viij[th] forbyddyth the to cownsayle
    Or to bare any fawls wyttines.    (76)  992

The ix[th] forbyddyth othys grett,
    In any wise *thou* schuldist nott sweyre.
The last wold *tho*u schuldist no[t][1] covett
    Tliy neyburs goodis, hym to apere;[2]    996
    And this Mosees, amonge vs here,[3]
Hathe declarid amonge all men,
    Aftur scripture *that* we schulde lere,[4]
How to kepe these *comm*andementis X.    1000

*The doctors express their surprise.*

I. DOCTOR.  Beholde, owre lawis how he dothe
      expownde,
    Thatt neu*er* larny[d][5] on boke to rede!
Then all we, he ys moche more *pro*fownde
    In all trawthis, yff we take hede.    1004
II. DOCTOR.  Brother, lett hym goo his weyis;
    For yff *thi*s abrode were knone p*er*fettly,
The peple wolde geve him more prese
    Then we[6] docturs for all owre clarge.    1008

III. DOCTOR.  Ye fryndis bothe, syth yt is soo,
    He knois no[7] farthur of owre lore;
But asse he c*um* soo let hym goo,
    For w*i*th vs he schall medyll no more.    1012

      *There cu*m*yth Josoff* and *Mare sekyng the chylde* and *Mare*
      *seyth :*

*Mary in great grief; she has spent three days in the search for Jesus.*

MARE.  A! dere Josoff, whatt ys youre redde?
    Of my grett dolor noo bote ma be;    (77)
My hart ys heyve as any leyd,
    My chylde ageyne tyll I ma see.    [f. 15]  1016
We haue hym soght in many a stede,
    Vp and downe these deyis iij;
And wheythur that he be quyke or ded,
    I do not kno thatt; woo ys mee!    1020

---

[1] *Corr. by* H.    [2] H. *changes to* impere.    [3] S. *omits two half lines:* amonge all men, / Aftur scripture.    [4] H. *changes to* ken.    [5] *So* H.    [6] H. *writes* us.    [7] H. *changes to* mo.

JOSOFF.  In sorro wasse there neyu*er* man more,

    But mornyng ma nott ytt amend ;

Mare, wyff, lett vs therefore

    Take the *grace* that God woll send.        1024

*[Joseph thinks Jesus may be about the temple.]*

Yff chyldurs cu*m*pany he haue coght,

    Abowt yondur tempull he ys full right.

                *[They turn toward the temple.]*

MARE.  A ! Josoff, I see that I haue soght !

    In this worlde wasse neu*er* soche a syght.    1028

See, husebond, where he syttyth aloft

    Amonge yondur masturs soo moche off myght.

*[Mary sees Jesus.]*

JOSOFF.  Now blessid be hym [1] thatt hethur vs

    broght,

    For now in hart I am full lyght !        1032

MARE.  Josoff, ye kno the ordur well,

    Goo ye *and* feyche youre chylde *and* myne.

Now I see hym owt of all p*er*yll,         (78)

    Whom he schall w*ith* vs ageyne.[2]    1036

*['Go and fetch our child !']*

JOSOFF.  Ey ! Mare, wyff, ye kno ryght well,

    Asse I haue tolde you many a tyme,

W*ith* men of myght durst I neyu*er* mell.

    Loo ! dame, how the sytt in there furis fyn !   1040

*[Joseph dares not appear before the doctors.]*

MARE.  To them youre arand for to sey,

    Therein, Josoff, *ther* ys no p*er*ell ;

The haue reygardid you alwey

    Because of age, this wott I well.        1044

JOSOFF.  To them, wyff, whatt schulde I sey ?

    In feythe, I do nott knoo full wele.

Surely, I schall be schamyde to-dey ;

    For I cane nothur croke [3] nor knele.     1048

MARE.  Then goo we theddur bothe to

    To them *that* sytt soo worthe in wede ;

Yff ye woll not the arrande doo,

    No reymedy but I mvst nede.         1052

*[She goes with him.]*

---

[1] H. *changes to* he.     [2] H. *substitutes* go hyne.

[3] S. troke, *corr. emend. by* H.

JOSOFF.   E ! dame, goo tell them *thi* tale furst ;

    For lyke *thou* art to do thatt dede.          (79)

I wold tell myne and I durst,

    [I come be-hynde] also God me spede.[1]          1056

        *[They go up toward the altar.]*

Mary re-<br>proaches<br>Jesus.

MARE.   A ! Ie*sus*, Ie*sus*, my sun soo swete,          [f. 15 a]

    Thy gooyng froo me soo suddenly

Hathe cawsid vs bothe for to wepe

    W*ith* byttur teyris abundantly.          1060

Thyn olde fathur here *and* I

    For thy sake, sun, hathe lykyd full yll.

Owre yis the were but seldum dry,

    But now thatt we ar c*um* the tyll.

He must<br>fulfil his<br>Father's will.

IE*SUS*.   Modur, why did you seek me soo ?          1065

    Hyt hathe byn oft seyde vnto you,[2]

My Fathurs wyll I mvst fullfyll

    In eyu*ere*[3] pwynt, for well or woo.[4]          1068

She does not<br>understand,<br>but she is<br>very glad to<br>have found<br>him.

MARE.   Sun, these talis thatt you me tell

    Ase yet I canot vndurstand ;

But my hart, this kno I well,

    Ys were glade I haue the fonde.          1072

I. DOCTOR.   Now truly, dame, no me*r*vell ys

    Thogh thow in hart were full woo

To lose soche a chylde asse this.          (80)

    How long, wyff, hathe he byn thee froo ?          1076

MARE.   Syr, yt ys now these dayis iij,

Syth *that* he depa*r*tid furst fro me ;

I am full [glade][5] here hym to see

    Alyve w*ith*owt[6] woo.          1080

Jesus bids<br>farewell to<br>the doctors.

IE*SUS*.   Now farewell, masturs of myght *and* mayne !

    For w*ith* my modur now must I nede

For to reycomford hyr ageyne,

    Wyche soo longe for me hath levid in drede.          1084

---

[1] *Bracketed words supplied from* Y 248; *following this line in* MS. *is a line erased and illegible:* My place . . . this tyme . . . behynd.

[2] H. *writes* you untill.     [3] *Contraction for* er.

[4] H. *rearranges according to* Y *and* T : My fathurs wyll for well or woo / In eyu*er*[y] pwynt I must fullfyll.

[5] *Corr. by* S.     [6] H. *writes* withowt[en].

I. DOCTOR.   Now thatt Lorde of lordis be thy spede,
  Where-eyu*er* thow goo in any quost![1]

They invite
him to stay.

But yff thow wolt tarre, thow schalt[2] not nede
Any more to put thy fryndis to cost.[3]      1088

III. DOCTOR.   How seyhst thow, fathur, for thy
  goo[d][4] wyll,
Wolt thow grant *th*i help thyre-tyll,     [f. 16]
  Awey thatt he do not goo?      1091

JOSOFF.   Noo, Si*r*, in good feyth, *th*a*t* I nyll,

Joseph and
Mary object.

Nor neyu*er* forgoo hym be my wyll,
  Nodur for frynde nor foo.    (81) 1094
A long whyle we have hym myst,
And gone he wasse, or thatt I wyst ;
But hade I hym wonis be the fyst,
  He schall noo more doo soo !      1098

MARE.   Now, lordyngis, of your curtesse,
Do[5] ye nott wyll my chylde fro me ;
For w*ith* my wyll yt schall nott be,
  Whyle thatt owre lyvis last.      1102

I. DOCTOR.   Then yt is noo bote for to intreyte,

More fare-
wells.

Thy chylde I see I canot gete ;
I tro yt be but wast to speyke,
  Thatt tyme I thynke ys past.      1106

IESUS.   Now lordyngis all, w*ith* youre lysence,
Good tyme yt ys thatt we were hence ;
I thanke [you][6] of youre hy sapence
  Thatt I w*ith* you haue hade.      1110

II. DOCTOR.   Now, sun, when-eyu*er* thow cum*y*st *th*is
  wey,

Invitation to
come again.

Be bold of hus, I the p*r*aye.[7]
Yff thow to age lyve may,
  Thy fryndis ma be full glade.      1114

MARE.   Now farewell, lordis of hy degre !    (82)
I take my leyve at you all three ;
Thatt Lorde thatt ys in Trenete,
  He kepe you all from care !      1118

---

[1] H. *alters to* chest.    [2] *So* H., S. schult ; MS. *vowel illegible.*
[3] H. *alters to* quest.    [4] *Corr. by* S.    [5] *So* H , S. De.
[6] *Supplied by* S.    [7] *Contraction for* ra.

JOSOFF. And for the fyndyng of this oure sun,[1]

. . . . . . . . . . . . . . . . . . .

In heyvynis blysse thatt we[2] ma wone,[3]

And geve you well to fare.         1121

*The weather is fair and they depart for Nazareth,*

Now, cu*m* on, Mare, w*ith* myrre chere,

And bry*n*ge youre chyld w*ith* you here ;

At Naza*r*ethe now I wold wee weyre.

MARE. S*ir*, in good tyme wee schall cu*m* there ;

The wey *and* weddur *and* all ys feyre,

Whereoff am I right fayne.        1127

JOSOFFE. In this place whyle we ar here,   [f. 16 *a*]

Loke thatt we haue all owre gere,

Thatt we cu*m* nott agayne.        1130

MARE. Josoffe, husebonde, we myse nothyng ;[4]

But at youre wyll lett vs be gooyng

Asse fast ase eyu*er* we can.        1133

*first taking leave of the company.*

Ande now att all this cu*m*pany,

My leyve I take *and tha*t full humbly ;     (83)

Vnto thatt Lorde most myghty

Now I betake you eyu*er*e mon.        1137

JOSOFFE. Now farewell, my fryndis all !

For I mvst goo whatt-eyu*er* befall ;

Nedis mvst *that* nedis schall,

Be me here may you kno.        1141

A ! thatt all you ma vse thatt weyis,

At all tym*is* youre wyvis to pleyse ;

Then schall you awoide moche dysees.

God grant thatt you ma do soo !        1145

[*They go out.*]

*The doctors comment*

I. DOCTOR. Now, ye lordis thatt hathe the lawis to leyde,

Marke well the wordis thatt hathe byn seyde

Be yondur chylde of wysedome grett,        1148

---

[1] *A line seems here to be omitted.*    [2] H. *changes to* yc.

[3] H. *supposes the line omitted here.*

[4] H. *supposes that a line is here omitted.*

Wyche at this tyme amonge vs here
Declarid owre lawis be clarge clere,
Wyche be his actis dothe apere,
  Thatt of God he ys eylecte !    1152

*upon the wisdom of the Child.*

II. DOCTOR. Now surely yt can no nothur be,
For he ys nott levyng *that* eyu*er* see
Soch hy knoleyge of exselence
  In soo tendur vthe ;    1156
For in owre moste hyist dysspecionis,[1]
To them he gawe tru solyssionys,  (84)
And also made exposysionis
  Acordyng to the truthe.    1160

III. DOCTOR. Ys not thys a wondurs case,
Thatt *thi*s yonge chylde soche knolege hase?
Now surely he hath asposschall[2] *grace*,
  Soo hy dowtis des*er*nyng ;    1164
Thatt we wyche nobull docturs be,
And gradudis gret of old[3] antequete,
And[4] now on this place w*ith* yonge[5] infance [f. 17]
  Ageyne ar sett to larnyng.    1168

I. DOCTOR. Now, bredur[6] bothe, be my consell
  These myghtte matters you sett on syde,
And in avoidyng of more p*er*ell
  Thatt here-apon myght betyde ;
  Therefore lett vs no lengur abyde
In these cawsis for to contende,
For this dey ys almost at an yende.    1175

*They set the mighty matters aside until another time;*

II. DOCTOR. Now, brethur bothe, syth yt ys soo,
  Ase vere nature dothe me compell,
Here my trowthe I plyght you to
  In hart for eyu*er* w*ith* you to dwell.  1179

III. DOCTOR. Now, masturs all, be won assent, (85)
  All owre matters reyjurnyd be,
Tyll thatt a dey of argument

---

[1] H. *writes* dysspu[ta]cionis.  [2] H. *writes* a spesschall.
[3] H. *omits* old.  [4] H. *omits* And.  [5] H. *omits* yonge.
[6] S. brodur

Ma be apwyntyd indyfferentle ;
the commonalty are invited to be present then.
Where all[1] you,[2] the comenalte,
You ma depar*te* on this condyssion,
Thatt ye atende at the next monyssion.                    1186

I. DOCTOR.  Now, fryndis, tochyng owre festefall dey,
Ys there oght els *that* I ma sey ?
II. DOCTOR.   No more now, bute evyn awey,
For the nyght drawis fast apon.                    1190
III. DOCTOR.   And of youre cu*m*pany I wold you p*r*a.
And here I take my leve at eyu*ere* mon.                    1192

Tys matter nevly translate be Robert Croo in the
yere of oure Lord God M[l]v[c]xxxiiij[te], then beyng meyre
Mastur Palmar, beddar ;  and  Rychard  Smythe  an[d][3]
[Herre][4] Pyxley masturs of the Weywars; thys boke
yendide the seycond day of Marche in[5] yere above seyde.

[SONG I.][6]        [f. 17 a]
Thomas Mawdycke.      (86)
Rejoyce, rejoyce, all that here be !
The Angell these tythyng[s][3] hath browght,
That Simion, before he dye,
Shalle se the Lorde w*hi*ch all hathe wrowght ;        4

Wherefore now let vs all prepare
Owre temple that yn order be !
For he hathe put awey owre care,
The Seconde P*er*sone in Trinitye.                    8
Rychard.

[SONG II.][7]

Beholde, now[8] hit ys come to pase,
That manye yeres before was tolde,
How *tha*t Christ, owre ryght Messyas,
By Jw*das scholde be bowght and solde !        4

---

[1] H. *transposes* all *and* you.
[2] H. *inserts* [teche] *and ends sentence with this line.*     [3] *So* H.
[4] *Supplied by* S.     [5] H. *inserts* [*the*].     [6] *In late hand.*
[7] *In contemporaneous hand, but unlike* MS.     [8] S. how.

For owre offence he man became,
    His fathers wrathe to pacyfye,
And after, mekely as a lamb,
    Vpon the crose there dyd he dye.        8

O Lorde! as *thou* hast bowght vs[1] all,
    And suffryd at Mownt Callverye,
Recownfort vs[1] bothe gret *and* small,
    That yn thy trewth we lyve *and* dye!      12

                     James Hewyt.

[1] *Contraction for* us.

H

# Appendix I.

### Extracts from the Coventry Leet Book.[1]

1424 (Oct. 25). Wevers ... Item. Arbitrati sunt et ordina-
verunt quod dicti jorneymen et eorum quilibet solvet dictis
magistris annuatim in futuro quatuor denarios ad opus de le
pagent eorundem, et quod ipsi le jorneymen habeant cum magistris suis potacionem sive collectionem [sicut] antea consuerunt, *etc.* 5
—f. 27.

1427–8 (Conv. St. Paul). Hit is to haue in mynde that at a
lete holden atte fest seynt Mich. the *y*er off kyng Herre the sixt
the vij the smythes of Coventre put up a bille foloweng in thes
wordes : To you full wurshipfull meir, recordour, bayles, and to 10
all your discrete counsell shewen to you the craft of smythes how
thei were discharged of the cotelers pachand be a lete in the tyme
of John Gote then meire, and quytances made be-twene the forseid craftes eder to oder, lik as hit is well knowen and redy for to
shewe, and nowe late Giles Allesley in his office of meyralte preyed 15
the forseid craft of Smythes to tak the governaunce of the seid
pachand as for his tyme and no forther. And the seid craft did
hit wilfully to his plesaunce for the whiche cause the forseid
pachand is yete put to the forseid craft, and thei han no maner of
dute to tak hit to hem ; wyche thei beseche that ye of your grete 20
goodnes discharge the forseid craft of smythes of the pachand
atte reuerence of God and of truthe, and orden hit elles where ye
ben better avised be your good discression.

The whiche bill[2] be the avise of all the wurthy of the seid lete
and all oder apon the same lete beeng was onsuered and endo[r]sed 25
in this wise : Hit is ordeyned that the smythes shall[3] ocupie the
seid pachand forthe euery yere apon the payne of x$^{li}$ to be payd
at euery defaute to the use of the chambur.—f. 45 *b.*

1435 (E.). The orden that the sadelers and the peyntours of
the city of Coventre be fro this tyme forward contrebetory unto 30
the paiont of the cardemakers ; and that they paye as the carde-

---

[1] *A Calendar of Books, Charters,* etc., *in the Muniment-room of St.
Mary's Hall, Coventry,* J. C. Jeaffreson. Coventry, 1896. A 3. *Leet Books*
(a) 8 Hen. V.—1 and 2 Philip and Mary. *Most of the following extracts are
given or referred to in Sharp's* Dissertation, pp. 4, 8–11, 43–5. *Insignificant
variations from Sharp's text have not been noted.* (E.) *Easter Leet,* (M.)
*Michaelmas Leet.*

[2] *MS.* bull.                [3] *MS.* shull.

makers don yerly uppon the peyne of C s to be payd to the use
of the chamburlens.—f. 88 *b.*

1435 (M.). Thei will that the carpynters be associate unto the
tilers and pynners to maynten her pagent and her lyvery that now
5 is; and that the maior call the substance of the crafte of carpynters
and sett hem to-gether as one felawshipe.—f. 92 *b.*

1441 (E.). Ordinatum est quod Robertus Eme et omnes alii
qui ludunt in festo Corporis Xpisti bene et suficienter ludant, ita
quod nulla impedicio fiat in aliquo ioco sub pena xx s cuiuslibet
10 deficientis ad usus muros levanda per majorem et camararios,
etc.—f. 102 *b.*

1443–4 (C.S.P.). For-alsomoche as the crafte of cardemakers,
sadelers, masons, and peyntours of the cite of Coventre be long
tyme y-past haue byn as oone fellauship in beryng costys charges
15 and all other dueties of old tyme to ther pagent and to the said
felauship longyng. And now late, that is to say in the tyme of
Ric. Braytoft maior of the said cite, the said felauship for certen
causes among hem movyd wer lyke to departe and to breke ther
felauship wherfor certen persons of[1] the said craftes, shewyng to the
20 maiour the causes of ther grevance, besought hym in this matter to
sett due remedye. And so by goodly leysur the maior, callyng
a-fore hym and his counsell all the said hoole fellauship, rehersid
unto them the grevouse complayntes that wern made to hym by
certen persons of the said felauship. The for-namyd felauship
25 willyng to be ruled compromytted hem to abyde the rule and
ordynaunce of the meire and his councell. And so by advyse of the
said meyr and his councell, hit is ordenyd that the said iiij craftes
shalbe oone felauship beryng costes, charges, and all other dueties
to her pagent and to ther felauship longyng. And that thei shall
30 yerely chose new masturs a-pon saynt Thomas day in Xpmas weke
in the forme and maner folowyng : That is to say, ther shalbe of
every of the said craftys iiij men in a place consuette within the
said cite; and ther in in the fest of Saynt Thomas thai shall chose
of every of the said iiij craftes oone master for the yer folowyng.
35 And if so be that any of the said craftes a monethe afore the said fest
be reasonable cause unfayned may excuse hyme that thei may not
be at that eleccion of the masturs at the said feeste. That then the
crafte or the craftes that may nott be ther shall bryng in iij menys
names of the crafte that may not be ther at the eleccion and what-
40 soever the iij personnes with other that shalbe a-pon the eleccion
doo, thei that ben awey to agre therto, and also sone as the
masturs be chosen that same day or thei departe the new masturs
so chosen shall take ther consuett othe. And allso every person of
the said craftys shall pay yerely to the masturs xijd and all other
45 dueties, customes, and laufull charges that long to the pagent and
to the said felauship and all money that shalbe reryd [b] for

---

[1] *MS. of of.*

makyng of new brethren or els in other wais to the craftes renued,
as hit is gadred hit shalbe put in a comen box ther to be kepte to
the use of the said felauship and to the wurship of this cite.
Allso every mastur of the seid iiij craftes shall haue due correc-
cion of his own crafte of all the priue poynts that long to his  5
crafte, without meddlyng or entermettyng of any vther craftys.
Allso that ther shall no man of the said iiij craftes play in no pagent
on Corpus Xpi. day save onely in the pagent of his own crafte,
without he have lycens of the maior that shalbe for the yer.  Allso that every man that hath any money of forfetts that have byn 10
made or els money for makyng of bredren afore this tyme in the
said craftes that hit be brought in be-twen this and the fest of All
Saynts next comyng, and that to the maior.  And also that all
the masturs of the said felauship that have not accompted a-fore
this tyme that thay mak ther acompte be-twene this and the fest 15
of All Saynts next comyng and all the arereage, if any be, that
hit be brought in the same day and delyveryd unto the comen
box.  And allso that all masturs that now byn and all the
masturs of the said felauship that shalbe herafter yerle, shall
make ther acompte, every mastur for his tyme at the fest of 20
Estur.  Provyded allwey that the crafte of masons, ne none of
hem, shall not be charged to com to noo buryeng, weddyng, ne
offryng of the said crafts on workedais.  And who of the said
felliship disobeith this ordynaunce, or forefettyth in any of them,
shall pay at every forfett x li to the maior of the cite of Coventre, 25
that tyme beyng withouten any grace.

Nomina consilij maioris in hoc casu : (list).—f. 109 a and b.

1457.  (The king came to Coventry on) Fryday the xj of
Feveryere the yere reynyng of kyng Herry the sixt the xxxv[ti]
. . . The quene (margin).  On Corpus Xpisti yeven at nyght then
next suyng came the quene (Margaret) from Kelyngworth to
Coventre ; at which tyme she wold not be met, but came prively
to se the play there on the morowe ; and she sygh then alle the
pagentes pleyde save domes-day, which myght not be pleyde for
lak of day.  And she was loged at Richard Wodes the grocer, 35
where Ric. Sharp some-tyme dwelled ; and there all the pleys
were furst pleyde.  At which tyme the meyre and his brethren
sende unto her a present which was sich as here suyth : That is
to wit, ccc paynemaynes, a pipe of rede wyne, a dosyn capons of
haut grece, a dosyn of grete fat pykes, a grete panyer full of pes- 40
codes and another panyer full of pipyns and orynges and ij
cofyns of connfetys and a pot of grene gynger.  And there were
with her then these lordes and ladyes that here folowen : That is
to sey, the duke of Bukkyngham and my lady his wyff and all
ther childern, the lord Revers and my lady hys wyf, the lady of 45
Shrowesbery the elder, and the lady of Shrowesbery the younger,
with other mony moo lordes and ladyes.  And the Friday then
next suyng she remeved to Colshull to her mete and so to Eculsale

to the prynce; at which tyme the seid meire and his brethern
with right a good feliship of the seid cite, which plesid her highnes
right well, brought her to the utmast syde of theyre fraunchise
where hit plesyd her to gyff them grete thank bothe for theyre
5 present and theyre gentyll attendaunce.—f. 173 *b*.

1460 (E.). Also hit is ordeyned that every craft that hath
pagant to pley in, that the pagant be made redy and brought furth
to pley, uppon the peyn of C s to be reased of iiij maisters of the
crafts that so offend.—f. 182.

10 1474 (E.). Hit is ordened at this present leete that every crafte
with-in this cite com with their pageaunts accordyng as hit haith
byn of olde tyme, and to com with their processions and ridyngs
also, when the byn required by the meir for the worship of this
cite [upon the] peyne of xli. at every defalte.—f. 227 *b*.

15 1493 (Apr.). Also hit was ordeyned at this present lete that
the tallowe chaundelers shuld be unyed unto the craft of smythes,
accordyng as hit hath be ordeyned be lete aforetyme, which they
nowe conferme uppon the peyn of every singler persone of the
seid tallowe chaundelers that refuse this order nowe confermed to
20 lese C s to this city, and his body to prison till he so will do.—f.
270 *b*.

1493 (Oct.). It. It is ordeyned at this lete that the chaundelers shuld pay *y*erely to the smythes ij s towards their paient.—
f. 271.

25 1494 (Apr.). Also hit is ordeyned, as hath be ordeyned and enacted be dyvers letes in tymes past, that the chaundelers and cooks
of this cite shall be contributory to the smythes of this cite and to
pay *y*erely towards the charge of ther preste and pageant, every
chaundeler and cooke ij s; every man faylyng of such payement
30 to lese at every tyme xl s and to have enprisonment till he paye the
seid ij s with the arrerages in that partie, if eny be, and the seid
peyn; the mair for the tyme beyng to haue a noble thereof,
and the craft of smythes another noble, and iiij nobles to the
wardeyns of this cite to the use of this cite. Provided that no
35 such persone which their wyfes occupie makyng and sellyng of
candell be constreyned to be master or keper with the smythes in
no wyse.—f. 272 *b*.

1494 (Apr.). For-asmoche as the unyte and amyte of all citees
and comenaltees is principully atteyned and contynued be due
40 ministration of justice and pollytyk guydyng of the same; for-
seyng that no persone be oppressed nor put to forther charge than
he convenyntly may bere and that every persone withoute favor
be contributory after his substance and facultees that he useth to
every charge had and growyng for the welth and worship of the
45 hole city; and whereso it is in this cite of Coventre that dyvers
charges have be continued tyme oute of mynde for the worship of
the same, as pagants and such other, whech have be born be
dyvers crafts whech crafts at the begynnyng of such charges were

more welthy, rich, and moo in nombre then nowe be, as openly
appereth; for whech causez they nowe be not of power to continue
the seid charges without relief and comfort be shewed to them in
that partie; and inasmoch as there be dyvers crafts in this cite
that be not charged with like charges; as dyers, skynners, fysshe-    5
mongers, cappers, corvisers, bochers, and dyvers other.  Therfor hit
is ordeyned be this present lete that the mayre and viij of his
counceill have auctorite to call all the seid crafts and other that
be not charged for the seid charges and them to adioyn to such
crafts as be ouercharged with the forseid pagants uppon peynes be   10
hym and his seid counceill to be sette.  And if eny persone refuse
such unyon and contribucion, or such resonable measne to be
taken be the discrescion of the seid mayre and his counceill, such
persone so refusing to forfet and paye such peyn in that partie so
to be sette be the seid mayre and his counceill.  And that such    15
resonable measne in the premisses so to be taken be the seid mayre
and his counceill to be of like force and effect as yf it had be
made at the present lete.—f. 273.

    1494 (M.).  Where hit was ordeyned at the laste lete that such
crafts that were not contributory to the crafts as bere yerely      20
charge in this cite to the worship of the same shuld be unyed
and adioyned to the crafts so charged be the discrescion of the
maire and his counceill, which ordenaunce hath not be put in
execucion caused be dyvers self-willed persones whech be their
willes wold obbeye no other rule ne ordre but after their owne      25
willes grounded without reason, which may not be suffred yf
this cite shulde prosper and contynue in welth.  Hit is therfore
ordeyned at this present lete that all maner crafts and persones
occupying eny crafte within this cite not beying charged to eny
yerely charge that is had and made in this cite for the worship     30
of the same, as paiants and such other, that they, betwixt this and
the fest of Seynt Martyn next comyng, of their toward-lovyng
disposicion applye them-self to joyn and unye themself or to be
contributory to other craft that is charged, as is aforseid, in relief
of their charge; which their so doyng shall principally please      35
God and contynue the gode name and fame that this cite hath
had in tymes past.  And that every craft and persone that woll
not of their goode willes be the seid fest applye them to such unyon
as is aforerehersed, that then such persone and crafte that refus-
yng obbeye, stand, and performe such order and direccion of the     40
maire and his counceill in that partie to be ordred and made, uppon
the peyn of every persone and craft that disobeieth to lose at the
first refusell C s, at the ij$^{de}$ x li, and at the iij$^{de}$ xx marc.—
f. 273 b.

    1494 (M.).  Also it is ordeyned, at the same lete, at the         45
request of the inhabitaunts dwellyng in Gosseford strete, that the
pageants yerely frohensfurth be sette and stande at the place
there of olde tyme used lymyt and appoynted, uppon payn of

every craft that doth to the contrary to lese at every defalt
vj s viij d to the use of the cite, to be levyed and paide.—
f. 273 b.

1494–5 (Jan. 12). Memorandum. That the feliship and mys-
5 terye of bochers in Coventre, remembryng the ordennaunce lately
made be auctorite of lete for contribucion to be had and made
be such crafts as be not charged to such ordinary charges and costs
as be yerely made and boren for the worship of this cite, callyng
also to theyr mynde the olde acqueyntaunce and amyte that of
10 long tyme hath be and contynued, be measne of entercours and of
bying and sellyng, betwixt them and the feliship of whittawers,
whech be overcharged to the charges above rehersed ; and for
their relief in the premisses, at Coventre aforeseid the xij^th day of
Januare the x^th yere of the reign of our soverayn lord king
15 Henre vij^th in the presence of Robt. Grene then beyng maire,
were agreable and ther graunted to bere and pay yerely frothens-
furth to the said feliship of whittawers towards the yerely charge
of their paiant as long as they ther shalbe charged with the seid
paiant xvj s viij d be the hands of the keper and maisters of the
20 seid feliship of bochers to be paide to the kepers and mastirs of the
seid feliship of whittawers yerely iiij s in the vigell of the Holy
Trinite withoute ferther delaye, without eny other or ferther
charge or besyness be them to be made or doon to the seid feliship
of whittawers.—f. 273 b.
25   1495 (Apr.). Also hit is ordeyned at the peticion and desire of
the craft of cardmakers towards their charge that they yerely ber in
kepyng their pageant that the crafts of skynners and barbors shall
yerely frohensfurth bere and pay to the seid craft of cardmakers
xiij [s] iiij d in the forme suyng : That is to sey, the maisters of
30 the crafte of skynners and the maisters of the barbors shall yerely
in the vigill of the Holy Trinite pay unto the maisters of the cardmakers, either of them, vj s viij d, and yf eyther of the seid crafts
fayle of payement at that day, they and every singler persone of
either of the seid crafts, that payement denying, to lese at every
35 default vj s viij d, and in default of payement, their bodies so for-
fetyng to be commytte to prison their to remayn unto the tyme
they have paide that fyn and over that to fynde suerte that eftsones he shall not defende in that partie.—f. 275.

1495 (Apr.). Also hit is ordeyned, etc., at the peticion of the
40 crafte of wrights and tylers and pynners that these persones whos
names here followen shalbe ioyned and contributory to the crafte
of wrights frohensfurth for ever, and to pay and bere yerely after
their porcion as other wrights doo towards the charge of their
pageant, uppon the peyn of every person doyng the contrarie to
45 lese at every defalt vj s viij d, and in defalt of payement of that
peyn, their bodies to prison till they have paide hit and over that
fynde suertee that he eftsones offende not in that partie. These
be the names : John Okley kerver, Rich. Percy wright, John

Cokkes wright, Nicholas Slough cartwright, John Norton whele-wright, and John Knyght whelewright.—f. 275 b.

1495 (Apr.). Also where hit was shewed at this present lete be bill put in be the girdelers that the crafte of cappers and fullers of their goode will were agreable to paye in the fest of the vigill of 5 the Holy Trinite to the master of the crafte of girdelers yerely xiij s iiij d towards the charge of their preste and pageant etc. Hit was ordeyned and stablisshed be auctorite of this present lete that that agrement and acorde shuld stande stable and to be per-formed & kept for frohensfurth for ever, with more that yf paye- 10 ment yerely be not made in this seid vigill then every person that denyeth such payement to lese at every defalt vj s. viij d with imprisonment, as is aboveseid in the crafte of carpenters.—f. 275 b.

1507 (Apr.). Memorandum. That it is ordeyned at this lete that the craft and feliship of bakers shalbe contributories and 15 charged from hensforth with the craft and feliship of smythes and to pay yerely to them toward theyre pagent at Corpus Xpisti tyde xiij s iiij d, and so to contynewe from hensforth yerely.—f. 297 b.

Itm. It is ordened at this present lete that the felisship of corvesers shalbe contributory and chargeable with the crafte of 20 tanners yerly from hensforth and to pay xiij s iiij d, and to begyn theyre payment of the hole at Corpus Xpisti tyde next comyng, and so forth yerly at every Corpus Xpisti tyde to pay xiij s iiij d. —f. 297 b.

It. It is ordened and agreed that from hensforth the feliship 25 and crafte of bochers shalbe yerly contributorye to the felyship of whittawers toward ther pagent at Corpus Xpisti tyde xvj s viij d, and so to continue yerly forthlyke as they dydde afore, etc.— f. 297 b.

1524 (Apr. 12). Item. It is enacted that so longe as the crafte 30 of shomakers fynde and keip ther priest, they shall reteyne and keipe in ther hands to ther own use yeirelie the marke of money which thei were wont to paye yeirelie by act of leete to the craft of tanners, and provided alwayes that the said craft of shomakers shall pay unto the said tanners at Corpus Xpisti tyde next ensuyng 35 vj s viij d.—f. 339.

1526. Item. It is enacted that all carvers within this citie frome hensfurth shalbe associat with the craft of peyntors and that every carver shall pay yeirelie to the peyntors towards the charges of their pagiaunt xij d without contradiction upon 40 peyn for every defaut to forfett vj s viij d to the seid craft of peyntors, and that the said carvers frome hensfurth shalbe dis-myssed and discharged frome the craft of carpenters, and that Richard Tenwyntor shall pay suche arrerages to the carpenters as he oweth theme for the xij d which he shuld haue payed theme 45 yeirelie in tymes past.—f. 344 b.

1529 (Apr. 8). Itm. It is enacted at this lete that the crafte of cappers of this citie frome hensfurth shalbe owners of the weyvers

pagiaunt with all the implements and apparell belongyng to the
same pagiaunt, and that the seid craft of weyvers shall yeirelie
frome hensfurthe pay unto the master of the seid crafte of cappers
vj s viij d ; and so the seid craft of weyvers frome hensfurth to be
5 clerlie discharged of the seid pagiaunt and of the name therof.—
f. 350 b.

1531 (Oct. 2). It. Wher as the company, feliship, and craft of
cardemakers and sadelers of this citie meny yeires and of longe
continuaunce have hadd and yet haue the cheif rule, governaunce,
10 reparyng and meyntenaunce, as well of a chappell within the
parishe churche of Seynt Michells in the seid citie, named Seynt
Thomas Cappell, and of the ornamentes, juells, and lightes of the
same, as also of a pagiaunt with the pagiaunt house and pleyng
geire with other appertenaunces and apparells belongyng to the
15 same pagiaunt. The meyntenaunce and reparacion wherof haithe
been and is yeirelie to the greit charge, cost, and expenses of the
seid company and crafte, beyng now but a fewe persones in nomber
and havyng but smale eyde of eny other craft for the same. So
that ther said charge is and like to be more ponderouse and
20 chargeable to theme then they may convenyentlie bere or susteyn
in shorte tyme to come, oneles provision for a remedy may be
spedilie hadd. In consideracion wherof and for-asmoch as the company, feliship, and craft of cappers within this citie, now beyng in
nomber meny welthy and honest persones, and have maid dyvers
25 tymes sute and request unto the meire and his brethern the aldermen of this citie to have a certeyn place to theme assigned and
lymyted, as dyvers other crafts have, to sitt to-gether in ther seid
parishe churche to here ther dyvyne service and bere suche charges
for the same as by master meire and his brethern the aldermen
30 shalbe assigned ; it is therefor by the mediacion of Mr. Richard
Rice now meire of this citie and of his seid brethern the aldermen at this present lete assembled and by auctoritie of the same
with the agrement, consent, and assent of all the seid parties, companyes, and crafts, enacted, ordeyned, and constituted that the
35 seid company and craft of cappers frome hensforthe shalbe associat,
joyned, and accompanyed with the seid crafts of cardemakers and
sadelers in the governaunce, reparyng, and meynteynyng, as well
of and in the seid Chappell, named Seynt Thomas chappell, and of
the ornaments and lights of the same, as of and in the seid pagy-
40 aunt [b] and pagiaunt house with the implements, appertenaunces,
pleaers, reherces, and pleyng geire accustumed, belongyng and
necessarie to and for the same, after suche maner or better as it
haithe been used and accustumed before tyme. And that every
housholder or shop-keper of every of the seid companyes and
45 crafts toward and for the charges and exspenses aboveseid shall
not onelie pay yeirelie to the maisters and kepers of the seid
crafts at such tyme and day as the seid crafts shall appoynt xij d ;
and upon Seynt Thomas day, named the Translacion of Seynt

Thomas, shall also offere yeirelie every of theme j d at the high masse seid in the seid chappell. But also the seid maisters, company, and crafts fromehensfurthe shall applie and bestowe to and upon the seid reparacions and charges all the revenues, rents, and profitts of all soche lands, houses, and tenements as they or eny of 5 theme now have or herafter shall have to the use and behove of the seid companyes and crafts; and the viij s of yerelie pencion which is yeirelie payed by the peynters and carvers unto the seid charges shall yeirelie be payed and go to the same charges. And that the seid maisters now electe and hereafter to be electe maisters 10 of the seid crafts shall yeirelie, upon suche a day as the seid maisters shall appoint and agre, accompeny theme-selfs to-gethers and bryng in and make a true and a full accompt every of theme to the other of all ther seid receites, revenues, and profittes. And the seid charges and the charges of the kepyng of harnes belong- 15 yng to the seid crafts with the weiryng of the same in the watches and other necessarie charges and busynes for the seid crafts allowed, payed, and performed, the overpluse of the seid money of the seid revenues, profitts, and money shalbe bestowed and put in a box with two locks and two keyes, the on key to remeyne with 20 the masters of the craft of cardmakers and sadelers, and the other key to remeyn with the maisters of the craft of cappers, sauelie to keip the seid money in the seid box untill they have nede to bestow it upon the seid charges or otherwise, as they shall thynk convenyent; and the seid box to remeyn in the said chappell 25 fastoned with a cheyne.

Also it is enacted by the auctoritie and consent aforseid that the maisters and compeny of the craft of cappers shall fromehensfurthe femyliarlie and lovynglie accompeny and sitt togethers in the seid chappell with the seid compeny and craft of carde- 30 makers and sadelers to here ther divyne service, and also shall go togethers in ther processions and watches too and too togethers; and that the seid compeny and craft of cardmakers and sadelers shall haue the preemynence and overhande in ther sittyngs and goyng together oon yeire, and the seid craft and compeny of 35 cappers shall lykewyse haue the preemynence and overhande in ther sittyng and goyng the other yeire, and so continew frome yeire to yeire lovynglie fromehensfurthe; so that the seid cardemakers and sadelers shall not lack ther rome nor sittyng in the seid chappell.—f. 357 a and b. 40

1531 (Oct. 2). Itm. It is enacted also that the company and craft of barbars of this citie shall yeirelie fromehensfurthe pay unto the company and craft of gurdelers of this citie vj s viij d toward ther charges of the pagyant and processions at suche day and tyme as they were wont to pay the seid some unto 45 the craft of cardmakers, upon peyn every of theme to forfeit for ther defaut xij d to be levyed by distresse to the use of the citie.—f. 358.

Itm.  It is also enacted that the compeny and craft of walkers
of this citie shall yeirelie pay unto the company and craft of weyvers
vj s viij d towards the charges of ther pagyant at such day and tyme
as it hathe be wont to be payed.   And that the company and
5 craft of skynners shall likewise pay unto the seid craft of weyvers
yeirelie v s towards ther seid charges.—f. 358.

1532 (May 14).  Itm.  It is enacted that the craft of peynters
shall pay yeirelie fromehensfurth iiij s of the viij s that they wer
wont to pay to a pagiaunt unto the craft of gurdelers and the other
10 iiij s of the seid viij s unto the craft of cardemakers.—f. 359 b.

1533 (May 6).  Also it is enacted, that such persones as be not
associat and assistant to eny craft which is charged with eny
pagiant of this citie, as fishemongers, bowyers, flechers, and suche
other, shall now be associat and assistaunt to such crafts as the
15 Mr. Meire shall assigne and appoynt theme.—f. 361.

1537 (Apr. 24).  Item.  Wher as the meire, aldermen, beileffs,
and cominaltie of this citie by ther wrytyng indented and sealled
with ther comen seall have graunted, given, and dymysed unto the
master, kepers, fraternitie, and company of the craft of cappers of
20 this citie the chappell, pagyaunt, and pagyaunt house which was
latelie surrendered and given upp by wrytyng to theme by the
fraternitie and company of cardemakers and sadelers.  It is nowe
enacted by auctoritie of this lete that the seid fraternitie and
company of cappers shall enjoy the seid pagiaunt, pagiaunt house,
25 and chappell accordyng to the tenour of the seid wrytyng
indented, etc.—f. 368 b.

1547 (May 3).  Item.  It is also enacted that the cowpers of
this citie shall fromehensfurth be associat with the tilers and
pynners and bere suche charges as thei haue doon in tymes past ;
30 and that the cowpers shalbe the hedd and cheffest of theim and
stand charged with the pagyaunt.—f. 400.

# Appendix II.

*Records and accounts of the trading companies of Coventry referring to the Corpus Christi Play.*[1]

## SMITHS' COMPANY.[2]

(13) *Characters.*[3]  God (Jesus), Caiaphas, Herod, Procula (Pilate's wife), beadle (or porter), the Devil, Judas, Peter and Malchus, Anna (or Annas), Pilate, Pilate's Son, two knights, four tormentors, two princes.

(14) *Machinery, dresses*, etc.[3]  The cross with a rope to draw 5 it up and a curtain hanging before it, two pair of gallows, four scourges and a pillar, gilding the pillar and the cross, scaffold, fanes to the pageant, mending of imagery (1469), a standard of red buckram ; two red pensils of cloth painted and silk fringe, iron to hold up the streamer ; four gowns and four hoods for the 10 tormentors (afterwards described as jackets of black buckram with nails and dice upon them), other four gowns with damask flowers, also two jackets party red and black. two mitres (for Caiaphas and Annas), a rochet for one of the bishops, God's coat of white leather (six skins), a staff for the demon, two spears, 15 gloves (twelve pair at once), Herod's crest of iron, scarlet hoods and a tabard, hats and caps—straw hats, cheverel (chevelure, peruke) for God, three cheverels and a beard, two cheverels gilt for Jesus and Peter, faulchion for Herod (gilt), scarlet gown, maces, girdle for God, a newe sudere to God vij d, a seldall for 20 God xij d., sceptres for Herod and his son, poll-axe for Pilate's son, (15) blue buckram 5 yds. and 6¾ yds. sattin purchased in 1501 [4] ; velvet hose were sold in 1590 at the breaking up of the pageant.  *Music.*  1584 (only), trumpet and bagpipe ; minstrels is a common entry, and the waits are paid for " piping." 25

---

[1] *Mainly reprinted from Sharp's Dissertation on the Coventry Mysteries and from the introduction to the Abbotsford Club edition of the* Weavers' Pageant. *Numbers in parentheses refer to pages in Sharp's* Dissertation ; *when preceded by A., to the Abbotsford Club edition.* H.-P. *refers to Halliwell-Phillips,* Outlines of the Life of Shakespeare, 7th edition, *from which some records have been quoted.  Graphic signs have been put in ordinary letters.  Direct quotations from Sharp are preceded by* Sh.

[2] *Sh.* The accounts of this company commence in 1449. . . 1585 [was] the last year of their exhibiting.

[3] Sharp's *list.*

[4] *Sh.* . . . the latter appears to have been used for Herod's gown, and most probably the buckram also.

(15) *Agreement.*[1] 1452–3. These men above writen wer
acordid and agreed on Munday next befor Palme Sonday, anno
H. (6th) xxxj., that Thomas Colclow, skynner, fro this day forth
shull have the rewle of the pajaunt unto the end of xij yers next
5 folowing, he for to find the pleyers and all that longeth therto all
the seide terme ; save the kepers of the craft shall let bring forth
the pajant and find clothys that gon abowte the pajant and find
russhes therto. And every Wytson-weke who that be kepers of
the crafte shall dyne with Colchow and every master ley down
10 iiij d., and Colchow shall have ʒerely for his labor xlvj s viij d
and he to bring in to the master on Sonday next after Corpus
Xpisti day the originall and fech his vij nobulleʒ ; and Colchow
must bring in at the latter end of the termes all the garments
that longen to the pajant as good as they wer delyvered to hym.
15 This was ordeyned in the time of Will. Melody, Th. Warner, and
Will. Byngley, then kepers of the crafte.

*Specimen of Pageant Expenses, Entry for* 1490. This is
the expens of the furste reherse of our players in Ester weke ;
inprimis in brede iiij d, it.[2] in ale viij d, it. in kechyn xiij d, it. in
20 vynegre j d ; summa[3] ij [s] ij d.

(16) It. payd at the second reherse in Whyttson-weke in brede,
ale, and kechyn ij s iiij d.—Inprimis for drynkynge at the pagent
in havinge forthe in wyne and ale vij d ob, it. in the mornynge at
diner and at sopper in costs in brede vij d ob, it. for ix galons of
25 ale xviij d, it. for a rybbe of befe and j gose vj d, it. for kechyn
to denner and sopper ij s ij d, it. for a rybbe of befe iij d, it. for
a quarte of wyne ij d ob, it. for an-other quarte for heyrynge of
Procula is gowne ij d ob, it. for gloves ij s vj d, it. spend at the
reparellynge of the pagantte and the expences of havyng it in and
30 furthe xiiij d, it. in paper ob. ; Summa xij s j d ob.

Mem.[4] payd to the players players for Corpus Xpisti daye ;
inprimis to God ij s, it. to Cayphas iij s iiij d, it. to Heroude iij s
iiij d, it. to Pilatt is wyffe ij s, it. to the bedull iiij d, it. to one
of the knights ij s, it. to the devyll and to Judas xviij d, it. to
35 Peter and Malkus xvj d, it. to Anna ij s ij d, to Pilatte iiij s, it.
to Pilatte is sonne iiij d, it. to an-other knighte ij s ; Summa
xxviij s ; the mynstrell xiiij d.

Mem. that these bene the garments that wer newe reparellyd
a-gaynste Corpus Xpisti daye ; inprimis iiij jakketts of blake
40 bokeram for the tormentors with nayles and dysse upon them, it.
other iiij for tormentors of an-other suett wythe damaske flowers,
it. ij of bokeram with hamers crowned,[5] it. ij party jakketts of rede
and blake, it. a cloke for Pilatte, (17) it. a gowne for Pilattes sone,

[1] *Sh.* A similar agreement was made in 1481 with Sewall and Ryngald.
[2] itm̄ *and below, sometimes* it'.
[3] Sm̄a *and below.*
[4] Md̄ *and below.*
[5] *Sh.* The arms of the smiths' company is three hammers crowned.

a gowne for the bedull, it. a hode for the bedull, it, twoo burlettis, it. a creste for Heroude, it. a fawchon for Heroude, a hatt for Pilatte, a hatt for pilatts sone, it. ij myters for the bysschoppis, it. ij hatts for ij princes, it. iiij hatts for the tormentors, it. other ij hatts for the tormentors, it. a poll-ax for Pilatts sone, it. a  5
septur for Heroude, it. a masse, it. a septur for Pilatts sonne, it. iiij scorges and a piller, it. ij cheverels gyld for Jhe and Petur, it. the devyls hede; the somme of all the costes and workemanschyp and colours drawyth to xv s.

(18) *The Pageant.*[1]  1578. ij new berars of yron for the seyt 10
in the padgand.  (19) 1440, it. p. cloth to lap abowt the pajent, payntyng and all iij s vj d ob.[2]

1471, expens for burneysshyng and payntyng of the fanes to the pageant xx d; 1553,[3] it. payd for payntyng of the pagent tope xxij d.[4]   15

(20) *Scaffolds for spectators.*  Making of a new post to the scaffold, tryndyll and theal to ditto, two new scaffold wheels 6s. 8d., iron pins and colters to the scaffold wheels, boards about the scaffold, three boards and a ledge for the scaffold, clamps and iron-work, setting in of the pageant and scaffolds, driving the 20
pageant and scaffolds.[5]

*Moving of the pageant, Stations.*[6]  1450, spend to bryng the

[1] *Sh.* . . . we may form some idea of the appearance presented by the smiths' pageant by a consideration of the following items : thus, the cross was painted and gilt ; there is a charge for setting up the "mortys of the crosse" and for a piece of timber to it ; also a rope to draw up the cross, and the cloth that hangs before it.  The pillar to which Christ was tied when scourged was also painted and gilt.

[2] *Sh.* These cloths were obviously hung round the pageant vehicle, so as to conceal from the eyes of the spectators the lower room in which the performers "apparelled themselves," as well as the machinery underneath the "rowme," or stage of action ; such as the hogsheads in the new pageant of this company, the windlass which in the cappers' pageant had three men to attend on it and in the drapers' had a rope three fathom long, the apparatus for representing the earthquake in the drapers' pageant, and hell-mouth, *etc.*  There are constant charges for nails, tenterhooks, rings, wire, thread, small cord, and similar articles, which of course were used for the curtains and in the machinery and dresses.  *See also* H.-P. II., 289 ; 1569, "halfe a yard of Rede Sea" 6*d* ; 1565, ("theatrical appliances of another company") three paynted clothes to hang abowte the pageant ; (2 Edw. VI.), payd for makyng of the hooke to hang the curten on iiij. *d.*  Some of the pageant accounts include payments "for curten ryngus."

[3] *H.-P.* 1554.

[4] *Sh.* . . . the use of pencils or streamers, or both, may be discovered in all the remaining accounts.  *They were also used in processions.*

[5] *Sh.* . . . the usual charges are for having out of the pageant, setting the scaffolds ; and setting in of the pageant and scaffolds to the pageant-house after the performance was over.

[6] *Sh.* The smiths' was usually "dryven" by a number of men not specified.  It appears that the *first station* of this pageant was in Gosford street, and as that is the first ward in point of precedency, it seems very probable that all the pageants commenced playing there ; another was at Much Park street end, most likely the corner of Jordan Well, in which case a third was at New Gate.  *See Introduction.*

pagent in-to Gosford stret; 1471, expens at Mikelparke strete ende for ale to the pleyers x d, it. at Richard Woodes dur for ale to the pleyers v d; 1486, it. for ale at the New ȝate j d ob; 1497, it. for the horssyng of the padgeant xij d; 1498, it. payd for ij
5 cords for the draught of the paygaunt j d; 1562, it. for settyng the padgande yn the first place vj d.

(21) *Rehearsals.*[1] 1466, it. in expense at the rehers in the parke iij d; 1576, pd for Sent Marye hall to reherse there ij d, spent on the comyanye after we had hard the second reherse ij d,
10 1579, pd to the plears rehersyng in the Palys[2] xij d; 1584, payde the players at the last reherse in Seint Nicholas hall iij d.[2]

*Dresser.*[3] 1474, pd for sweepyng the pagent and dressyng vij d.

*Ale and wine.*[4] 1450, it. payd for a pynt of wyne for Pilatt
15 jd; 1480, pd for a quart red wyn for Pilat ij d; 1494, it. in expence on the pleares for makyng them to drynke and hete at every reste iij d.

*Men about the pageant.* 1469, it. for iiij jaked men about the pagent iiij d; 1564, pd for a chassyng stafhed 6 d.[5]

20 *The oath of the masters* of the company : They swear to " kepe unto the uttermasse all suche laudable customs as pagans, quart-rage, weddings, burings, and such other like thinge as hathe be in timis past usyd and customyd."

(22) *Annual pageant pence.*[6] 6. Edw. VI., reseyved of the craft
25 for pagent pencys iij s iiij d.

*Journeymen.* 13. Hen. VII., *Rules of the Smiths' Company:* Also that they wate upon the hede mayster upon Corpus Xpisti daye to goo upon prossession, also to wate upon the maysters and attende upon the pageaunt to the worsshipe of this cite and
30 the crafte; in like wyse to wate upon the maisters of the crafte and so likewise to goo upon wache on Myssomer nyȝht and Santte Peter nyȝght.

(26) *Characters. God.* 1451, it. payed for vj skynnys of whit leder to Godds garment xviij d, it. payed for makyng of the
35 same garment x d; 1490, it. a cheverel gyld for Ihē; 1498, it. payd for mendyng a cheverel for God and for sowyng of Gods kote of leddur and for makyng of the hands to the same kote

---

[1] *Sh.* Annual rehearsals (usually two in number) took place before the respective companies.

[2] *Sh.* The "palys" was the bishop's palace, part of which was rented by the company for their quarterly and occasional meetings. The smiths' company had their annual dinner on St. Loy's day in St. Nicholas Hall.

[3] *Sh.* A person was appointed *dresser* of each pageant.

[4] *Sh.* . . . ale was given both to the players and drivers. Pilate being the principal character in the smiths' pageant, the performer was allowed wine.

[5] Sh. *conjectures that these entries refer to officials stationed in the street to prevent intrusion by the spectators. He says that no such charge occurs in the accounts of the other companies.*

[6] *Sh.* This varied from 2s. 2d. to 3s. 4d. and sometimes more.

xij d; 1501, it. pd for a newe sudere for God vij d; 1553, it.
payd for v schepskens for Gods coot and for makyng iij s; 1560,
it. for a selldall for God xij d; 1565, pd for payntyng and gyldyng
(*inter alia*) Gods cote, pd for a gyrdyll for God iij d.

Caiaphas and Annas. 1486, it. for a tabarde and an hoode 5
[the hire of] iiij d; (28) 1487, it. paid for hyryng off a skarlet
hood[1] and a raygete[2] for on off the bisshoppis v d; 1499, it.
payde for colours and gold foyle and sylver foyle for ij myttyrs;
1544, payd for a bysschops taberd of scarlet that we bowght in
the Trenete Church x s.                                            10

(28-9) *Herod*.[3] 1477, it. to a peynter[4] for peyntyng the
fauchon and Herods[5] face x d. It. for assadyn, silver papur and
gold paper, gold foyle and grene foyle ij s j d, it. for redd wax
ij d, it. payd to Thomas Suker for makyng the crests xxij d;[6]
1478, it. for assaden for the harnes x d; 1480, expense for a slop 15
for Herod (*inter alia*), pd for peyntyng and dressyng Heruds
stuf ij d; 1487, it. for mendyng of Arrodes crast xij d;[7] 1489,[8]
it. paid for a gowen to Arrode vij s iiij d, it. paid for peyntyng
and steynyng[9] ther-off vj s iiij d, it. payd for Arroddes garment
peynttyng that he went a prossasyon in xx d[10]; 1490, a fawchon, 20
a septur, and a creste for Heroude repaired; 1494,[11] it. payd for
iij platis to Heroddis crest of iron vj d, it. payd for a paper of
aresdyke xij d, it. payd to Hatfield for dressyng of Herods creste
xiiij d; 1499, it. payd to John Hatfelde for colours and gold foyle
and sylver foyle for the crest and for the fawchen (*inter alia*); 25
1501, it. for vj ʒards satten iij quarters xvj s x d, it. for v ʒardus
of blowe bokeram ij s xj d, it. pd for makyng of Herodus gone
xv d[12]; 1516, it. payd to a peynter for peyntyng and mendyng of
Herodes heed iiij d; 1547, pd to John Croo for mendyng of
Herrods[13] hed and a myter[14] and other thyngs ij s; (*H.-P.* II. 290) 30
1554, payd to John Hewet payntter for dressyng of Erod hed and
the faychon ij s.

---

[1] *Sh.* wood [hood].           [2] *Sh. adds* [rochet].
[3] Sh. *points out that the smiths' pageant followed* S. Luke 23. 6 *ff.*
[4] *H.-P.* peyntour.           [5] *H.-P.* Herodes.
[6] *Sh.* The (last three) items *anno* 1477 follow each other in the account
book. They relate to the ornamenting of crests, of which most likely
Herod's was one; no other instances of crests occur in the smiths' pageant
accounts. Two would therefore probably belong to the knights, who would
be clad in armour, of which the company had three suits.
[7] *Sh.* Many similar entries occur in subsequent years.
[8] *H.-P.* 1490.
[9] *H.-P.* peynttyng and stenyng.
[10] *Sh.* (164). By this and the preceding item (1476, it. for hors hyre to
Herod iij d), it appears that the character of Herod . . . joined the (Corpus
Christi) procession, being the only instance of this nature that has been
observed.
[11] *H.-P.* 1495.
[12] *Sh.* (30). A satin gown (probably) blue was provided for this character,
whereas in other instances a painted dress sufficed.
[13] *H.-P.* menddyng of Herrode.           [14] *H.-P.* mytor.

*Additional items concerning Herod.*[1] 1490, item paid for mendyng off Arrodes gauen to a taillour viij. *d*; item paid for mendyng off hattes, cappus, and Arreddes creste with other smale geyr belongyng iij. *s*; 1508, item paid for colour and coloryng of
5 Arade iiij. *d.*

(30) *Pilate's wife Procula.*[2] 1477, it. for sowyng of dame Procula wyff shevys iij d; 1478, it. for mendyng of dame Procula garments vij d; 1487, it. to reward to Maisturres Grymesby for lendyng off her geir for Pylatts wyfe xij d; 1490, it. for a
10 quarte of wyne for heyrynge of Procula is gowne ij d ob; 1495, Ryngold's man Thomas thatt playtt Pylatts wyff; 1498, it. paid to Pylatts wyffe for his wages ij s.

*Beadle or porter.*[3] 1480, expense for a jaket for the bydull (*inter alia*); 1490, it. a gowne for the bedull, it. a hode for the
15 bedull, repaired.

(31) *Two knights.*[4] 1449, it. ij spears iiij s iij d.

*The devil.*[5] 1451, it. payd for the demons garment makyng and the stof v s iij d ob, it. payd for collyryng of the same garment viij d; 1477, it. for mendyng the demons garment (*inter
20 alia*), it. for newe ledder to the same garment xxij d; 1490, it. the devyls hede (repaired); 1494, it. paid to Wattis for dressyng of the devells hede viij d; 1498, it. paid for peynttyng of the demones hede (*inter alia*); 1567, it. payd for a stafe for the demon iiij d.

25 *Judas.*[6] 1572, pd for canvys for Judas coote ij s, pd for the makyng of hit xd.

(32) *Peter.*[7] 1490, it. a cheverel gyld for Petur.[8]

*Malchus.* 1477, the performer received 4d.

*Pilate.*[9] 1480, pd for mendyng Pilats hat iiij d; 1490, it.

[1] *H.-P.* II. 290.
[2] *Sh.* Few traces of her dress are to be discovered; and it appears to have been considered of little importance, as not one new article of apparel belonging to her has been noticed.
[3] *Sh.* Only two items occur applying to his dress.
[4] *Sh. conjectures that the knights wore armour with which of course the smiths were well provided. As two or three suits were used at the Mid-summer-eve processions, the expenses of cleaning and repairing it might occur in that connection rather than here. He appropriates to them also two crests and the two spears of the entry.*
[5] *Sh.* The devil in the Smiths' pageant had a dress made of leather and coloured in all probability black; he had also a painted vizor, which was frequently repaired or new painted, and a staff.
[6] *Sh.* The following (*entry for* 1572) is all that appears respecting his dress. In conformity with the well-known popular belief that Judas had red hair and beard, there can be little doubt of this character being so represented in the mysteries. In the enumeration of articles belonging to the pageant, we find " 3 cheverels and a beard," besides those for Jesus and Peter, which were gilt.
[7] *Sh.* A single entry decisively belonging to this character is all that occurs. Sh. *remarks that* 4d. *was paid to the performer in* 1477.
[8] Sh. *conjectures that Peter also wore a gown and a beard.*
[9] *Sh.* Few traces of his dress are discoverable. The performer was paid

I

a cloke for Pilatte, it. a hatt for Pilatte (repaired); 1494 it. paid
for braband to Pylatts hate v d and for canvas ij d ob.

(33) *Pilate's son.* 1490, it. a gowne for Pilatts sone, it. a
hatt for Pilatts sone, it. a poll-ax for Pilatts sonne, it. a septur
for Pilatts sonne.                                                                 5

*Tormentors.* 1451, it. payed for makyng of iiij gownnys and
iiij hodds to the tormentors and the stof that went therto xxiiij s
x d ob; 1490. Mem. that these bene the garments that wer
new reparelleyd a-gaynste Corpus Xpisti daye: inprimis iiij
jakketts of blake bokeram for the tormentors with nayles and 10
dysse upon them, it. other iiij for tormentors of another
suett wythe damaske flowers, it. ij of bokeram with hamers
crowned,[2] it. ij party jakketts of rede and blake; 1501, it.
for makyng off iiij jaketes ij s, it. for iiij ellne cloth for the
jakkets and the hatts xviij d, it. pd to the paynter for hys 15
warkemonchipe xxj s vij d.[3]

(34) *Two Princes.* 1490,[4] it. ij hatts for ij princes (repaired).

(35) *Miscellaneous.* 1489, mendyng of hatts, cappis, with
other smale geyr iij s; 1490, it. twoo burlettis (repaired); 1494,
it. paid for a strawen hate ob, a leffe of roche clere j d; 1497, 20
payntyng of the players harnys xx s; 1499, it. for colours and
gold foyle and sylver foyle for iiij capps (*inter alia*); 1501, it.
for borrowyng off a skerlet gone and a cloke ij d, mendyng the
massus; 1564, it. payd for iij cheverels and a berde xij d; 1584,
it. payd for ij beards vj d.                                                        25

*Gloves.* 1477, it. xij peyr glove₃ to the pleyers xviij d, (under
the head soluciones ad le pleyers) inprimis to Jh's for gloves and
all xxij d[5]; 1505, pd for a dos' off whyght gloves xij d, pd for
ij payr off reed gloves viij d.

*Painting faces.* 1498, it. paid to the peynter for peyntyng of 30
ther fasses viij d.[6]

*Music.*[7] 1451, it. payed to the mynstrells viij s,[8] it. spend on
mynstrells dinner and their soper on Corpus Xpisti day xx d;
1471, it. paid to the waytes for mynstrelship vj s; 1477, it. paid

---

3s. 4d. in 1477 ; afterwards it was advanced to 4s. being the highest sum
paid in this pageant.

[2] *Sh.* Perhaps these dresses might be appropriated with more probability to the two princes.

[3] Sh. *remarks that these charges are relatively very great referring to
the miscellaneous entry for* 1497.

[4] *Sh.* . . . this is the only . . . occurrence.

[5] Sh. *points out that the garment worn by that character had gloves of the
same material attached to the sleeves.*

[6] *Sh.* It is evident that those characters which were not played in masks
or visors, as was the case with Herod and the devil, were represented with
the faces of the performers painted. Indeed many other similar entries
occur.

[7] *Sh.* In general the entries of this portion of expenditure are confined to
the following items (1451, 1471, and 1477).

[8] *Sh.* Two and sometimes three are specified as the number of minstrels.

to the wayts for pypyng v s ; 1549, it. payd to the waytes for the
pagent ij s viij d ; 1554 (164), pd to the mynstrells for prosessyon
ij d and pageants ij s vj d.

(36) *The play-book.* 1494, it. paid to John Harryes for beryng
5 of the orygynall that day vj d[1] ; 1495, payd for copyyng of the
ij knyghts partes and demons ; 1506 (15), resevyd amonge bredren
and other good felowys toward the orygynall ij s ix d[2] ; 1563, it.
to Robart Croo for ij leves of ore pley boke viij d.

*Additional items referring to the pageant, dress, etc.*[3] 1462,
10 item expende at the fest of Corpus Christi yn reparacion of the
pagent, that is to say, a peyre of new whelys the pryce viij. *s*,
item for naylys and ij. hokys for the sayde pagent ij. *d*, item for
to have the pagent ynto Gosford strete xij. *d* ; 1467, item in met
and drynk on mynstrelles and on men to drawe the pagent xxij. *d* ;
15 1470, item rysshes to the pagent ij. *d*, item clampys of iron for the
pagent viij. *d*, item ij. legges to the pagent and the warkemanship
withall vj. *d* ; 1471, expenses to brynge up the pagent into Gosford strete amonge the feliship viij. *d*, expenses for burneysshyng
and peyntyng of the fanes to the pagent xx. *d*, item cloutnayle and
20 other nayle and talowe to the pagent and for waysshyng of the
seid pagent and ruysshes vj. *d ob*, item at bryngyng the pagent
owt of the house ij. d, item nayles and other iron gere to the
pagent viij. *d ob*, expenses to a joyner for workemanshipp to the
pagent vij. *d* ; 1480, item for havyng furth the pagent on the
25 Wedonsday iij. d, item paid for ij. peyre newe whelis viij. *s*,
expenses at the settyng on of hem vij *d*, item for byndyng of
thame viij *d*, paid to a carpenter for the pagent rowf vj *d* ; 1498,
item for the horssyng of the padgeantt and the axyll tree to the
same xvj. *d*, item for the hawyng of the padgeantt in and out and
30 wasshyng it viij. *d* ; 1499, item paid for ij. cordes for the draught
of the paygaunt j. *d*, item paid for shope and gresse to the whyles
j. *d*, item paid for havyng oute of the paygant and swepyng therof
and havyng in and for naylles and ij. claspes of iron and for
mendyng of a claspe that was brokon and for coterellis and for a
35 bordur to the pagaunte xix. *d* ; 1547, paid for dryvyng of the
pagent iiij. *s* iiij *d*, paid for russys and soop ij. *d* ; 1554, item payd
to payntter for payntyng of the pagent tope xxij. *d* ; 1570, paid
for laburrars for horssyng the padgang xvj. *d*, spent abowt the
same bessynes xvj. *d*, for takyng of the yron of the olde whele
40 x. *d*, paid for poyntes and paper iij. d ; 1572, paid for canvys for
Jwdas coote ij. *s*, paid for the makyng of hit x. *d*, paid to too
damsselles xij *d*, paid for a poollye and an yron hoke and mendynge the padgand xvj. *d*, paid for cowntters and a lase and
pwyntes for Jwdas iij. *d* ; 1573 (*new play*), paid for pleyng

---

[1] *Sh.* In 1491, a certain writing is called in their accounts "the new
rygenale."

[2] *Sh. adds* in sums of 1d. and 2d. each.

[3] *H.-P.* I. 338–41.

of Petur xvj d, paid for Jwdas parte ix d, paid for ij. damsylles xij d, paid to the deman vj. d, paid to iiij. men that bryng yn Herod viij. d, paid to Fastoun for hangyng Jwdas iiij. d, paid to Fawston for coc-croyng iiij. d, paid for Mr. Wygsons gowne viij. d ; 1574, Paid for pleynge of Petur xvj. d, paid for Jwdas 5 ix. d, paid for ij. damselles xij. d, paid to the deman vj. d, paid to iiij. men to bryng yn Ilerode viij. d, paid to Fawston for hangyng Jwdas and coc-croyng viij. d, paid for Herodes gowne viij. d ; 1576, a payment of 18 d. " for the gybbyt of Jezie"; 1577 (new play), "for a lase for Jwdas and a corde" 3d.; (old 10 pageant) paid to the plears at the fyrst reherse ij. s vj. d, paid for ale iiij. d, paid for Sent Marye Hall to reherse there ij. d, paid for mendyng the padgand howse dore xx. d, paid for too postes for the dore to stand upon iiij. d, paid to the carpyntur for his labur iiij. d, paid to James Beseley for ij. plattes on the 15 post endes vj. d, for great naylles to nayle on the hynge ij. d, paid to vj. men to helpe up with the dore vj. d ; 1578, (new play) paid for the cokcroing iiij. d, paid to Thomas Massy for a trwse for Judas ij. s viij. d, paid for a new hoke to hange Judas vj. d, paid for ij. new berars of yron for the new seyt in the padgand 20 vij d.; 1502,[1] item paid for gloves to the pleyares xix d, item paid for pyntyng off ther fasus ij d ; 1548, payd to the paynter for payntyng the players facys iiij d.

*Smiths' New Play.*[2] 1573, pd for pleyng of Petur xvj d, pd for Judas parte ix d, pd for ij damsylls xij d, pd to the deman 25 vj d, pd to iiij men that bryng yn Herod viij d, pd to Fawston for hangyng Judas iiij d, pd to Fawston for coc croyng iiij d, pd for Mr. Wygson's gowne viij d [3] ; 1576, for the gybbyt of Jezie xviij d ; (37) 1577, for a lase for Judas and a corde iij d ; 1578, pd for a trwse for Judas ij s viij d ; pd for a new hoke 30 to hange Judas vj d ; 1579,[4] pd for a gowne to the tayllers and sheremen x d.

*Destruction of Jerusalem,* a new pageant performed 1584.[5]

Items from the *charges attending the rehearsals* : It. payd to Cockram in earnest for to playe on his bagpypes iiij d, it. payd to 35

---

[1] *H.-P.* II. 290.
[2] *Sh.* In 1573, after the usual entry of payments to performers and other expences of the pageant as heretofore, a short break occurs, and in the margin is written "New pley," after which follow these items. *Most of these items are given in the preceding paragraph also.*
[3] *Sh.* This was a gown belonging to Sir William Wigston, as appears by other entries, and was frequently borrowed by the smiths for their pageant. The charge of 8d. is for wine given in return for the use of the gown, which was worn by Herod.
[4] *Sh.* This new performance was continued (except in 1575 when no play was exhibited) until 1580, and seems to have been acted after the old pageant. During the years 1580-3, the smiths did not exhibit their pageant.
[5] *Sh.* No less than six rehearsals took place previous to the public exhibition of this new pageant.

a trumpeter in earnest at Seynt Nycholas hall iiij d, it. payde to
John Deane [1] for takynge paynes abowte the pageant ij s ij d.

Literal copy of the *entry of expenses* : Expencys and paymentes for the pagente : Inprimis payd to the players for a
5 reherse ij s vj d, it. payde to Jhon Grene for wrytynge of the
playe-boke v s, it. payde to the trumpeter for soundynge in the
pagent v s, it. payde to hym that playde on the flute ij s vj d, it.
payde to Jhon Foxall for the hyer of Irysshe mantylls viij d, (38)
it. gyvyn to the dryvers of the pagent to drynke iiij d, it. payde
10 for sope for the pagent wheles iiij d, it. payde to Cookeson for
makynge of a whele to the skaffolde viij d, it. payde for a iron
pynne and a cotter for the skaffolde whele iiij d, it. spent on the
companye on the pley even ij s viij d, it. payde to Will'ms for
makynge of ij payre of galleys ij s (Under the head *other*
15 *paimentes and exspences* . . . it. payde for lace for the ij payre
of galleys xv d,[2]), it. pd for the masters breakfast on the playe
daye xx d, it. pd for the players drynke to the pagent ij s, it. pd
for starche to make the storme in the pagente vj d, it. pd for
carryenge of our apparaill from pagent to pagente vj d, it. pd for
20 drynke for the muʒiʒions ij d, it. pd to Hewette for fetchynge of
the hogges-headds vj d, it. pd to the souldyers for waytynge on
the captaynes ij s, it. pd for a pottell of wyne to the pagente x d,
it. pd to the muʒicions for playenge on theyre instruments in the
pagente v d, it. pd for the M*aster* and the players sowper viij s vj d,[3]
25 it. pd to Jhon Deane for hys dyner sowper and drynkynge xij d,
it. pd for russhes packthryd and tenter hookes viij d, it. pd to ij
drumme players x d, it. pd to the dryvérs of the pagente iij d, it.
pd to Hewet for his paynes ix d, it. pd to Reignolde Headley for
playenge of Symon and Phynea v s, it. pd to Gabryel Foster for
30 playenge of Justus Ananus Eliaʒar and the chorus vj s viij d,
it. pd to Jhon Bonde for playenge of the capteyne Jhoannes and
and the chorus vj s viij d, it. pd to Willm̄ Longe for playenge of
Ms̄yers Jacobus Hippenus and the chorus vj s viij d, it. pd to
Jhon Hoppers for playenge of Jesus and Zacharyas iij s, it. pd to
35 Henry Chamberleyne for playenge of Pristus, a pece [4] of Ananus,
and Zilla iij s iiij d, it. pd to Jhon Grene for playenge of Mathias
and Esron ij s, it. pd to Jhon Copestake for playenge of Esron
his parte xx d, (39) it. pd to Lewes Pryce for playenge of Niger
his parte xvj d, it. pd to Frauncys Coccks for playenge of Solome
40 xij d, it. pd to Rich*ard* Fitʒharbert and Edward Platte for
playenge chyldren to Solome xij, it. pd to Xpofer Dygbye for his
ij drummers vj s viij d, it. pd to the awyntyente berer xij d, it.
pd to Robert Lawton for kepynge of the booke ij s, it. pd to

---

[1] *Sh.* John Deane was the company's sumner.
[2] *Sh. suggests these were merely tressels to support the pageant floor.*
[3] *Sh.* s.
[4] *Sh.* apece.

Edmund Durrant for payntynge ij s, it. pd to Thom's Massye for
the temple and for his beardes iij s ; Soṁ is v li iij s vij d.[1]

*Pageant and pageant-house sold.*   1586, it. recd of Mr. Pyle
for the pageante howse xx s, it. recd of Henry Bankes for the
pageant xl s.                                                          5

In 1591 the smiths *paid instead of performing.*   1591, it.
payd to Mr. Mayor towards the playes of the pageantes xx s.

*Additional Items*[2] *concerning the Pageant-House.*   1571, paid
for a lode of cley for the padgyn howse vj. *d*, paid for iij. sparis
for the same howse vj. *d*, paid to the dawber and his man  10
xiiij. *d*, paid to the carpyntur for his worke iiij. *d*, paid for
a bunche and halfe of lathe ix. *d*, paid for vj. pennye naiylles ij. *d*;
1576, spent at Mr. Sewelles of the company about the pavynge of
the pajen house vi. *d*, payd for the pavynge of the pagen house
xxij. *d*, payd for a lode of pybeles xij. *d*, for a lode sande vj. *d* ; 15
1586, item paide to James Bradshawe for mendynge the pageant-
howse doores iiij. *d*, item to Christofer Burne for a key and settynge on the locke on the doore v. *d*, item paide to Baylyffe
Emerson for halfe yeres rente of the pageant-howse ij. *s.* vj. *d*,
item gyven to Bryan a sharman for his good wyll of the pageante- 20
howse x. *d*.

*The putting down of the pageants.*[3]   1580, *(MS. Annals)* The
pageants were again laid down.[4]   1584, *(id.)* This year the new
play of the Destruction of Jerusalem was first played.[5]

(40) *City Accounts* : Paid to Mr Smythe of Oxford the xvth 25
daye of Aprill 1584 for his paynes for writing of the tragedye xiij
li vj s viij d.   1591,[6] (12) At a Council House held 19th May :
It is agreed by the whole consent of this house that the Destruction of Jerusalem, the Conquest of the Danes, or the historie of
K[ing] E[dward] the X., at the request of the Comons of this cittie 30
shalbe plaied on the pagens on Midsomer daye and St. Peters

---

[1] Josephus, *The Jewish War*, iv.          [2] *H.-P.* I. 337–8.

[3] *Sh.* (37, 39) *says that no company whose accounts have been preserved*
(*smiths, cappers, drapers, and weavers*) *exhibited a pageant during the years*
1580–3, *and attributes the discontinuance to the influence of the Protestant*
*religion.*   He says, " The good men of Coventry, who in 1574 amused Queen
Elizabeth at Kenilworth castle with their Hox Tuesday performance, com-
plained that although there was no papistry or superstition in it, yet owing
to the zeal of certain of their preachers, it had been of late laid down."

[4] *Sh. says that the pageants generally are here alluded to, and that* " again "
*is used in consequence of the Hox Tuesday shows having been put down in*
1561.   1561, (*MS. Annals*) This year was Hox Tuesday put down ; *cp. also*
1575, (*Id.*)   This year the pageants or Hox Tuesday that had been laid
down 8 years were played again.

[5] *Sh.* All of the companies (exhibiting pageants) whose records of the
period exist, performed this new one, whence it may be inferred that appli-
cation was made for a revival of the pageants, and that they were willing to
gratify the people in their favourite amusement ; also at considerable charge,
provided them with a new subject, free from the objections raised against
their former representations.

[6] *Sh.* This elaborate performance was not repeated until 1591.

daye next in this cittie and non other playes. And that all the mey-poles that nowe are standing in this citie shalbe taken downe before Whit-sonday next and non hereafter to be sett up in this cittie.—*Com. Council Book.*

## THE CAPPERS' COMPANY.

5    (42) *History.* *Sh.* speaks of a very curious book of accounts belonging to the cappers' company which commenced in 1485. The first charge for exhibiting their pageant occurred in 1534. (43–5) Until 1530 they had been contributory to the girdlers' pageant. In 1529 also by act of leet, the cappers had been authorised to
10 possess the weavers' pageant; the weavers' accounts show however that the order was not carried out. In 1531, an act of leet associates the cappers with the cardmakers and sadlers in chapel and pageant.[1] The first time the cappers' company exhibited their newly acquired pageant was in 1534, when it appears that
15 31s. 5½d. was expended in "reparacions made of the pageant and players ger," and 30s. 4d. for rehearsals and charges of playing. From this period until 1580 the pageant was regularly exhibited; a pause then ensues until 1584, when in conjunction with the sheremen and taylors, a new pageant, the Destruction of Jerusa-
20 lem, was performed. In 1591 they played once more " at the mayors commandment."
    *Contributory pageantry.* (43) 1532, payd for dyvers besynesse aboute the cardemakers iijs xjd; 2nd quarter, idem vij s. In 1574 and for subsequent years the cardmakers and sadlers con-
25 tributed 13s. 4d. annually to the cappers towards their pageant, likewise the company of walkers 6s., skinners 4s., painters and joyners 3s. 4d.
    (47) *Machinery, Dresses,* etc.[2] Wind rope and a locker to the wind, requiring a man sometimes three men to "tend" it;
30 hell-mouth; boards about the sepulchre side of the pageant; apple-tree; two ledges for the pageant, two standers for the same, charges for " setting up " the fore part of the pageant and timber to bear the side of it. Cloak for Pilate, coat for Mary Magdalen, coat made of buckram for the spirit of God, coat for the demon,
35 surplices or albs for the angels, gowns for the bishops, hoods and mitres for ditto, "roles" for the Maries, gloves, stars, diadems, censers, our Ladies crown, the Marie's crowns, flowered, mall or club for Pilate, balls for Pilate, mall or club for the demon, the demon's head (or vizor), rattle, spade, two crosses, poleaxe, bow,
40 four white harness, two streamers and pensells, thread, cord, wire, " white incoll," nails, tenter hooks, rings, points, rushes.
    *The pageant.* (Inventory of ornaments, jewels, goods, *etc.* be-

---

[1] *Sh.* In January 1536, the cardmakers and sadlers conveyed the afore-named chapel and pageant to the mayor, aldermen, *etc.*, and in the same month they were re-conveyed to the cappers.
[2] Sh.'s *list.*

longing to the cappers' chapel) 28 Henry VIII. (1536, 1537): it. ij pajiont clothes of the passion ; *Accounts* (no date), it. pd for lynen clothe to paynt v s, it. pd to Horseley the paynter xxxiij s iiijd.[1]

1597. *Inventory of goods belonging to the cappers' company*[2] includes ij. pawles, sixe cressittes, ij. streamars and the poles, ij. bisshopes myters, Pylat·s dublit, ij. curtaynes, Pylates head, fyve Maries heades, one coyff, Mary Maudlyns gowne, iij. beardes, sixe pensils, iiij. rolles, iij. Marye boxes, one play-boke, the giandes head and clubbe, Pylates clubbe, hell-mowth, Adams spade, Eves destaffe.

(48) *Play-books.* Pd for making of the new[3] plea book v s; 1540, pd for the matter of the Castell of Emaus xiij d[4]; pd for writyng a parte for Herre Person j d.

*Usual expenses of performing.*[5] Dressing the pageant 6 d.; a person going with it 10 d.; the clerk for bearing the book or "the keeper of the playe-book " 12 d.[6]; spent at the first rehearsal, to the players 18 d., on the company 7 s. 4 d.; spent at the second rehearsal to the players 18 d, on the company 7 s.; players' supper 2 s.; drink to the drivers of the pageant 12 d.; twelve (sometimes eight or ten) men driving it 2 s.; drink to the players between the play times 13 d.; pd Pilate, the bishops and knights to drink between the "stages" 9 d. The annual charge for playing the pageant was about 35 s. until 1550, afterwards 45 s. to 50 s.

(49) *Illustrative Charges.* Payd for the players drynkynge at the Swanne dore ij s viij d ; p'd for our supper on the play day for ourselves, goodman Mawpas, the minstrull, the dresser of the pagent, and the somner and his wyfe iiij s ; p'd for havyng the pagent in and out xij d ; p'd for four whit harnesse xvj d ; p'd for v dossan poyntes iiij d ; p'd for rysshes j d ; p'd for sope and gres ij d.; 1553, pd to the carpenter[7] for tendyng on the pageant xij d ; 1554, pd the carpenter for tendyng the pageant (and some repairs) xvj d.

*Entire entry for* 1565. Costes and charges of the pagyande : it. payd to Pylate iiij s, it. payd to the iiij knyghts iiij s viij d, it. payd to the ij. bysshopes ij s, it. payd to God xx d, it. paide to the sprytt of God xvj d, it. payd to the ij angelles viij d, it. payd to the iij Maryes ij s, it. payd to the demon xvj d, it. payd to the mynstrell viij d, it. payd for vj dossyn of poyntes xij d, it. payd

---

[1] *Upon the basis of these entries and the relatively large sums paid,* Sh. *conjectures that these cloths were displayed on the vehicle, or used for covering the lower room at the time of representation.* He points out that a painting of the passion would agree with the subject of the cappers' pageant.

[2] *H.-P.* I. 342.      [3] Sh. *new of the.*

[4] Sh. *conjectures that the* Appearance to the Travelers *was added to the cappers' pageant this year, the parts of Caiaphas and Luke being taken by performers playing other parts earlier in the pageant.*

[5] Sh.'s *list.*

[6] Sh. *points out that this was probably the prompter.*

[7] Sh. *says that it was not unusual to have a carpenter in attendance.*

for rep[a]rasyons of the pagyand tymber nayles and iren vij s viij d,
it. p'd for the hyer of iiij harnes and scorrynge of our harnes iiij s,
it. p'd for dresynge and colorynge the bysshoppes hodes ij s, it.
p'd for makynge the hoodes and mendynge Maudlyn coate xij d,
5 it. spent at tavern xij d, it. payd for a hoke of iren xvj d, it. payd
for one whelle ij s ij d; som xlj s x d. (50) More charges of the
pagyand : it. spent at the first rehearse at the brekefast of the
companye v s vij d, it. spent at the second reherse vj s ij d, it. payd
to the players at the second reherse iij s, it. payd at the havynge
10 out and settynge in of the pageand xij d, it. payd for dressynge
the pagiand and kepynge the wynde xij d, it. payde to the dryvers
iiij s, it. payde to the dryvers in drynke viij d, it. payde to the
players betwene the stages viij d, it. payd for the players sopper
ij s viij d, it. payd for rosshes and small corde iij d, it. payd for
15 balles x d, it. payd for iij gawnes of ale in the pagiand xij d, it.
payd to the syngers xvj d, it. payd for a payre of gloves for Pylate
iiij d, it. payd for grece iij d, it. payd for our sopper at nyght iij s,
it. payd for furrynge of the hoodes viij s ; som xxix s x d.

*Other entries.* (37) 1543, pd for a lace of jorne to compas the
20 beame xj d; (48) 1548, rec'd. from the whittawers for the " hyer
of our pageand " 3 s. 4 d. ; (22) 1562, rec' of the fellowship for
pageant xxxij s iiij d [1]; (20) 1565, it. spent at the first rehearse at
the brekefast of the companye v s viij d, it. spent at the second
reherse at the brekefast of the company vj s ij d; 1584, pd the
25 dresser of the pagent; (21) (no date) payd for dressynge the pagyn ;
(no date) pd for drynkyng for the playars betwen the play tymes
xiiij d (sometimes betwen the stages), pd for drynk in the pagent,
drynkynge at the Swanne dore ij [s] viij d. (66) 1544, payde for
drynk in the pageant for the plears for bothe days viij d.[2]
30 *Additional items concerning the pageant.*[3] 1562, item spent
on the craft when the overloked the pagyand ij. *s*, item payd for
iiij. harneses hyrynge iij. *s*, item payd to the players betwene the
stages viij. *d*, item payd for dressynge the pagyand vj. *d*, item
payd for kepynge the wynd vj. *d*, item payd for dryvyng the
35 pagyand iiij. *s*, item payd to the dryvers in drynke viij. *d*, item
payd for balls vj *d*, item payd to the mynstrell viij. *d* ; 1568, item
paid for a ledge to the scafolde vj. *d*, item paid for ij. ledges to
the pagiand viij. *d*, item paid for grett naylles vj. *d*, item for
makynge clene the pagiand house ij. *d*, item paid for washenge
40 the pagiand clothes ij. *d*, item for dryvinge the pagiand vij. *s* vj. *d*,
item paid to the players at the second stage viij. *d*.

1567,[4] item payd for a cloutt to the pagiand whelle ij. *d*,
item payd for a ponde of sope to the pagiand iij. *d*, item payd
to the players at the second stage viij. *d*, item payd for balles
45 viij. *d*, item payd to the mynstrell viij. *d*, item payd to Pilat for

---

[1] *Sh.* No other entry of a like nature has been observed.
[2] Sh. *supposes from this item that the pageants were occasionally exhibited for two days.*  [3] *H.-P.* I. 33–40.  [4] I. 340.

his gloves ij. *d*, item payd for assyden for Pilat head ij. d, item
payd to Jorge Loe for spekyng the prologue ij. *d* ; 1568, item
paid for balles viij. *d*, item paid for Pylatt gloves iiij. *d*, item paid
for the spekynge of the prologe ij. *d*, item paid for prikynge the
songes xij. *d*, item paid for makynge and coloringe the ij. myters   5
ij. *s*. iiij. *d*, item paid for makynge of hellmothe new xxj *d* ;
1571, item paid for mendynge the pagiand geyre iij. *d*, item paid
for a yard of bokeram xij. *d*, item paid for payntynge of the
demons mall and the Maris rolles vj. *d*, item for makynge the
roles ij. *d*, item paid to the players att the second stage viij. *d*.   10

    *The characters.  Pilate.* (50) Item for "a skeane of grene silke"
to mend Pilate's cloak, and the "mendyng" 6 d.[1]; makyng of
Pylatts malle xxij d[2]; A new malle xx d ; ditto ij s j d ; pd Richard
Hall for makyng Pylates clubbe xiij d; pd for ij pounde and
halfe of woole for the same clubbe x d ; pd for mendyng of Pylatts   15
malle iij d.[3]; pd for balles for Pylatt iij d, lether for balles ij d,
balls iiij d—xij d ; pd for makyng of xvj balls and for ij skyns of
lether v d ; pd for a skyn for balls for makyng and sowyng v d ;
pd for balls and for mendyng of Pylatts cloobe iiij d ; (51) p'd for
a payre of gloves for Pylate iiij d ; p'd for assyden for Pilat head   20
ij d ; p'd for canvas vj d and the makyng of Pylats doblet xvj d—
xxij d.

    *God.*[4] (53) There is a charge for painting *inter alia* the rattel,
the spade, and ij crossys, and hell mowthe and also an item of
expenses for boards used about the sepulchre side of the pageant.  25

    *Mother of Death.* (54) *Sh.* gives no information.

    *Four Knights. Sh.* For these characters four suits of white
(or bright) armour were procured for which a regular entry of 16d.
occurs, being the sum paid for the use of them.

    *Spirit of God.* It. payd for the spret of Gods cote ij s, it.  30
payd for the makyng of the same cote viij d, it. payd for ij yardes
and halfe off bockram to make the spirits cote ij s j d, it. payd for
makynge the same cote viij d.[5]

    *Our Lady.* (55) It. paide for mendyng our ladys crowne.

    *Two bishops.*[6] It. paide for makyng the ij byschoppes gownse   35
xxj d, it. p'd for furrying the sayd gownse ij s iiij d, it. payd to
Mr Warynge for the rest of the bysshoppes gownse vij d, it. an
ell of bockram for one of the bysshoppes xiij d, it. pd for makyng

---

    [1] Sh. *supposes from this that Pilate's cloak was green.*
    [2] *Sh.* (51) *states that about* 1790 *in an antique chest within the cappers'
chapel he found* (*together with an iron cresset and some fragments of armour*)
*a club or mall stuffed with wool, the covering of which was leather; the
handle, then broken off, had evidently been of wood.*
    [3] *Sh.* There is a charge for painting the mall.
    [4] *Sh.* No article of dress explicitly intended for this character appears in
the account.
    [5] *Sh.* Very many instances of painted buckram dresses occur in these
accounts.
    [6] Sh. *conjectures that the two bishops were Jewish priests,* probably
Caiaphas and Annas as in the smiths' pageant.

a whod for on of the byschopps iiij d, it. payd for dressynge and
colorynge the bysshoppes hodes ij s, it. payd for furrynge of the
hoodes viij[d], it. paide for makynge and colorynge the ij myters
ij s iiij d, it. payd for payntyng the bisshoppes myters; likewise a
5 charge of 6 d. " for mendyng of ij senssars."

*Two angels.* It. payd for waschyng the angells albs ij [d], (56)
it. pd for mendynge the angells surplisses and wasshyng iij d.[1]

*The three Maries.* It. p'd for mendynge Maudlyns cote iiij d,
it. payd for skowryng of Maryes crowns j d, it. for payntynge the
10 Maries rolles iiij d, it p'd for a yard of bokeram xij d, it. p'd for
makynge the roles ij d, it. p'd for mendyng the Maries rolles ij d,
paid for mendyng the Maries heare viij d.

*The demon and hell-mouth.*[2] It. payde for mendynge the
devells cote and makyng the devells heade iiij s vj d, it. payd to
15 Harrye Benett for mendynge the demons cote and makyng the
head v s, it. pd for making the demons head xviij d, it. payd for
a yard of canvas for the devells malle and for makyng viij d, it.
payd for payntyng the devells clubbe (several entries). (57) *Sh.*
" selects " the following entries referring to hell-mouth : It. p'd
20 for mendyng hellmowthe ij d, it. payd for payntyng of hell-
mought iij d, it. payd for makynge of hell-mothe new xxj d, it.
paide to Horsley (*inter alia*) for pentyng hell-mowthe.

*Deadman.* Entries in 1574 and 1576 only.[3]

*Prologue.*[4] It. p'd for the spekynge of the prologe ij d, it. paid
25 to Jorge Loe for spekynge the prologue ij d; in 1573 4 d. is paid for
speaking the preface, and the same sum in 1574 for the prologue.

*Singers and minstrels.*[5] *Sh.* (48) A customary charge is " paid
to the minstrell " usually 8 d. There also occur these items : " for
makinge the songe " and " for prikynge the songes xvj d." It. p'd
30 to the singyngmen xvj d, it. p'd to the singers and makyng the
songe ij s iiij d.

*Miscellaneous entries.* (64) It. p'd for vj payr of gloves iij s iiij d,
it. a staf for a polax ij d, it. payd for mendynge of the bowe iij d., it.
p'd for halfe a yard of rede sea vj d ; (46) it. pd for a pece of tymber
35 for an apeltrie ij s iij d, it. pd for ij cloutes, a clamp and other yron
work about the apeltre xij d[6] ; (16) mendyng the players reparell.
1569, payd Thomas Nyclys for prikinge the songes xij d.

[1] Sh. *suggests that* "ij starrs" 12d. *and* "a dyadem," 4d. (sic) *be appropriated to these characters.*

[2] *Sh.* This character (the demon) was furnished with a vizor or mask,
and a club made of buckram and painted.

[3] Sh. *suggests that it was a person delivered from hell.*

[4] *Sh.* Preface or more frequently prologue.

[5] *Sh.* Singers and singing men is an article of regular entry after the
term "minstrell" is discontinued. 6d. and 8d. was the accustomed fee to
the minstrell.

[6] *Sh.* Adam and Eve, though not particularized in the list of performers
in the cappers' pageant (in consequence probably of these parts being taken
by persons who had played other characters in an earlier portion of the
pageant) were nevertheless indispensable requisites, and the introduction of
this appropriate and distinguishing symbol is thus readily accounted for.

*The Destruction of Jerusalem.*  *Sh.* gives the following as an exact copy of the entry for the pageant of the Destruction of Jerusalem in 1584, when the cappers were at joint expense with the shearmen and taylors :

1584.  Paymentes for our partes for the pagyn and acte :  Payd for fyve reherses v s ; spente at the same reherses xx s ; spente at Thomas Robynsons bytymes at the appointing off thinges x d ; paide for our partes at the settinge and drivinge of the pagyn and skaffoldes ij s vj d ; payd for dressynge the pagyn vj d ; paide towards the hyre of a drum xij d ; payde for playinge of the same drum iiij d ; payde for mendynge of the skaffolds vij d ; payde for iij beardes ij s vj d ; paide sixe musicissions ; payd for the hyre of a trumpet vj d ; payd for mendynge of the players reparrell vj d ; paide towardes the players breakfast and drynke in the pagyn and a-nyght[1] when the had played v s vj d ; paide for more[2] ale that was droncke at the settinge in of the pagyn and skaffolds iiij d ; payde for makinge in of oure pagyn dores and small cordes iiij d ; (65) payde for oure suppers and the iiij masters of the sharmen and tayllers and the clarkes and sumners iiij s ; the some is xxviij s ix d. Paymentes to the players :  Payde to Owton v s, payde to Thomas Symcoxe v s, payde to the barber iij s vj d, payde to the butler iij s vj d, payde to Hollande iij s vj d, paide Xpoffere Tayller ij s x d, payde to Hawkes xvj d, payde to Mathewe ij s iiij d, payde to Hawmon xvj d, payde to Mr Myles sonne xvj, payde to Holbage xvj d, payde to Jhon Shewels man viij d, payde to the captaynes lackies xij d, payde to xij souldyars to were red cotes ij s, payde for iij garlande made of bayes vj d, payde for the temple xij d, payde to Jhon Grene for makynge the booke v s[3] ; payde for the kepynge the boke xij d ; the some is xliiij s ij d ; the some of our parte is xxij s j d.

*Last records.*  1591, payd to Thomas Massey towards the playes xx s.[4]  In 1589, the company had sold the lead and tile off their pageant house ; in 1596, "furrs of players gowns" were sold for 14 d., also rd of Ric. Dabson for byshopps hodds viij s.[5]

*The pageant-house.*  *Sh.* mentions numerous items for repairing the pageant-house and for securing the doors, and states that it was situated in Mill-lane.

## DRAPERS' COMPANY.[6]

*The Pageant-house.*  In 1392–3 (16 Richard II.), a tenement in Little Park street (*Cartulary of St. Mary's*, leaf 85 b) is described

---

[1] *Sh.* anyght.          [2] *Sh.* more ffor.

[3] *Sh.* He furnished copies of the play to the smiths' and mercers' companies on the same terms.

[4] Sh. *says that the cappers lent their pageant, dresses, and other apparatus, contracting with Massey for the exhibition.*

[5] *Sh. says* (66) *this is* the last trace of the pageant history of the cappers' company.          [6] *Sh.* The oldest book of accounts of this company now to be found commences in 1534.

as *inter ten*ementum *prior*um et *conven*t*us ex* parte *una* et *domu*m
pro *le pagent panna*rum *Coventre ex alt*era.[1]

In 1520, the Trinity Guild sold to this company timber "to
make their pageant" value 7s. 7d.; 1534, an entry occurs in their
5 accounts of 4s. received for the rent of "the old pagent howse,"
the new one being also mentioned in the same account. The
orders and rules of the company "gathered owt off oulld and
anssyent boukes" in 1534 contain an order that the masters shall
"se the prossecyon kept on Corpus Cristy daye, the pageond and
10 play well broughte forth with harnessyng of men and the watche
kept at Mydsomer on Seynt Peters nyght with oder and good
custumes usyd in old tyme to the lawde and prays of God and
the worschypp of thys cytte" (160).

*Characters.*[2] God, two demons, three white (sometimes saved)
15 souls, three black (sometimes damned) souls, (67) two spirits, four
angels, three patriarchs, two worms of conscience, prologue, two
clarks for singing, one to sing the basse, Pharisee.

*Machinery,*[2] etc. Hell-mouth—a fire kept at it; windlass and
three fathom of cord; earthquake, barrell for the same, a pillar
20 for the words of the barrel painted; three worlds painted and a
piece that bears them; a link to set the world on fire[3]; pulpits
for the angels; cross, rosin, a ladder.

*Dresses.*[2] God's coat of leather, red sendal for God; demon's
head (or vizor); coats, hose, and points for the demon; coats for
25 the white and black souls, hose and points for them; suit for
angels—gold skins, wings for angels; three cheverels and a
beard; four diadems; black, red, and yellow buckram; hair 3 lb.
for the demon's coat and hose; hat for the Pharisee.

*Music*, etc.[2] Trumpets, organ, regalls. 1566, payd to Thomas
30 Nycles for settyng a songe xij d.

*Play-books.* 1557, paid to Robart Crowe for makyng of the
boke for the paggen xx s.

*Pageant.* 1540, it. for mendyng the bateling yn the toppe of
the pagent viij d; 1567, payd for carvyng bords and crest for the
35 toppe of the padgen iij s; (68) 1561, pageant driven by ten men
who received 2s. 6d.

*Miscellaneous items* (77). 1538, p'd to hym that drove the
pagent ij d, it. for pakke thrydde and sope ij d ob; 1556, payd for
nayllys, ressys and rosyn vj d; 1557, payd to the plears when the
40 fyrste paggen was pleyd to drynke ij s; 1569, payd for alle at
the Swanne dore ij s.

*The charges of performing* vary from 21s. to £4 8s. 6d.

*Payments to Performers.*[4]  1538, it. payd to hym that

[1] *Sh.* It may be remarked that this is the first instance of pageants in
Coventry that has been discovered.  [2] Sharp's *list.*
[3] *Sh.* The worlds were provided annually, and the number three seems to
indicate that the performance was limited to as many representations on
Corpus Christi day.
[4] *Sh.* The character of God commences the list in payments to performers.

playeth goddes parte iij s iiij d, it. payd to iiij angeles xvj d, it.
payd to iij patriarches xij d, it. payd to iij white soules xviij d,
it. payd to iij blakke souls ij s, it. payd to ij demons iij s, it. payd
for kepyng the wynde vj d ; 1556, it. payd to God iij s iiij d, it.
payd to ij demons iij s, it. payd to iij whyte sollys (1565, savyd    5
sowles) v s, it. payd to iij blake sollys (1565, dampnyd sowles) v s,
it. to ij spryttys xvj d, it. payd for the prolouge viij d, it. payd to
iiij angellys ij s, it. payd to iij pattryarkys xviij d, it. payd to
ij clarkys for syngyng ij s, it. payd to the trompyttar iij s iiij d
(afterwards 5 s.), it. payd for playng on the reygalles vj d ; 1557, 10
it. payde to Jhon to synge the basse iiij d ; 1566, it. payd to the
pageant players for their songs iiij d ; 1560, it. payd to Robert
Cro for pleayng God iij s iiij d ; 1561, it. payd for playeing of
the protestacyon viij d, it. payd to ij wormes of conscience xvj d ;
1562, it. payd to ij wormes of conscyence xvj d ; 1569, pd for alle 15
when thei (the players) drese them iiij d.

(69) *The characters. God.* 1556, payde for vij skynnes [1]
for Godys cote (*inter alia*); 1557, paid for a peyre of gloves
for God ij d ; 1562, payd for a cote for God and for a payre
of gloves iij s ; 1565, p'd for iiij yards of redde sendall for 20
God xx d.

*Demons.* 1536, it. for mendyng the demones heed vj d ; 1540,
it. for peyntyng and makyng new ij damons heds (*inter alia*) ;
1556, payd for a demons face ij s ; 1560, payd to Cro for mendyng the devells cottes xx d ; 1568, payd for makyng the devells 25
hose viij d, payd for poynts for the demon (*inter alia*), payd for
canvas for one of the devells hose xj d, payd for makyng the ij
devells facys x s, payd for makyng a payre of hose with heare
xxij d, paid for iij li. of heare ij s vj d ; 1572, it. pd for ij pound
of heare for the demons cotts and hose and mendyng.            30

*White and black souls.* (70) 1536, for mendyng the white
and the blake soules cotes viij d ; 1537, it. for v elnes of canvas
for shyrts and hose for the blakke soules at v d the elne ij s j d, it.
for coloryng and makyng the same cots ix d, it. for makyng and
mendynge of the blakke soules hose vj d, it. for a payre of newe 35
hose and mendyng of olde for the whyte soules xviij d ; 1543, it.
p'd for the mendyng of the whytt solls kotts with the ij skyns
that went to them xvj d ; 1553, payde for a dossyne of skyns for
the sollys cottys iiij s vj d, p'd for makyng the sollys cottys iij s ;
1556, p'd for canvas for the sollys cottys xix ellys xiiij s iij d, 40
p'd for ix elys of canvas made yellow xij d, pd for x elys of canvas
made blacke xd, payd for ij pessys of yallow bokeram vij s vj d,
payd for iiij yards of rede bokaram ij s viij d, payd for makyng
the sollys cotts vj s viij d, p'd for blakyng the sollys fassys
(*inter alia*); 1565, p'd for ix yards and a halfe of bukram for 45
the sowles coates vij s ; 1566, p'd for the poynts for the souls
(*inter alia*); 1567, p'd for iij elnes of yelloo canvas ij s x d,

---

[1] *Sh.* refers to smiths' accounts, pp. 85-6.

it. for collering the solles cotts yellow xvj d, p'd for a solles
cote xij d.[1]

(71) *Two spirits.*[2] 1556, payd for iij elys of lynyne cloth for
the playars gownys iij s viij d, payd for makyng of iij gownys and
5 a cotte vj s.[3]

*Four angels.* 1538, it. for makyng an angells scytte xij d;
1540, it. for peyntyng and makyng new iiij peire of angells
wyngs (*inter alia*); 1556, payd for iiij pere of angyllys wyngys
ij s viij d; payd for iiij dyadymes ij s vij d, payd for vj goldyn
10 skynnes; 1565, payd for iiij yards of boorde to make pulpytts for
the angells viij d, payd for a pece of wode to make feete for them
iiij d, payd to the carpenters for makyng ij pulpytts *etc.* iiij s.[4]

(72) *Three patriarchs.* 1556, payd for iij chefferellys and a
berde of here iij s x d.[5]

15 *Two worms of conscience.* Introduced in 1561.[6]

*Prologue.*[7] 1561 (only), it. payd for playeing of the protestacyon viij d.[8]

*Pharisee.* 1562, it. payde Robert Croo for a hat for the
Pharysye vij d.[9]

20 *Machinery*, etc. *Windlass.* 1538, it. for mendyng a rope to
the pagent thre fedom longe v d; 1543, payd for a new roppe for
the wynd xviij d; 1556, payd for dryvyng of the pagand kepyng
the wynde iiij s; (73) 1568, payd for a cord for the wynde ij s
vj d, payd for mendyng the wynde ij d.

25 *Hell-mouth* (61). 1537, it. paide for payntyng and makyng
newe hell-hede xij d; 1538, it. payd for mendyng of hell-hede
vj d; 1542, payde for makyng helle-hede viij s ij d; 1554, it. payd
for payntyng hell-hede newe xx d; 1556, payde for kepynge hell-
hede viij d; 1557, it. payd for kepyng of fyer at hell-mothe
30 iiij d; 1565, p'd to Jhon Huyt for payntyng of hell-mowthe xvj d;
1567, p'd for makyng hell-mowth and cloth for hyt iiij s.

---

[1] Sh. *suggests that the damned souls wore a parti-coloured dress which
represented flames.*

[2] Sh. *says that the two spirits were first introduced in* 1556 *in which year
many new dresses and properties were acquired.*

[3] Sh. *assigns these entries to the two spirits because of the linen material.*

[4] Sh. *appropriates for general reasons the diadems and the six golden skins
to the angels; the latter item he says immediately follows the former in the
original entry.* Sh. (77). In 1565, Aug. 17, Queen Elizabeth visited
Coventry; on which occasion the drapers' pageant stood at the cross; it
appears from their accounts that pulpits for the angels and other special
preparations were made for that exhibition.

[5] *This also is* Sh.'s *assignment.*

[6] Sh. There is no entry of dress or apparatus that can be applied to them.

[7] Sh. This was amongst the additions made in 1556.

[8] Sh. This might probably (as well as the prologue, for both were introduced subsequently to the Reformation,) be spoken for the purpose of *pro-
testing* against any papistical notions, notwithstanding they played the
pageant as it had been accustomed.

[9] Sh. In the payments to performers no such character appears, and
besides the above there is only one other notice of it.

*Earthquake.*[1] 1556, payd for the baryll for the yerthequake (*inter alia*), payd for the pyllar for the wordys of the baryll iij s iiij d, payd for payntyng the pyllur (*inter alia*); 1557, payd for kepyng the baryll (*inter alia*), it. payd for tyntyng the yerthequake iiij; 1556, payd for keveryng the erthequake to porter ij s. 5

*Three worlds.* 1556, payd to Crowe for makyng of iij worldys ij s, payd him more for same iij s viij d; 1560, paid to him for the worlds 3s. 8d.; (74) 1558, payd for iij worldys iij s viij d, payd for payntyng of the worldys (*inter alia*), payd for settyng the world of fyer v d, payd for kepyng fyre (*inter alia*). 10

*Cross.* 1537, it. for makyng of the crosse and coloryng yt ij d.

*Ladder.* 1557, payd for a larthar iiij d; 1566, payde for fetchyng and kepyng the ladder ij d.

*Music.* 1538, it. payd for mendyng the trumpetts vij d; 1557, it. to the trumppeter iij s iiij d, payd for fechyng a pere of horgens 15 and the carrege of them whoume ij s; 1558, p'd for beryng of the orgens vj d; 1556, it. payd for playng on the reygalles vj d; 1565, it. payd to James Huyt for the rygalls xij d.

*Extra entry* 1572. *Sh.* After the usual entry of particulars of the pageant charges for 1572 occurs the following : The chargys 20 of iiij new gownes and iiij surplesses ; payd to Wyllm̃ Walden for stufe xliiij s j d, payd to John Grene for canvas lj s iiij d, payd to John Gosnell for furryng the gowns xx s, payd for makyng the gownes x s, payd for makyng the surplesses xvj d, payd for wryttynge the booke x s; sm̃a vj li xvj s ix d.[2] 25

*Destruction of Jerusalem.* 1584, cost of £6 4s. 9d.[3]

*Last entries.* 1591, payd Thomas Massye[4] for the pagent xl s, payd for corde and horssyng the pagen vj d,[5] 1595, Recd. for the hyer of our players clokes with other such stufe iiij s.

## MERCERS' PAGEANT.[6]

(77) 1579, Charges of the pagante : Paide for olde ordinarye 30 charges aboute the pagante for plaieres wages and all other thinges the some of iij li vij s viij d.

---

[1] *Sh.* The representation of an earthquake was first introduced in 1556 ; all the items are given.

[2] *Sh. suggests that this may have been a supplementary pageant, but inclines to think it a play performed before the company at their dinner.*

[3] *Sh.* Not particularized, only a general entry.

[4] *Sh.* Massye seems to have been a general contractor for managing the pageants that year ; the cappers and mercers as well as the drapers agreed with him. It will be seen by referring to the accounts of 1584 that he furnished the "temple & beards" to the smiths' company, and probably did the like as to the "temple" for the cappers. He was certainly paid 16d. for services toward the mercers' pageant in 1584.

[5] *Sh.* One instance only occurs of horses in the drapers' pageant, viz. 1591, the very last time of their performing (20).

[6] The oldest account book of the mercers' company now remaining commences in 1579, the last year of a regular performance of the pageants.

*Trinity Guild accounts.* 1473 (13 Edward IV.), *R' Joh'e Trumpton et Thoma Colyns custodibus de mercers pro redditu de pagent house* lij s vj d.[1] *MS. annals.* 1525, The mercers' pageant gallantly trimmed stood in the Cross Cheaping this year, when 5 the Lady Mary came to Coventry.[2]

(78) *Destruction of Jerusalem.*[2] 1584, Charges of the pagante and the playe[3] : Pd for hieringe apparell for the playeres and for carrig xxxiij s, p'd for makinge ij greene cloks x s ij d, p'd Green for the playe booke v s, p'd for mendynge the skaffolde iiij s 10 iiij d, p'd Digbyn for dromminge vij s, p'd iij boyes that plaied xvj d, p'd for mussike v s iiij d—p'd the trumppeter iij s iiij d— viij s viij d, p'd the painter iij s, p'd 12 souldiours iiij s iiij d— p'd a standard bearer xij d—v s iiij d, p'd for drivinge the pagante and skaffolds v s iiij d, p'd for settinge up the pagant viij d. One 15 performer received 6s. 8d.; others 5s., 4s., and 3s. each.

1588, "pagante stufe" sold to the amount of 59s. 8d.; the only article specified "a copper chayne" produced 2s. 4d.

1591, p'd Thomas Masseye towards plainge the pagants xxxiij s iiij d.[4]

20 PINNERS' AND NEEDLERS', TILERS', AND COOPERS' PAGEANT.[5]

*Harl. MSS.* 6466, *the Tilers' Book of Rules and Orders, copied by H. Wanley.*

(79) 1453 (Rich. Wood Mayor). Also yt ys ordeynyd bye a general counsel of all the crafte and craftes[6] that the wryghtes craft of Coventre schall paye to the pageant x s uppon Whytsonday or else by Corpus Christi daye uppon the payne of xx s halfe to the 25 mayor and halfe to the crafte and by cause they to haue no more to do wythe the pageant but payeyng there x s.—f. 5.

Be hyt knone to all men be thys writeng in the tyme of Richard Jacksson then beyng meire of Coventre be a wolle concell

---

[1] *Sh.* a like payment occurs so late as 1516.

[2] *Sh. gives the sum of the expenditure as* £8 9s. 6d. to which the girdlers contributed 52s. 2d.

[3] *Sh. speaks of these charges as a selection from the entry.*

[4] *Sh. suggests that this was contributed in aid of a pageant exhibited by some other company.*

[5] *Sh.* (78) The rules and orders of the company of pynners and nedelers, agreed upon 2 Henry V. (1414) before Laurence Cook then mayor of Coventry and others, "evermore for to stonden and to lasten," recite *inter alia,* that the said craft are to bear the charges and reparations of "her pagent callyd the takyng down of God fro the cros for evermore amongs hem ;" and to eschew faults and mischiefs of false men of the same craft, they agree that they shall be clothed in one livery against Corpus Christi day, from year to year, and ride on that day with the mayor and bailiffs, "all in asute in worshep of the citee on pain of 2s. each, and every member of the company who intends having a livery against Corpus Christi feast, to bring 40d. to the master on the 25th of March, and the remainder when he fetches his livery, and if he has an hood, then to bring 6d. more on the 25th of March and the remainder when he takes his livery.

[6] *MS.* and also that.

K

made at a let that all the tylle-makers of Stoke schall pay to crafts of pinnars, tyllars, and cappars of Coventre every yere,[1] 8d a man,[2] how many so euer [3] be, and hyt to be payd apone Corpus Christi day, apone the pene of 20 s halff to the mere and halffe to the crafte and thys ordeynd [4] and grauntyd in the tyme of Rycherd 5 Cokke then beyng merre of Coventre, tyn beyng kepper of the seyd crafts Thomas Thenell, John More; Henry [    ], wittenes therof.—f. 6.

1501 (R'd Jackson mayor). Also yt is ordeynd and agred by the wholl body of the craft of the bowyers[5] and fletchers of the 10 citie of Coventre in this behalfe and by ther on will that what stranger that is mad brother to them after ther ordonaunce aforseid, that 6s 8d of his brotherhode to remayn to the cost and reparacion of the pagent of the pynners, tyllers, and coupers of Coventre in payne of 20s halfe to the maire and halfe to the crafte.—f. 7. 15

Also hit is ordeynd and agred by the woll body of the craft of bowyers & fletchers of Coventre in the tyme of John Duddesbury beynge meyre of the citie of Coventre and by the wholl councell of the same at Estur lett ther holden, that the keperis of the craft aforseid shall pay to the maisters of the pynners, tyllers, and cowperis 20 of Coventre for the yere beyng, and to ther successours for ever yerely, the 12th day aftur the fest of Corpus Christi 3s 4d, apone the pene of 20 s half to the meyre and halfe to the craft of pynners, tyllers, and cowpers a-for-seid ; and mor-over the wholl body of the craft of pynners, and tyllers, and coupers of Coventre graunteth that 25 the wholl body of the craft of bowyers and fletchers of Coventre be at ther liberte not to come amonge them, nother to weddyngs, nor byrryngs, nor to wache, nor to no other costom, but be at ther liberte for ever.—f. 7.

1502. Also hit is ordeyned and a-grede by the wholl body of 30 the craft of the tylmakers of Stoke in the tyme of Richard Jackson beynge meyre of the cittie of Coventre and be the wholl councell of the same at Estur lett then holden, that the maisters for the yere beyng of the tyl-makers shall pay to the craft of the pynners, tylers, and cowpers at Coventre and to ther successours for 35 ever 5 s, ther to be delyverd to the maisters of the craft for the yere beynge apon Corpus Christi daye, appon the peyn of 20 s, halfe to the meyre and halfe to the craft, and this ordinance was confermyde afor master Richard Cooke in hys meyralte and afor other of his worshippfull brethurun.—f. 8. 40

1504 (John Duddersbury mayor). Also hit is ordeynde and a-grede by the wol body of the craft of the tylmakers of Stoke by ther one will that what stranger that is made brother with them after ther ordinaunce, that 6s. 8d. of his brotherhode to remayn to the cost and reperacion of the payant of the pynners, and 45

---

[1] MS. herre.   [2] MS. in one.   [3] MS. money to every.
[4] MS. orffyn.   [5] MS. err. Cottyers, here and throughout ; so Sh.

tyllers, and coupers of Coventre in payne of 20 s, halfe to the major and halfe to the crafte.—f. 8.

*Carpenters contributory.* 1448, *it. solutum ad le pinneros pro le pagent* x s. 1461, payd to pynners and tylers for the pagent x s.
5 Similar regular entries occur in their *Book of Accounts* now in the Muniment-room in St. Mary's Hall.

## TANNERS' PAGEANT.[1]

1517. *Sh.* (80) Wm. Pisford of Coventry by a will dated this year gives to the tanners' company his scarlet gown and his crimson gown to make use of at the time of their plays. Also to
10 the craft of tanners and to every other craft finding priest or pageant, to the augmentation of the service of God and upholding of the laudable custom of the city 3s. 4d. each.

## OTHER PAGEANTS.

Other pageants considered by *Sh.* (80–2) are :
*Girdlers' Pageant.* No information except that derived from
15 the Leet Book.

*Whittawers' Pageant.* 1548, the cappers "receved of the crafte of the whittawers for the hyer of our pageand iij s iiij d." The butchers were contributory and *Sh.* gives these entries from their account book : 1562, paid to the whittawers towards theyr
20 pagand xiij s xiij d.[2] 1591, it. pd at Mr Mayors commaundement towards the pageants xxij s iiij d.

*Painters' Pageant.* The authority for supposing that the painters had a pageant is the order of leet 1526 requiring the carvers to contribute 12d. each to the painters' pageant. But in
25 1532 another order commands the painters to contribute 4s. yearly to the girdlers. The 1526 order refers to the cardmakers' pageant in which the painters were associated.

*Cardmakers' Pageant.* Various orders of leet are the only records preserved. In 1537 their pageant passed into the hands
30 of the cappers.

*Shearmen and Taylors' Pageant.* *Sh.* (66) A deed 19 Hen. VII. (1503) describes the pageant house belonging to the shearmen and taylors as situated there (in Mill-lane) betwixt the pageant houses of the pinners' and weavers' companies.[3] In 1579 the
35 smiths hired a gown of the shearmen and taylors for the use of their pageant.

---

[1] *Sh. states that the account books and other documents belonging to the company have been destroyed.*
[2] *Sh.* This payment was regularly made, with the exceptions of the years 1566, 1580–3, until 1584 when they paid 20s.
[3] *See also account of weavers' pageant-house below.*

## The Weavers' Pageant.[1]

1453. Also it is ordenyd that the jorneymen of the seyd crafte schall haue yerely vj.*s* viij.*d* and for that they schall have owte the paggent and on Corpus Christi day to dryve it from place to place ther as it schal be pleyd and then for to brynge it ageyn into 5 the paggent howse without ony hurte nyther defawte and they for to put the master to no more coste.—*Ordinances of the Company of Weavers.*[2]

1523, spend on Corpus Christi[3] day xxij s viij d ob[4]; 1525, same item xxx s viij d ob. 10

Entry for 1525. Expencys on Corpus Christi day : It.[5] payd for met and drynk for the players ij s x d, it. payd to Symyon for hys wagys ij s iiij d, it. payd to Joseph xiiij d, it. payd to Mare x d, it. payd to Sodden for Ane x d, it. payd to Symyons clark x d, it. payd to J̄hu xx d, it. payd to the angles 15 xx d, it. payd for glovys viij d, (A. 20) it. payd to the synggers xvj d, it. payd Homon for dryving of the pagent v s iiij d.[6] Under the head of receipts occurs for this year only : It. res.[7] of the masters for the pagynt money xvj s iiij d.

*Subsequent History. Sh.* No other than general entries occur 20 until 1541. The charges for Corpus Christi day regularly occur in the accounts from their commencement in 1523 to 1533 inclusive ; after which no payment is found until 1537. From 1537 the weavers' pageant was regularly performed until 1579. 1566, (Queen Elizabeth's visit), weavers' pageant at Much Park street 25 end.[8] (A 21) 1587, r.[9] of John Showell for the padgant xl s, payd at James Ellidges when we sold our padgent xiij s, payd at Pyringes when we sold the payntynge of the . . . xvj d ; 1591, it. payd to Mr. Mayor for the padgantes xx s ; 1593, it. payd when we reseved the moneye for the players aparell xij d ; 1606, it. p*d*. 30 at Pyringes when we hired our aparel to Thomas Masie xvj d ; 1607, it. p*d*. when we lente our players aparell ij d.

(A. 22) *Players.* 1544, it. pd to Symyon iij s iiij d, it. payd to Joseph ij s iiij d, it. pd to Mare xx d, it. payd to J̄hu xx d, it. payd to Symyons clark xx d, it. payd to Ane xx d, payd to the ij angells 35 viij d, payd to the synggers xviij (1550, synggers for the pagent); 1551, it. payd to the woman for her chyld iiij d ; 1553, it. payd to the letell chylde iiij d. *Sh.* remarks that in 1523 five performers became love-members of the weavers' company and paid on admis-

---

[1] *Sh.* The most ancient account-book of the weavers' now called the clothiers' company commences in 1523. *In a footnote in which* Sh. *explains that the weavers must have had a pageant long before that, he refers to an agreement between the masters and journeymen wherein it is stipulated that every journeyman shall annually contribute* 4d. ad opus de le pagent. *All references to* Sh. *in the account of this pageant refer to Abbotsford Club edition* 1836 (A.).   [2] H.-P. 1. 339.   [3] *Sh.* corpus xp̄i *and below.*
[4] *Sh.* s̄, d̄, ob̄, *and below.*   [5] *Sh.* Ītm *and below.*
[6] *Sh.* Four leaves are here wanting in the account-book ; so that the entry is not completed.   [7] *Sh.* res̄ *and below.*   [8] A. 27.   [9] *Sh.* R ~ *and below.*

sion 10d. each : 1523, res. of Symons clarke x d, res. of Jochop̄
x d, res. of Our Lady x d, res. of J͞hu x d, res. of Anne x d.

*Fines.* 1450, r. of Hary Bowater of hys fynys beyng Symeons
clerke x d, r. of Crystover Dale playing J͞hu of hys fyne x d, r. of
5 Hew Heyns pleynge Anne for hys fyne vj d.

*Pageant Dresses.* 1523, it. pd for makyng of a whyt ford
prelatt for J͞he viij d ; 1541, payd for a amys for Symyon ij d ;
1542, payd for makyng of Symonys mytor viij d ; 1543, it. payd
for hyre of the grey ames iiij d ; 1570, it. paid for the hyer of ij
10 beards to Hary Benet ij d ; (A. 23) 1576, it. payd for ij beards
and a cappe vj d ; 1578, it. payd for mendyng of the two angelis
crownes ij d.

*Music.* 1536, payd to the mynstrell for Corpus Crysty day
and myssomer ny3ght ij s ; 1554, payd to James Hewet for hys
15 reyggals viij d ; 1556, payd to James Hewett for playing of hys
rygols in the paygent viij d ; 1561, it. payd James Hewett for his
rygols and synggyn iij s iiij d ; 1586, payd to Mr. Goleston for
mendyng our instruments xvij d.

*Play-book.* 1535, it. payd for makyng of the playe-boke v s.
20 *Pageant Vehicle.* 1535, paid to the wryght for mendyng the
pagent iiij s ij d, payd to Rychard Walker for a theyll v d, payd for
smale pesys of tymber v d, payd to the whylwryght for mendyng
the whyle vij d, payd for iron worke to the pagent x d (1542, xij d),
payd for gret naylys to the whells iiij d, payd for v pene nayle
25 and vj pene nayle viij d, payd for bordys to the pagent xij d ;
1542, payd to the wryght for makynge the ij lytyll whellys iijd ;
1563, payd for payntyng of the vane iiijd ; 1569, it. payd for
smythy worke belongyng to our pagent xx d, it. payd for hangyng
up our pagyent doore vij d ; 1570, it. paid for mendyng of a
30 prentyse broken with the pagyent x d.

(A. 24) *Sundries.* 1535, payd for russys pynnys and frankyn-
sence ij d (*Sh.* sometimes 4d.—and soap is occasionally added) ;
1546, it. pd for rosshes and pake thread ij d (tenterhooks sometimes) ; 1556, it. pd for the wast of ij tapars iij d ; 1558, it. pd
35 for the wast of ij tapars and insence ij d ; 1570, it. paid to John
Hoppers for ij rehersys in the halle iiij d. *Sh.* says that charges for
rehearsals were of regular occurrence, and that "there is good reason
to believe" that the hall here referred to was St. Nicholas' hall
which the company usually attended.

40 *Specimen Entry.* 1563, in primis for ij rehersys ij s, it. payd
for the dryving of the pagente v d, it. paid to Symeon iij s iiij d,
it. paid to Josephe ij s iiij d, it. paid to Jesus xx d, it paid to
Mary xx d, it. paid to Anne xx d, it. paid to Symeons clarke xx d,
it. paid to the ij angells viij d, it. paid to the chylde iiij d, it. paid
45 for russhes packthryd and nayls iiij d, it. paid to James Hewete
for his rygoles xx d, it. paid for syngyng xvj d, it. paid for gloves
ij s ij d, it. paide for meate in the bocherye x s ix d, it. paid for
bread and ale vij s viij d ; summe xliiij s iij d.

(A. 25) *Pageant house.  Sh.* From deeds belonging to the now
Clothiers' company it appears that, so early as 13th Hen. VI.,
1435, a parcel of land in Mill Lane, adjoining the " tailour paiont,"
being 30½ feet wide and 70½ long, was granted and let for 80 years
to John Hampton and 7 others, paying 3s. 8d. rent, and covenant- 5
ing to erect thereupon during that term " *unam domum vocatur* a
paiont hows " and to keep the same in good repair during the said
term.  By another deed dated 12th May, 17th Hen. VI., 1439,
Richard Molle, weaver, and others, demise to Wm. Gale and Wm.
Flowter masters of the Cardmakers' company, Richard Twig master 10
of the company of Saddlers, John Ward master of the Painters'
company, and Henry Stevons and Henry Clerk masters of the
Freemasons' company, and their successors, a void piece of ground
in Mill Lane, adjoining certain land held by the master of the
weavers, for 101 years, paying 4s. rent during the life of Thomas 15
Wutton and 2s. afterwards during the lives of the granters,
covenanting also to keep in repair any building erected thereon.
On the 6th October 1455 the same parties convey to Richard
Cokkes and 5 others, weavers, in fee, " a place of land, built
upon, called wevers' pagent-howse in Mill Lane," reserving 1d. 20
yearly rent to the master and brethren of St. John's Hospital.
On the 10th of the same month the above-named Cokkes and
others grant a rent charge of 4s., during his life, to Thomas
Wutton, payable out of the weavers' pageant house ; and on the
6th June 1458 Cokkes and Pace release their interest in the 25
same to John Tebbes and 3 other cofeoffees.  On the 18th Dec.
1466 the surviving feofees grant the pageant house to Wm. Jones
and Laur. Hyron, weavers, in fee.

(A. 26) *Repairs*, etc., *to pageant house.*  1531, payd for
mendyng of the pagent-howse wyndo ij s ; 1537, pd for makyng 30
of a hynge to the pagent-howse dore viij d.

*New building on the site of pageant house.*  1587, r. for the
journe of the padgent house x s vj d ; paymentes for bulding of
the paygente house in the Myl Lane : Item in prymis payd at
takinge doune of the house and the tilles, for hieryng of a rope 35
and caryinge the leade to the store house, and for drynk to the
worke-men that same day ij s x d, it. payd to carpenters for ther
wages iij li iiij s iiij d, it. payd to the masones for ther wages viij s
iiij d, it. payd to the tilers for tiling and daubing xvij s viij d, it.
payd for stone and for carying of stone xij s, it. payd for sand 40
and claye v s ij d, it. payd for lyme and for heare to make mortar
ix s viij d, tiles 9s. 6d., timber 30[25] s. 8d., spars and stoods
11s. 8d., it. payd for a hundred and halfe of bryckes ij s ij d, it.
payd at the rearyng of the house and on the nyght befor x s vj d ;
Summe is xj li xvij s x d. 45

*Pageant.*  1535, payd to the journeymen for dryvyng the
pagent iiij s ij d, spend between the plays vj d ; (A. 27) 1564, it.
for mendyng of the pagyon viij d, it. for payntyng of the vane

iiij d, it. pd for nayls for the pagente v d, it. paid for iij carte
nayls for the whells iiij d; 1566, it. payd for a whele for the
pagente iiij s, it. payd for byndyng the whele and for carte nayles
and other workemanshype that belongyth unto hym iij s iiij d, it.
5 payd for a spoke [1] for the whele xij d, it. payd for naylls and sope
and a clowte for the axetre xij d; 1568, it. paid for greate nayles
for the pagent wheles ij s, it. payd for makyng of iij trestles and
mendyng the pagent xiiij d; 1570, it paid for makyng an exaltre
for the pagyante xij d, it. paid for a trendell for the scaffold and
10 the makyng iij d; 1572, it. pd for a trendyll for the scaffoll iiij d;
1573, it. paide for mendinge the pageand x d.

(A. 27) *Miscellaneous.* 1564, it. paid for settynge one of
Jhesus sleues ij d, it. paid for payntyng of Jesus heade viij d,
it. paid for solyng of Jesus hose j d, it. paid to John Dowley to
15 make oute the money for his gowne viij d; 1566, it. payd for
mendyng of ij poleaxes viij d.

(A. 21) *Destruction of Jerusalem.* 1584, item paide for
rehearses ij s, item paide at the settinge out of the pagion vj d,
item paide on the pagion daye for bread and drincke iij s viij d,
20 item paide for nayles and rushes vj d, item paide to John Smythe
xvj s, item paide for drivinge of the pagion v s, item paide to
Robert Baggesley for mending of the pagion vj d; rentgatherer's
account: payd for that whych belongeth to the pagyaunte xij s,
payd for nayles and mendyng of the pagyent iij d.

# Appendix III.

*Pageants on Special Occasions.    Extracts from the Coventry*
*Leet Book.*

25    *Reception of Queen Margaret in* 1456.[2]    Md.[3] That the
Thursday next aftur the fest of seynt Bartholomewe the postyll,
the yere reynyng of Kyng Herry the sixt aftur the Conquest
xxxiiij, Richard Braytoft *then* beyng meyre, was made assemble
yn seynt Mary Halle, of worshipfull persons, whos names
30 folowen :— (*List of* 90 *persons.*)
    The wheche p*er*sones aboven rehersyd then ordyned *and*
provyded, that *ther* shold a C marke be levyed by the wardes yn
Coventre, wherof L marke to be *y*even to oure souerayne lady the

---

[1] *Sh.* stroke.    [2] *Leet Book*, ff. 168–170 b.    *Sh.* Diss. pp. 145–151.
[3] f. 168.

quene *and* other L marke to the prynce, at her next comyng to
Coventre.

Afturward, that ys for to sey at the fest of the Holy Crosse
the xxxv yere of Kyng Herry the sixt, at Coventre, L marke
was yeven to oure soverayn lady the quene; and the xx day of 5
January then next folowyng, he the seyde meyre and his counsell,
the other L marke of the seyd C marke, was relivered to the
collectours of every warde after the rate, as hit be endentures
severally made be-twix the seyde meyre *and* the collectours
apereth, savely to kepe to the use of the prynce, when he comes 10
to Coventre.

Md. That the demene *and* rule that was made *and* shewed
un-to oure soverayn lady the quene, at Coventre, was thus as it
foloweth yn wrytyng; that is for to sey, furst at Bablake there
was made a Jesse over the yate right well [arayed], and there were 15
shewed too speches, as foloweth :

YSAY.   Princes most excellent, born of blode riall,[1]
 Chosen quene of this region, conforte to all hus,
I, Ysay, replete with the spirite propheticall,
 Wordes to your magnificens woll I say thus :[2]    20
 Like as mankynde was gladdid by the birght of Jhsus,
So shall this empyre joy the birthe of your bodye ;
The knyghtly curage of prince Edward all men shall joy to se.

JEREMY.   Emprece, quene, princes excellent, in on person all iij,
 I, Jeremy the prophete trew, theis wordes of you wyll say :25
This reme shall joye the blessyd tyme of your nativyte ;
 The mellyflue mekenes of your person shall put all wo
  away.
 Unto the rote of Jesse[3] likken you well I may ;
The fragrante floure sprongon of you shall so encrece *and* spredde, 30
That all the world yn ich party shall cherisshe hym, love *and*
  drede.

Afturward with-inne the yate at the est yende of the chirche,
was a pagent right well arayed *and* therin was shewed a speche
of seynt Edward *and* an-other of seynt John the Evaungelist, 35
as foloweth :

[4]S. EDWARD.   Moder of mekenes, dame Margarete, princes
 most excellent,
 I, kyng Edward, welcum you with affeccion righ[t] cordiall,
Certefying to your highnes mekely myn entent.    40
 For the wele of the kyng *and* you hertely pray I shall,
 And for prince Edward, my gostly chylde, whom I love
  principall,

----

[1] f. 168 b.  [2] *This and the preceding line inverted in* MS.
[3] MS. rote of Jesse rote.  [4] f. 169.

Praying the, John evangelist, my helpe *ther*in to be ;
On that condicion right humbly I gif *th*is ryng to the.

JOHN EVANGELIST.   Holy Edward, crownyd kyng, brother in
     virginyte,
5     My power playnly I wyll prefer thi wyll to amplifye.
Most excellent princes of weymen mortall, yo*ur* bedeman wyll
     I be.
     I knowe yo*ur* lyf so vertuus *th*at God is plesyd therby ;
     The birth of you un-to *th*is reme shall cause grete melody.
10  The vertu*us* voyce of pr*in*ce Edward shall dayly well encrese ;
     Seynt Edward, his godfader, *and* I shall pr*a*y *ther*fore dowtelesse.

Afturward the cundit yn Smythforde strete was right well
arayed *and* there was shewed iiij speches of iiij cardynall v*er*tues,
as foloweth :

15  RIGH[T]WESNES.   I, Righ[t]wesenes, that causeth treuth to be
          had,
     Mekely as a maydyn my langage wyll I make,
     And welcu*m* you, pr*in*ces right cherefull *and* glad ;
     With you wyll I be dwellyng *and* never you forsake.

20  TEMPE*R*AUNCE.   I, Temp*er*aunce, to plese you warly wyll wake,
          And welcome you as most worthy to my power,
     Besechyng youre highnes this langage to take ;
          I wyll feythfully defende you from all man*ner* daunger.

     STRENGH.   I, Strengh *th*e iij^e vertewe, wyll playnly appere,
25        Clerely to conseyve yo yn yo*ur* estate most riall,
     And welcu*m* yowe, pr*in*ces, gladly w*it*h chere ;
          For to do *th*at mowe plece you, aray ws we shall.

     P*R*UDENCE.   I, Pr*u*dence, of the iiij vertewes highest in degre,
          Welcu*m* you, dame M*a*rgarete, quene crowned of this
30        lande.
     The blessyd babe *th*at ye have born, pry*n*ce Edward is he,
          Th*u*rrowe whom pece *and* tranquilite shall take *th*is reme
          on hand ;
     We shall endowe both you *and* hym clerely to understonde ;
35  We shall pr*e*s*er*ve you p*er*sonally *and* nev*er* fro you dissev*er*.
     Doute not, pr*in*ces most excellent, we iiij shall do our dev*er*.

[1] Afturward at the crosse yn the Croschepyng, there were
ordeyned div*er*se angels sensyng a-high on the crosse, *and* there
ranne out wyne at mony places a long while.
40     Afturward betwix the seyde crosse *and* the cundit bene*th*e
that, were sette ix pagentes right well arayed *and* yn ev*er*y
pagent was shewed a speche of the ix conqueroures ; yn the furst
was shew*ed* of Hector, as foloweth :

[1] f. 169 b.

HECTOR. Most pleasaunt princes recordid *that* may be,
    I, Hector of Troy, *that* am chefe conquerour,
Lowly wyll obey yowe *and* knele on my kne,
    And welcum yowe tendurly to yo*ur* honoure
      To this conabull cite, the p*r*inces chambur ;      5
Whome ye bare yn youre bosom, joy to *th*is lande,
Thro whome in p*r*osperite *th*is empyre shall stand.

In the secunde pagent was shewed a speche of Alex*ander*, as
foloweth :

ALEX*ANDER.* I, Alexander, *tha*t for chyvalry berith *th*e balle,   10
    Most cura*giuos* [1] in conquest, thro *th*e world am y-named,
Welcu*m* yowe, p*r*inces, as quene p*r*incipall.
    But I hayls you ryght hendly, I wer worthy to be blamyd ;
    The noblest p*r*ince *that* is born, whome fortune hath
      famyd,      15
Is yo*ur* sovereyn lorde Herry, emp*er*our *and* kyng ;
Unto whom mekely I wyll be obeying.

In the thridde pagent was shewed of Josue as foloweth :

JOSUE. I, Josue, *that* in Hebrewe reyn p*r*incipall,
    To whome *that* all Egipte was fayn to inclyne,     20
Wyll abey to yo*ur* plesur, p*r*inces most riall.
    As to the heghest lady *that* I can ymagyne.
    To the plesure of yo*ur* p*er*sone, I wyll put me to pyne,
As a knyght for his lady boldly to fight,
Yf any man of curage wold bid you unright.     25

In the fourthe pagent was shewed of David, as followeth :

DAVID. I, David, *that* in deynte [2] have led all my dayes,
    That slowe *th*e lyon *and* Goly thorowe Goddys myght,
Will obey to you, lady, youre p*er*sone prayse
    And welcu*m* you curtesly as a kynd knyght,     30
    For the love of yo*ur* lege lorde, Herry that hight,
And yo*ur* laudabull lyfe that vertuus ev*er* hath be ;
Lady most lufly, ye be welcu*m* to *th*is cite !

[3] In the fyth pagent was shewed a speche of Judas, as
foloweth :     35

JUDAS. I, Judas, *that* yn Jure am callid the belle,
    In knyghthode *and* conquest have I no pere,
Wyll obey to you, princes, ell*es* did I not well
    And tendurly welcum you yn my manere.
    Yo*ur* own soverayn lorde *and* kynge is p*r*esent here,   40
Whome God for his godenes p*r*eserve in good helthe,
And ende you w*ith* worship to this landys welthe !

[1] MS. cur*ius*.    [2] S. deyntes, MS. deyntes.    [3] f. 170.

In the sixt pagent was shewed a speche of Arthur,[1] as foloweth :

ARTHUR. I, Arthur, kynge crownyd *and* conquerour,
    That yn this lande reyned right rially ;
5  With dedes of armes I slowe the emp*er*our ;
      The tribute of this ryche reme I made downe to ly—
      Ihit unto [you], lady, obey I mekely,
As youre sure s*er*vande ; plesur to yo*ur* highnesse,
For the most plesaunt p*ri*nces mortal that es !

10   In the vij pagent was shewed a speche of Charles, as foloweth :

CHARLES. I, Charles, chefe cheftan of t*h*e reme of Fra*un*ce
    And emp*er*our of grete Rome, made by eleccion,
Which put mony paynyms to pyne *and* penaunce ;
      The holy relikes of Criste I had in possession—
15      Ihit, lady, to yo*ur* highnes to cause dieu refeccion,
Worshipfully I welc*um* you after yo*ur* magnificens ;
Yf my s*er*vice mowe plese you, I wyll put to my diligence.

In the viij pagent was shewed a speche of Julius, as foloweth :

JULIUS. I, Julius Cesar, sov*er*ayn of knyghthode
20      And emp*er*our of mortall men, most hegh *and* myghty,
Welc*um* you, p*ri*nces most benynge *and* gode ;
      Of quenes t*ha*t byn crowned so high non knowe I.
      The same blessyd blossom, t*ha*t spronge of yo*ur* body,
Shall succede me in worship, I wyll it be so ;
25  All the landis olyve shall obey hym un-to.

In the ix pagent was shewed a speche of Godfride, as foloweth :

GODFRIDE. I, Godfride of Bollayn, kynge of Jerusalem,
    Weryng t*h*e thorny crowne yn worshyp of Jh*es*u,
Which in battayle have no pere under the sone beme ;
30      Yhit, lady, right lowely I loute unto yowe.
      So excellent a p*ri*nces, stedefast *and* trewe,
Knowe I none c*ri*stened as you in your estate ;
Jh*es*u for hys m*er*ci incresse *and* not abate !

[2] Afturward *and* last the cundit yn the Crossechepyng was
35 arayed right well with as mony virgyns as myght be t*h*eruppon,
and there was made a grete dragon *and* seynt Marg*ar*et sleyng
hym be myracull, *and* there was shewed full well this speche
that foloweth :

S. MARGARET. Most notabull p*ri*nces of weymen erthle,
40     Dame M*ar*garete t*h*e chefe myrth of t*h*is empyre,
Ye be hertely welc*um* to t*h*is cyte.

---

[1] *Smiths' Accounts*, 1455(6), Item. To have owght the pagent at the
comyng of the quene, that ys the parell to the pagent and harneste men and
the harnes to [harnes] hem wyth and a cote armyr for Arture and a creste
with iij grevyes, xvijs xi d ob.—*Sh.* loc. cit. p. 149.     [2] f. 170 b.

To the plesure of *your* highnes, I wyll sette my desyre ;
   Bothe nature *and* gentilnes doth me require,
Seth we be both of one name, to shewe you kyndnes ;
Wherefore by my power ye shall have no distresse.

I shall *pray* to the P*ri*nce that is endeles                                   5
   To socour you w*ith* solas of his high *grace*.
He wyll here my peticion this is doutles,
   For I wrought all my lyff *tha*t his wyll wase ;
   Therfore, lady, when ye be yn any dredefull cace
Calle on me boldly, *ther*-of I p*ra*y you,                                    10
And trist to me feythefully, I woll do *tha*t may pay yow.


Md. Payde to John Wedurby of Leyces*ter* for *the* p*ro*vicion
*and* makyng of these p*re*misses of the welcomyng of our sove*ra*yn
lady the quene, *and* for his laboure inne *and* out xxv s.

Itm. payde for a tonne of wyne that was *y*even to our 15
sove*ra*yn lorde the kynge viij li iiij d ; itm. for ij gilt cuppes, of
the which on was *y*even to our sove*ra*yn lady the quene *and* the
other is kepte for our lorde the p*ri*nce unto his comyng, the whiche
cuppes weyen xliiij oz. qrt. *and* dr., p*ri*ce le oz. iiij s viij d, sma.
x li vij s j d, and ov*er* that, for giltyng of the fete of *th*e seid 20
cuppes with-inne iij s, sma. tot. x li x s j d ; itm. the meyre *y*afe
by the avyse of his counsell to diverse p*er*sones of the kynges
house xx s ; itm. he payde for a glase of rose-wat*er* that my lord
Ryvers had ij s.

*Reception of Edward IV. in* 1460.[1]   One hundred pounds 25
and a cup was given by the city to Edward IV. " to his welcome
to his cite of Coventre from the felde yn the north." [2]

*Receavynge Prynce Edwarde* [*in* 1474].[3]   Memorandum*. That
the xxviij. day of the moneth of Aprill cam oure lorde prince
Edward out of Walys so by Warrewik to Coventre and the meire 30
and his brethern w*ith* the div*er*s of cominalte of the seide citie,
clothed in grene and blewe, metyng oure seid lorde prince, upon
horsbake by-yonde the Newe Crosse, in a chare, beyng of age of
iij yere, ther welcomyng hym to his chaumber and *y*eyving hym
ther a C mark in a gilt coppe of xv ounces w*ith* a kerchyff of 35
plesaunce upon the seid coppe ; and then comyng in-to [the] citie.
And at Babulake *y*ate ther ordeyned a stacion, therin beyng Kyng
Richard w*ith* xiij other arrayed lyke as dukes, mark*i*ses, erles,
vicouns, and barons, *and* lordis w*ith* mynstrallcy of the wayts of
the cite, and Kyng Richard ther havyng this speche her folowyng : 40

---

[1] *Leet Book*, f. 184 *b*.    *Sh.* loc. cit. p. 151.
[2] *Smiths' Accounts*, 1460, Item for the havyng owght of the pagent, when
the pryns came, yn brede and ale, and to Samson wythe his iij knyghtys,
and to an harper iij s vj d ; it. for golde for Samsons garments and poyntys
iij d.—*Sh.* loc. cit. p. 152.
[3] *Leet Book*, ff. 222, 222 b.    *Sh.* loc. cit. pp. 152–154.

REX RICHARDUS. Welcom, full high and nobull prince, to us
    right speciall,
    To this your chaumber, so called of antiquite !
The presens of your noble person reioyseth our[1] harts all ;
5      We all mowe blesse the tyme of your nativite.
    The right lyne of the royall blode ys now as itt schulde be ;
Wherfore God of his goodnes preserve you in bodily helth,
To us and your tenauntes here, perpetuall ioy ; and to all londis,
    welth !

10    Also at the Condite afore Richard Braytoft the elder, a-nother
stacion with iij patriarkes ther stondyng upon the seid Condite,
with Jacobus xij sonnes with mynstralcy of harpe and dowsemeris, and ther rennyng wyne in on place ; and there on of the
seid patriarkes havyng this speche writtyn :

15    [PATRIARCH.]  O God most glorious !  Grounder and Gyver of
    all grace !
    To us iij patriarkes thou promysed, as scriptur maketh
    rehersall,
That of our stok lynially schuld procede and passe
20      A prynce of most nobull blode and kyngs sonne imperiall ;
    The wich was full-fylled in God. And nowe referre itt we
    schall
Unto this nobull prynce that is here present,
Wich entreth to this his chaumber, as prynce full reverent.

25    Also at the Brodeyate a pagiont ; and seint Edward beyng
therin with x a-states with hym, with mynstralcy of harpe and
lute, and Kyng Edward havyng this speche next foloyng :

[KING EDWARD.]  Nobull prynce Edward, my cossyn and my
    knyght,
30      And very prynce of our lyne com yn[2] dissent !
    [3] I, seint Edward, have pursued for your faders imperiall right,
    Wherof he was excludid by full furious intent.
Unto this your chaumber, as prynce full excellent,
Ye be right welcom ; thanked be Crist of his sonde !
35    For that that was oures is nowe in your faders hande.

    Also at the Crosse in the Croschepyng, were iij prophets stand-
yng at the crosse seynsyng, and upon the crosse a-boven, were
Childer of Issarell syngyng and castyng out whete obles and
floures, and iiij pypis rennyng wyne.
40    Also in the Croschepyng a-fore the Panyer, a pagent[4] and iij
Kyngs of Colen therein with other divers arraied and ij knyghts

---

[1] MS. your.    [2] MS. comyn.    [3] f. 222 b.
[4] *This was perhaps the shearmen and taylors' pageant. Smiths' Accounts,*
*1474, Expense for bryngyng furth the pagent a-yenst the comyng of the*
*quene and the prince vj d.—Sh. loc. cit. 154. The shearmen and taylors*
*would have the necessary costumes for the kings.*

armed wi*th* mynstralsy of small pypis, and one of the Kyngs
havyng this speche under writtyn :

[A KING OF COLOGNE.]    O splendent Creator! In all our
     speculacion,
       More bryghter then Phebus, excedent all ly*ght*!          5
We thre kyngs beseche the, wi*th* meke mediacion,
       Specially to p*re*serve this nobull prynce, *th*i knyght,
       Wich by influens of thy grace p*ro*cedeth a-right.
Of on of us thre lynnyally, we fynde,
       His nobull moder, quene Elizabeth, ys comyn of *th*at kynde.    10

     Also upon the Condite in the Croschepyng, was seint
George armed; and a kynges dough*ter* knelyng a-fore hym wi*th*
a lambe ; and the fader *and* the moder, beyng in a toure a-boven,
beholdyng seint George savyng their doughter from the dragon ;
and the Condite rennyng wyne in iiij plac*es*, and mynstralcy of 15
orgonpleyinge, and seint George havyng this speche under
wryttyn :

[SAINT GEORGE.]    O myghty God! Our all Socour celestiall !
       Wich *th*is reyme hast geven to dower
To thi moder, and to me, George, p*ro*teccion p*er*petuall,      20
       Hit to defende from enimies fere *and* nere ;
       And as this mayden defended was here,
Bi thy gra*ce*, from this dragon devour,
So, Lorde, p*re*serve this noble prynce, and ev*er* be his socour!

    [1] *Reception of Prince Arthur in* 1498.[2] Md. That this *y*er the 25
Wensday the xvij day of Octob*er* A*n*no xiiij° R. H. vij, p*ri*nce
Arthur, the first begoton son of kyng Henre the vij[th], then beyng
of *th*e age of xij *y*ers *and* mor, cam first to Coventre *and* ther
lay in *th*e p*ri*ory fro Wensday unto *th*e Munday next suying, at
which tyme he removed towards London. A*y*enst whos comyng 30
was *th*e Sponstrete *y*ayte garnysshed with the ix worthy[s], and
kyng Arthur then havyng this spech, as foloweth :

[KING ARTHUR.]    Hayle, prynce roiall, most amyable in sight !
       Whom the Court et*er*nall, thurgh p*ru*dent gov*er*naunce,
Hath chosen to be egall ons to me in myght,          35
       To sprede our name, Arthur, *and* acts to ava*u*nce,
       And of meanys victorious to have such habundaunce,
That no fals treito*ur*, ne cruell tirrant,
Shall in eny wyse make profer to your lande

And rebelles all falce quarels schall eschewe,         40
       Thurgh *th*e fere of Pallas, that favoreth y*our* lynage
And all outward enmyes laboreth to subdue,
       To make them to do to yewe as to me dyd homage.
       Welcome therfor, the solace *and* comfort of my olde age,

---

           [1] f. 281 b.
      [2] *Leet Book*, ff. 281-282. *Sh.* loc. cit. pp. 154-157.

Prince pereless, Arthur, icome of noble progeny,
To me *and* to your chamber, with all *th*is hole companye !

And at the turnyng into *the* Crosschepyng befor Mr. Thrump-
ton's durr, stode *the* barkers paiant well appareld, in which was
5 the Quene of Fortune with dyve*rs* other virgyns, which quene
has *th*is spech folowyng :

[Queen of Fortune.] I am dame Fortune, quene called, full
expedient
To emprours *and* princes, prelats, with other moo ;
10 As Cesar, Hectour, *and* Fabius, most excellent,
Scipio, exalted Nausica, *and* Emilianus also,
Valerius, also Marchus, with sapient Cicero.
E and noble men, brevely the truth to conclude all,
My favou*r* verily had, as storys maketh rehersall ;
15 With-oute whom, sithen non playnly can prosp*er*,
That in *th*is muitable lyfe ar nowe pr*o*cedyng,
I am come thurgh love. Trust me intiere
To be with yewe *and* yours evirmor enduryng,
Prynce, most unto my pleasure of all *that* ar nowe reynyng;
20 Wherfor, my nowne hert *and* best beloved treasur,
Welcome to *th*is your chaumbe*r* of whom ye be inhabitur.

And the Crosse in the Croschepyng was garnysshed, *and*
wyne ther rennyng, and angels sensyng *and* syngyng, with
orgayns and other melody *etc.*[1] And at *the* Cundyt, ther was
25 seynt George kyllyng the dragon, and seynt George had this
speche folowyng :

[Saint George.] O most sove*r*aign lorde, be divyne pr*o*vision
to be
The ruler of cruell Mars *and* kyng insupe*r*able !
30 Ye reioyce my corage, trustyng hit to se,
That named am George, yo*ur* patron favorable ;
To whom ye are *and* ev*er* shalbe so acceptable,
That in felde, or cite, wher-so-ever ye rayne
Shall I neve*r* fayle yewe, thus is my purpose playne.
35 To protect yo*ur* magnyficence myself I shall endever,
In all thyngs that yo*ur* highnes shall concerne,
Mor tenderly then I *y*it did ever ;
Kyng, duke, yerle, lorde, also berne,
As ye be myn assistence in pr*o*cesse shall lerne,
40 Which thurgh yo*ur* vertue, most amorous knyght,
I owe to yo*ur* presence be due *and* very right.

[1] *Chamberlains' Accounts, made up* anno 1499, It. pd. for settyng of the
posts in *the* Croschepyng, when *the* kyng was here, in gret ij s ; it. for takyng
down of *the* same posts a-geyn x d ; it. for pavyng in *the* Cros-chepyng ther
as the posts stode, of viij yards viij d.—*Sh.* loc. cit. p. 156.

Like-wyse as I *th*is lady be grace I defended,
  That thurgh myschaunce chosen was to dye,
Fro thys foule *ser*pent whom I sor wonded ;
  So ye in distresse *p*reserve ever woll I
  Fro all parell and wyked veleny,                                5
That shuld y*our* noble *per*sone in eny wyse distrayn,
Which welcome is to *th*is y*our* chamb*er and* to me right fayn

And this balet was song at the Crosse :

Ryall *p*rince Arthur, ⎫
Welcome newe tresur, ⎬ to *th*is y*our* cite !                    10
W*ith* all our hole cur, ⎭

Sithen in vertue der, ⎫
Lorde, ye have no per, ⎬ as all we may see.
Of y*our* age tend*er* ; ⎭

Cunyng requyred, ⎫                                                15
All hath cont*r*ived, ⎬ y*our* intelligence.
And so receyved— ⎭

That Yngland, all playn, ⎫
Maye nowe be right fayn ⎬ to their extollence.
Yewe long to remayn, ⎭                                            20

Syng we *ther*for all ; ⎫
Also let us call ⎬ that he yewe defend !
To God immortall ⎭

In this breve beyng ⎫
Your astate supportyng, ⎬ to y*our* lyfes yend !                 25
And vertue ay spredyng, ⎭

# Appendix IV.[1]

*Fragments of another version of the Weavers' Pageant.*

I. PROFETA.  Ye gret astronemarris now awake,
　　With youre fam*us* fadurs of phelossefee
Into the orrent aspecte you take,
　　Wherre in nevis *and* strangis aperid latele,
　　Ase towching the fracis off the wholle p*ro*fesse,
Afirmyng *tha*t a star schuld appere
Evin in Yseraell amongist vs here !　　　　　　7

II. PROFETA.  Bredur all, then be off good chere,
　　Those tythingis makis my hart ful light !
For we haue desirid many a yere
　　Of *tha*t star to haue a sight,
　　And speschalle off that king off myght
Off whose cu*m*yng we haue had warnyng
Be *th*e seyd star of p*ro*fettis deser*n*yng.　　　14

Yet furthurmore for owre larnyng,
　　Let us naue su*m* comm*en*ecasion
Of this seyd star be old p*ro*gnostefying
　　How hyt apperud *and* vndur what fassion.　　18

I. PROFETA.  Aftur a wondurfull strange demonstracion
　　Ase be the exp*er*ence p*ro*ve yt I con ;
For this star be interp*re*tacion
　　Singnefith the natevete of a mon ;　　　　22
　　Ase the profet [Balam] [2]
Be the spret off God affirmithe well
*Orreetur stella ex Jacob, et exurge homo de Yseraell.* 25

He seyd of Jacob a star schuld spryng,
　　Wyche singnefis only this same king
Wyche amonst vs now ys cu*m*
　　And ase towching the lettur folloing,
　　*Et ipse dominabitur om*ni *generacione.*　　30

[1] *See* Introduction, pp. XXXV. ff.　　[2] *Obliterated in* MS.

L

II. P*rofeta*.  Here be your fav*our* wold I move a questeon
    Of this p*r*incis high geneloge,
Wyche ou*er* the gentilis schuld haue domeneon,
    Where *and* off what sort born be schuld be.
    I. P*rofeta*.  Ase ye schall here right worthele
Be devin powar off a v*ir*gin pure,
Affirmyng the p*r*ofettis agenst all nature.        37

II. P*rofeta*.  Where fynd you *th*at in wholle scripture
    Of any right awter wyche that woll mencion?
I. P*rofeta*.  Isae the p*r*ofet wrytith full sure,
    *Ecce virgo concepith aparet fillium!*
    Balam seying of *th*e heyvinle wysedom
A man schuld be reysid here in Yseraell,
    In confirmyng the seyd questeon
*Et vocatur nomen eius Emanevell.*        45

II. P*rofeta*.  Yet to me yt ys moche marvell,
    Vndur whatt sort *th*at men schuld tell
Soche high mysteres before *th*e fell,
    He being but a mortall creature.        49
I. P*rofeta*.  Be Godis p*r*ovedence ye ma be sure
    The espret of God to them was sent,
And lafft to vs in wholle scripture
    And them-selvis not knoyng what hit ment.    53

II. P*rofeta*.  Presid be to hym wyche that espret sent
    Vnto vs pore wrechis of loo symplessete.
He beying the lord owre God om*n*ipotent
    In this his workis to make vs preve!
I. P*rofeta*.  Did not that p*r*ofett man callid Malache  58

. . . . . . . . . . . . .

[S*emeon*][1]
    With fysche, fowle, and best *and* eue*re* odur thing,
Vndur man to haue there naturall curse *and* being.    183

Yet owre anceant parence at the beginnyng
    Through *th*is dissabeydence had a grevas fall
From the abowndant blis euerlasting

        [1] *See* WCo, *line* 182.

Down into the vale off this mezerabull mundall;
Owre nature creatid be hym to be inmortall,
*And* now throgh syn fallin into [1] mortallete
And vtturle distroid wit*h*owt the gret marce                    190

This ded most dolor*us* ofte doth me constreyne
    Inwardle to sigh *and* bytturle to weepe,
Tyll t*h*at I remembur the gret *com*ford agein
    Off anceant *pro*fetis wit*h* t*h*e sentencis swete,
    Whose fructuos sencis off profonde larnyng depe
Wyche apon anceant awters grondid constantle,
Off Iȝae, the Sebbelis, Balam *and* Maleche.                    197

O Lord off lordis! yff thy swet wylbe
    Off t*h*is thi infynit worke send me t*h*e tru light,
Justle to expond t*h*is thy whole mystere,
    *And* that I wonse ma se that only king of myght,
    And thatt we ma walke in his weyis uppright
At whose cu*m*yng ase t*h*e *pro*fettis do expres
The right ungcion off Juda schall seyse.                    204

Oh Lord, fullfyll t*h*at hy tyme off pes!
    For my crokid age dravys fast apon.
Fane wold I see thatt wholle off whollenes,
    Or this mortall lyff fro*m* me were gon.
    O Lord, remembur thy doghtur Syon,
Releve hir, Lord, in t*h*is hir mezere
Reyleysche hyr *gr*aceose God off hir callamete                    211

Oh Lord, at t*h*i wyll all thing mvst be,
    Yet, Lord, thy *gr*ace to vs do exstend
The to serve wit*h* all vmyllete,
    And wit*h* thy *gr*ace huse rule *and* defende;
    Owre solis *and* bodeis to the we com*m*end
Ernystle loking for thy wholle *pro*mes
Owt off danger Yseraell *and* Jvda to reles.                    218

Oh Lord, reylev owre inbesyllete
    *And* thy only sun off lyff to us do send
Hym to reseyve wit*h* all vmyllete
    *And* off t*h*is mortall lyff thou to make amend.

[1] MS. to inmortallete.

O Lord, thy powar no man ma comprehend,
Yet grant me my peytission to obteyne
Not to dy till *th*at I thatt solam sight have seyne.  225

ANE.  Oh suffrent Semeon, wi*th* all vmylete,
    Wyche art owre gide in gostle gou*er*nance,
Wi*th* all due reverence beseche I the
    Thy humble obedient off longe contenevans
    Yet haue me, Semeon, in thy rememburrans,
When it schall plese that hy Messe
Vnto Yseraell *and* Juda reveylid to be.  232

Amongst the othur remembur me
    Wyche this iiij skore yeris *and* more
In this tempull contenevalle
    Thatt lord owre God eu*er* loking fore
    Wyche Yseraell *and* Juda schall restore
From dredfull bonde vnto lyberte
As well apperis be anceant *p*rofece  239

SEMEON.  Systur An, welc*u*m to me!
    Youre hoope ryght hyle I do com*m*end
Wych wyll appere ondowtedle
    When thatt Lord the tyme doth send  243

. . . . . . . . . . . . . .

cetera desunt.

# GLOSSARY.

A, 19/544, he.

accompted, 74/14, rendered an account.

actoris, 36/76, authors.

adioyn, 76/9, join to, unite; *pp.* 76/22.

afecte, 63/973, effect.

aferde, 28/812, afraid.

aleonde, 19/523, alien.

all-myght, 3/51, almighty.

amacid, 3/54, amazed.

ames, 107/9; amys, 107/7, amice.

anssyent, 99/8, ancient, old.

antem, 58/805 f., anthem.

apere, 64/996, *for* apair, impair.

asaye, 55/701, essay, attempt.

aspecte, 119/3, consideration, view.

asposschall, 69/1163, especial.

assadyn, 86/12; assaden, 86/15, *etc.*; aresdyke, 86/23, arsedine, gold coloured alloy.

associat, 78/38, 79/35, associated.

augent, 21/594, *prob. for* and gent (noble), *or for* argent (white); *third king was a* black-amoor.

awe, 60/887, away.

awter, 120/39, 121/196, author.

awyntyente, 91/42, ancient, flag.

Bassche, 22/643, shrink back abashed.

bayles, 72/10, bailiffs.

bayne, 22/636, ready, inclined.

beforne, 21/613, before.

bedull, 83/33, 84/1, beadle, crier (?).

berars, 84/10, bars.

berne, 117/38, baron.

besse, 61/902, busy.

betake, 68/1137, commend, commit.

be-teyche, 4/97, commit.

be-traye, 26/738, betrayal.

bewey, 53/652, boy.

ble, 22/643, complexion.

bloo, 50/550, blow, to take breath and rest.

bokeram, 83/42, *etc.*, buckram.

bordyng, 61/892, jesting, trifling.

bote, 64/1014, 67/1103, boot, remedy, profit.

braband, 88/2, brow-band.

brere, 46/399, brier.

brethur, 22/637, *etc.*, brethren.

breyde, on breyde, 63/962, (open) widely.

bronde, 17/491; brond, 18/497, brand, sword.

burlettis, 88/19, padded rolls of cloth for head or ruff.

bwey, 56/753; bweye, 61/902, boy.

byddyng, 63/965, commandment.

bydull, 87/13, beadle.

byrryngs, 104/28, buryings.

Can, 25/719, can do.

charge, 62/940, import, value.

chassyng, 85/19, chasing, hunting.

chefferellys, 101/13, chevelures, wigs.

cheverels, 84/7, *for* chevelures.

childur, 2/21, *etc.*, children; man-chyldur, 29/841.

clarge, 60/870, 61/905, *etc.*, knowledge, learning.

clowte, 109/6, clout, iron plate.

cofyns, 74/42, boxes, cases.

colters, 84/18, *for* cotters, bolts.

comenalte, 70/1184; cominalte, 114/31, commonalty.

comon, 19/542; comen, 19/547; comyn, 21/605, *pp.* come.

compromytted, 73/25, bound themselves mutually.

conabull, 112/5, convenient, suitable.

connfetys, 74/42, comfits, sweetmeats.

consuett, 73/43; consuette, 73/32, accustomed.

cost, 20/572, 30/873, *etc.*, coast, region.

cost, 4/98, way.

coterellis, 89/34, cotters, bolts.

cowntters, 89/43, counters, things used in reckoning.

coyff, 94/8, coif, head-dress.

cun, 29/828, sort, kind.

cundeture, 37/129, conductor, guide.

cundit, 111/12, 40, conduit.

cur, 118/11, heart.

customyd, 85/23, accustomed, wont.

Decryis, 60/864, decrees.

defende, 77/38, appear in court (?).

deformacion, 34/19, *ignorantly used to mean* form.

deme, 20/558, deem, judge ; *pp.* 2/20.

deserte, 35/66, desert or wilderness (?).

dever, 111/36, duty.

deynte, 112/27, *for* dainty, honour (?).

dissent, 115/30, descent.

dowsemeris, 115/12, dulcimers.

dresse, 6/178, direct one's steps.

dresser, 95/24, person who prepared or tended the pageant.

dressyng, 86/31, *etc.*, making ready, preparing.

dyght, 21/615, 43/321, *etc.*, dight, ready.

dyssepyssions, 60/869 ; dysspecionis, 69/1157, *for* disputisouns, disputations.

dysse, 88/11, dice, ornamental beads (?).

E ! 60/864, 61/900, *etc.*, ay ! alas !

eder, 72/14, either.

eftsones, 77/37, again, a second time.

ellne, 88/14 ; elnes, 100/32, ells.

enderes, enderes night, 31/1, night recently past.

entermettyng, 74/6, intermeddling.

espret, 120/51, 54, spirit.

eyvin, 4/108, *quasi sb.* equal or like.

Fanes, 82/8, 84/13, *etc.*, vanes.

fawchon, 84/2 ; fauchon, 86/12 ; faychon, 86/32; fawcun. 18/511 (?), *etc.*, falchion, sword.

fayne, 2/29, 5/145, *etc.*, fain, glad ; 28/816, *sb.* gladness.

fedom, 101/21, fathoms.

fere, in fere, 22/642, 24/700, in company.

fet, 11/293, fetch.

fetemanscipe, 55/702, footmanshid, action of walking.

feyrear, 55/725, fairer.

feymyne, 14/404, feminine.

for-alsomoche, 73/12, forasmuch.

ford, 107/6, furred.

for-do, 27/785, undo, ruin.

for-wachid, 25/720, weary with watching.

for-were, 49/518, tired out.

foteman, 57/780, traveller on foot.

fowndatur, 39/178, founder.

fracis, 119/5, phrases (?).

frute, 27/799, fruit, offspring.

fryght, 30/882, freighted.

fryth, 10/290, frith, wooded country; *assoc. w.* field.

fyndis, 3/79, fiend's.

Gawdis, 48/479, gauds, jests.

gawnes, 95/15, gallons.

gere, 68/1129, *etc.* ; geire, 79/41 ; geir, 87/9 ; geyre, 96/7, *etc.*, gear, goods, apparel, properties.

giandes, 94/9, giant's.

glede, 27/780, fire.

gostely, 25/716, spiritually.

gradudis, 69/1166, graduates.

grece, haut grece, 74/40, fat, wellfed.

groue, 7/183, grue or shudder (?).

gysse, 14/402, guise, custom.

Haft, 60/888, business.

har, 28/802, harrow, denunciation.

har, 63/958, higher.

hareode, 19/521 ; harrode, 21/614, herald.

harie, 22/646, S. *connects w.* harry, distress.

hayls, 112/13, greet, salute.

heddur, 11/293, *etc.*, hither.

hell-hede, 101/26-8, hell-mouth.

hem, 72/20 ; ham, 28/817 ; hyme, 73/36, *etc.*, them.

hendly, 112/13, gently.

hent, 29/843, seize.

heyrynge, 83/27, *etc.*, hiring.

horgens, 102/15, organs.

hy, 21/614, hie, go.

hyle, 122/241, highly.

hight, 112/30, hight, is called.

hyght, on hyght, 3/74, on high.

hylist, 18/514, most mighty (?).

hynd, 11/297, *etc.*, gentle, kind.
hyndly, 7/188, kindly.

Ihit, 113/7, 15, yet.
incoll, 93/41, inkle, tape.
in-fere, 22/642, *see* fere.
insampull, 5/133, example.

Jeseyne, 26/765 ; jesen, 24/698 f.,
gesine, childbed.
Jesse, 110/15, Jesse, genealogical
tree of Christ.
jubbarb, 47/433, jeopard, risk
danger.
journe, 108/33, journey, day's work.

Kast, 3/70, cast, form a purpose.
katyffis, 19/535, captives.
kerne, 27/784, vagabond, term of
contempt.
keveryng, 102/5, covering.
knytt, 4/94, tied.

Lange, 36/103, language.
large, 62/938, freely.
larthar, 102/12, ladder.
lede, 27/789, S. fame, popularity.
lere, 60/873, learn.
leyche, 4/99, leech, saviour.
leygence, 60/879, ligeance, alle-
giance.
leygis, 7/180, leagues.
lend, 7/192, remain.
link, 99/21, link, torch.
loggyn, 11/315, lodging.
londe, 49/520, plough furrow in
pasture land, *Warw. prov.*
looe, 8/214, 218, hill.
losyngere, 30/859, flatterer, de-
ceiver.
lett, 63/963, desist, forbear ; *pp.*
62/937.

Make, 21/607, do.
males, 18/497, malice.
markises, 114/38, marquises.
mede, 47/440, meed, merit.
mell, 65/1039, mix, meddle.
mellyflue, 110/27, mellifluous.
merle, 47/433, marl.
mete, 74/48, meeting or assembly (?).
meyne, 26/748, be disposed.
meve, 2/37, move.
moght, 7/189, might.
molde, 22/626, the earth, the ground.

mon, 2/33, man, one.
monyssion, 70/1186, monition, sum-
mons.
moo, 57/762, *etc.*, more.
mote, 3/50, *etc.*, may, must.
mowe, 111/27, *etc.*, may.
mvndall, 39/187 ; mundall, 121/187,
the world (?).
mvse, 61/907, consider, or wonder
at (?).
myddis, 8/208 ; meddis, 18/508,
midst.
myght, 18/516, mighty.
myttens, 12/323, mittens, gloves.
myre, 25/710, myrrh.

Nar, 50/553, nearer.
ne, 74/21, 76/25, nor.
Neowell, 16/474, Noël, Christmas.
nothur, 4/108 ; nodur, 67/1094,
neither.
novellis, 12/332, 336, news, tidings.

Obles, 115/38, obleys, little cakes of
bread.
obskevre, 13/352, obscure.
occupie, 75/35, follow a business.
oder, 72/14 ; odur, 120/182, other.
oddur, 44/362, odor, perfume.
olyve, 113/25, olive.
onpossibull, 4/87, 13/381, impossible.
on-sunder, 17/491, asunder.
or, 21/616, *etc.*, ere, before.
originall, 83/12 ; orygynall, 89/5 7,
play-book.

Page, 56/734, boy.
pardy, 59/832, parde, verily.
parfettle, 13/380, perfectly.
parrage, 14/395, family, descent.
parties, 25/730, parts, regions.
pay, 25/723, content, satisfaction.
paynemaynes, 74/39, paindemaines,
white bread.
paynyms, 113/13, pagans.
pensils, 82/9 ; pensells, 93/40, pen-
cels, streamers.
pipyns, 74/41, apples.
platt, 62/947, plain, clear.
poollye, 89/42, pulley.
pottell, 91/22, pottle, measure.
postyll, 109/26, apostle.
prelatt, 107/7, a garment (?).

premises, 114/13, what has been stated above.

prentyse, 107/30, *for* prentice, penthouse.

preve, 2/39, prove.

prikynge, 96/4, 97/29, setting to music (?).

probate, 37/109, proof.

produstacion, 36/93, protestation.

prognostefying, 34/17, 119/17, prophesying; *pp.* 34/39.

protestacyon, 100/14, protestation, declaration of dissent (?).

pyle, 16/453, edifice; pallays, *prob. better reading.*

pyne, 112/23, 113/13, pain, torment.

pyrie, 8/226, gust of wind.

pwynt, 66/1068, point; *plu.* 63/972.

pwyntis, 89/44, points, laces.

pyght, 43/320, arranged, set in order.

pytt, 12/323, put.

Quere, 9/265, choir.

quost, 67/1086, quest, search.

quyke, 64/1019, quick, alive.

Raygete, 86/7, rochet, garment worn by bishop.

recownfort, 71/11, recomfort.

rede sea, 97/34, cloth (?).

rede, 63/965, 966, interpret, or recite.

red, 27/786; rede, 28/822; redde, 64/1013, rede, plan, counsel.

reherces, 79/41; reherse, 85/8, *etc.*, rehearsal.

reycomforde, 42/282, *etc.*, recomfort, give new strength to.

reygalles, 100/10, *etc.*; rygols, 107/16, rigolls, musical instruments.

reygend, 12/344, region.

reygur, 63/985, rigor, violence, fury.

reyjurnid, 69/1181, adjourned.

reyleyshe, 121/211, release.

reymeve, 44/349, remove.

reparellyd, 83/38, *etc.*, repaired; *pres. part.* 83/29.

reryd, 73/46, raised, contributed.

reypriff, 14/385, *for* reprief, reproof.

roche, 88/20, rock (?).

rysshes, 89/15; ruysshes, 89/21; rosshes, 95/14; ressys, 99/3, *etc.*, rushes.

Sabett, 63/979, Sabbath.

saluer, 62/956, healer.

sapence, 67/1109, sapience.

schapp, *plu.* (?) 26/741, **shape**, figure.

scytte, 101/6, S. suit (?).

sede, 12/345, seed (?).

seldall, 82/20, 86/3, settle or seat (?).

sendal, 99/23, 100/20, sendal, silken material.

senssars, 97/5, censers.

sertes, 59/835, certes, in truth.

serviture, 37/128, servitor.

seynsyng, 115/37; sensyng, 111/38, *etc.*, burning incense in censers.

shevys, 87/7, shoes.

shope, 89/31, soap.

singler, 75/18, *etc.*, single.

sith, 4/106, *etc.*, since.

sithen, 117/15, *etc.*, since, because.

slop, 86/15, an outer garment.

soferent, 39/177, sovereign; *plu.* sufferntis, 2/28.

sond, 4/109; sonde, 19/540, *etc.*, messenger; message.

sparis, 92/9, spars, pieces of timber.

spede, 43/311, make haste.

spere, 12/348, spear; cp. *holy lance.*

spret, 119/24, spirit.

spretis, 3/53; spryttys, 100/7, spirits.

stablisshed, 78/8, established.

stoods, 108/42, studs, posts, joists.

strangis, 35/49, *sb.* news.

styde, 29/850, stead place.

stynt, 51/576, stop.

sudere, 82/20, 86/1, sudary, handkerchief.

suyng, 77/29, 116/29, following.

syn, 23/651, since.

syth, 6/178, *etc.*, since.

syngnefocacion, 9/260, signification, manifestation.

Tabarde, 86/5; taberd, 86/9; tabard, tunic or mantel.

tabulis, 60/866, tables.

tane, 60/862, taken.

tast, 31/899, explore, examine.

tent, 61/891, heed, attend to.

theal, 84/17; theyll, 107/21, *etc.*, thill, shaft.

thee, 50/557, thrive, prosper.

this, 36/90, thus.

thrall, 2/32, bondage.

thyddur, 8/231, *etc.*, thither.

thynke, me thynke, 20/562, *etc.*, methinks.

thyre-tyll, 67/1090, thereto.

till, 37/121, *etc.*, to, unto.

toocuns, 20/559 landmarks.

toward-lovyng, 76/32, docile.

translate, 70, revised, presented in a new form.

trayne, 6/147, treachery, deceit.

trendell, 109/9; trendyll, 109/10; tryndyll, 84/17; trindle, small wheel.

trone, in trone, 2/35, 3/63, on throne.

troo, 4/105, *etc.*; tro, 30/883, trow, believe.

truage, 19/524, tribute.

truse, 5/129; 51/577, truss, bind up; trwse, *sb.* 90/120.

turtill, 3/75, turtle, term of endearment.

turtuls, 45/376; turtillis, 46/421, *etc.*, turtledoves.

twynke, 18/506, wink.

tyll, 66/1064, to, unto.

tyntyng, 102/4, attending to.

Umellete, 20/556, humility.

untill, 63/966, unto.

unye, 76/33, unite; *pp.* unyed, 75/16, *etc.*

Velen, 28/802, villainous, servile.

verabull, 14/394, *for* venerable (?); S. valuable; M. *suggests* renable.

viallis, 19/538, viols.

vpsoght, 28/809, sought out (?).

vthe, 56/751, *etc.*, youth.

Warly, 111/20, cautiously, warily.

waxun, 49/511, waxed, grown.

waynis, 30/882, wains, wagons.

wede, in wede, 26/768, costume.

wedurs, 8/209, skies (?), clouds (?).

well-awey, 59/829, welaway, alas!

wene, 58/819, ween, think.

were, 12/341, *etc.*; werie, 49/513; werre, 58/793, very.

wheddur, 50/560, whether, which of two.

whyddur, 8/230; whedder, 21/595, *etc.*, whither.

where, 76/19, whereas.

whomly, 47/445, homely, rudely.

wode, 30/866, mad.

wodkoce, 47/432, woodcock.

wone, 68/1120, dwell, abide.

worthe, 5/137, betide.

wott, 65/1044, know.

wyddurde, 29/839, widowed (?), *or* withered (?); *women would be bending over as if old to conceal the children they were carrying.*

wyle, 59/840; wyll, 67/1100, wile, allure.

wynde, 6/168; wynd, 7/200, *etc.*, go.

wynd, 101/22; wynde, 100/4, *etc.*, windlass.

Yche, 47/437, I.

ycheone, 5/137, each one.

yhit, 113/30, yet.

yeyre, 37/126, air.

yonglyng, 61/899, youth.

yorth, 20/560; yarthe, 36/79, *etc.*, earth.

# INDEX OF NAMES AND MATTERS.

Note:—The characters in the pageants are referred to only at their first appearances. Insignificant names of craftsmen and places, also names used for dating, are not included at all. Names are in ordinary spelling except where there would be difficulty in recognising the word. Cap. signifies Cappers' Accounts; Dr., Drapers'; Mer., Mercers'; Sm., Smiths'; W., Weavers'.

PRINTED IN GREAT BRITAIN BY
RICHARD CLAY AND COMPANY, LTD..
BUNGAY, SUFFOLK.

Date Due